Away

Away

Maritimers in Massachusetts, Ontario, and Alberta: An Oral History of Leaving Home

GARY BURRILL

McGill-Queen's University Press
Montreal & Kingston • London • Buffalo

© McGill-Queen's University Press 1992
ISBN 0-7735-0899-6

Legal deposit third quarter 1992
Bibliothèque nationale du Québec

Printed in Canada on acid-free paper

This book has been published with the help of a grant from the Canada Council through its block grant program and with the aid of funds from the Nova Scotia Department of Culture and Tourism.

Canadian Cataloguing in Publication Data

Burrill, Gary Clayton, 1955–
  Away: Maritimers in Massachusetts, Ontario and
  Alberta
  ISBN 0-7735-0899-6
  1. Maritime Provinces – Biography. 2. Maritime
  Provinces – Social conditions. 3. Migration, internal –
  Maritime   Provinces.   4.   Maritime   Provinces   –
  Emigration   and   immigration.   5.   Massachusetts   –
  Emigration and immigration.
  I. Title.
  FC2029.B87 1992   971.5'04'0922   C92-090209-X
  F1035.8.B87 1992

Material previously published as "With Billy MacGillivray in Boston," *Cape Breton's Magazine* 53 (1990); "Stan Myers: A PEI Fiddler in Boston," *New Maritimes* 5, no. 10 (1987); and "First the West and then the Rest: Maritimers Remember the Harvest Excursions, New England, and Home," *New Maritimes* 8, no. 5 (1990) are published by permission. Lyrics from "The Idiot," © 1980 by Stan Rogers are used by permission of Fogarty's Cove Music.

For Debbie

Contents

Preface xi

Introduction 3

PART ONE: MASSACHUSETTS

The Maillets from Mavillette
11 Leo Maillet
13 Louis Maillet

From the Harvest
18 Ken Ring
22 Owen Caldwell
31 Donald "Danny" Cameron
35 Angus Crowdis
38 Louis Bannister

Dances, Dancers, and Fiddlers
41 Ralph MacGillivray
44 Elizabeth and Donald "Danny" Cameron
49 Stan Myers

Never Done
57 Agnes Gillis and Constance Kroha
63 Ann Hyde
67 Gladys McCoy

Local 67
70   Herbert G. Vickerson
73   Billy MacGillivray

The Biologist
80   Ralph Wetmore

Sisters
87   Villa Easton
89   Gertrude Dixon
95   Myrtle Richardson

Members
99   Alta Holmes
100 Angus Crowdis
102 Christine MacKay Carmichael
104 Isabel Morrison

Boats Down the Bay
107 Lloyd and Merle Merriam

PART TWO: ONTARIO

Parliament and Gerrard
113 Bruce and Molly Greenlaw

It Owns You
122 Bud MacLeod

Up and Down the Road
126 Jim Ormond
133 Bud and Essie Davidson
138 James Clarke
141 Billy King

Pulpits
147 Robert Mumford
149 Ian MacLean

Kicking It Around
150 Brad Elliot
154 Allan Cooper
157 Jean Andrews
162 Greg Kavanagh
164 Ted Ring

A Banker and a Politician
166   Arthur Crockett
168   Flora MacDonald

Here to Stay
170   Mary Johnston
171   Phyllis Trenholm
174   Myra Jones
176   Lois Veniot

The Prince of Wales
177   Stuart, Vivian, and Beth Walsh

PART THREE: ALBERTA

A Miner, a Mechanic, and a Driver
185   Donald MacDonald
188   Don Bishop
192   Ron MacNeil

*The Maritime Reunion Association
of Alberta*
200   Keith McElwain
204   Danny Batherson
207   Jeff Miller
209   Larry MacDonald

Of Jobs
215   Alan Waddell
221   David Bona
222   Shawn Mulherin

Halifax Sells Alberta
227   Laureen Bowness
230   Mike Hasler
236   Colin Logan

2506 4th Avenue NW
239   Lloyd Wallace
241   Alan Shaw
244   Duane Lee
248   Vince Buchanan

Preface

A few words about the places, the process, and the people of this book.

Massachusetts, Ontario, and Alberta were selected as the areas for this project because, while Maritimers have gone to many other places in great numbers, these three areas have been a main focus of the exodus from home for one or more generations in this century. Take my own age group (I'm thirty-six) as a point of reference: my great-grandparents' generation looked primarily to Boston for work when they made the decision to leave home in the years between the turn of the century and World War I; their children, my grand-parents' generation, did the same in the 1920s; people my parents' age looked primarily to the Toronto area when they decided to leave for work after World War II and into the 1960s; and Maritimers of my generation, and younger, thought first of Alberta in the late 1970s and early 1980s, before the collapse of the western oil economy. Not all the people whose accounts appear here arrived in these areas during these particular years, nor are they all of the specific age groups outlined above; but the Massachusetts–Ontario–Alberta framework provides at least the broad outlines of an inter-generational map of migration from the Maritimes.

All of the personal accounts here were recorded in Massachu-setts, Ontario, or Alberta; references of direction like "back there," "down there," and the like refer, therefore, exclusively to the Mari-times throughout. (And let us take passing note of the prepositional anomalies by which Maritimers refer to home. The consensus is that you go "up" to Boston from the Maritimes, and "down" when you're travelling home. "Down" and "home" feel right together, but there's something jarring about going "up" to Boston when your finger is following the Mercator Projection, for a good part of the trip, pretty well straight south. Some people say this has to do with the prevailing winds, a holdover from a time when "up" and "down" were used more to refer to sails and seawinds than stocks and securities. Others claim it has to do with the numbering system of longitudinal degrees: the numbers decrease, "go down," as you move east. The whole matter is thrown into confusion when Alberta – unquestionably "up" relative to the Maritimes in terms of both sea level and northerliness on the map – is referred to as "out" west. But Maritimers go "down east" wherever they're leaving from – and usages of these prepositions have been standardized here in the interests of consistency.)

No attempt has been made to be geographically or otherwise representative as far as the origins of the people who speak here are concerned. I met most of the authors of these accounts through relatives and friends, either theirs or mine. Often a person would have one or two friends from home whom they knew well enough to talk these things over with, and then, having spent some time with me, one thing would lead to another. Areas of the Maritimes like Yarmouth County, Moncton, Halifax, and industrial Cape Breton, where I have lived, worked, or otherwise spent some time, or where I have family, are much better represented here than, say, Prince Edward Island or northern New Brunswick, where I know fewer people. The absences in this collection – for example, of a great deal of the most profound Maritime experience of exile, that of the Acadians, or of the experience of Maritime Native people – therefore reflect not my views on what's important in Maritime history but rather the limitations of my experience.

The accounts that make up this volume were all recorded in 1981 – in May and June in Ontario, July and August in Massachusetts, and November and December in Alberta. This has made for unavoidable inconsistency in the time references between the Alberta section and the rest of the book. Although the oil boom was to come to an abrupt halt not long after these conversations were recorded, Alberta was still very much in "boom mode" in 1981, and that period is here referred to exclusively in the present, unlike the past tense that people use elsewhere in the book to talk about the postwar expansions in Massachusetts and Ontario. Part Three, "Alberta," also reflects the issue that was on many Maritimers' minds in Alberta in 1981 – the resentment in the West against the influx of "easterners," who were associated in a lot of discussion at the time with an increase in crime.

A word on the process. These accounts are not "interviews' in the sense of structured sets of questions and answers. Rather, time and time again, as I introduced myself and my subject by explaining something about the theme of leaving home in Maritime history, some kind of chord was struck in the self-understanding of those I spoke with, and we then spent an hour, an afternoon, or a day recording a conversation about the place of leaving home in their lives and in their thinking. Sometimes these accounts are short, sometimes they are lengthy. Some are chronologically quite complete, to 1981; others evoke the experiences of a particular period. Together, they stand as a general picture of the life of the Maritimes-in-exile, the hundreds of thousands of people from home, away.

Spoken and written language have very different rhythms and ways of conveying things, and in the shift from the conversational nature of talk to the more linear logic of the page, the inner continuity of a spoken account can, without care, largely be left behind. And so each of these accounts has been edited in an effort to preserve its conversational unity within the world of the written word. All of the people whose self-explanations appear here have been consulted about the faithfulness of these altered accounts to their original forms of expression. Another round of editorial revisions has usually ensued. This process has the obvious disadvantage of being extremely time-consuming; it has taken years. But it also has the benefit, in my view, that the end product speaks with an integrity that otherwise could prove elusive.

I have only this regret: many of the people who were kind enough to share something of their lives with me in 1981, especially in the Boston area, have passed away before the completion of the project. To their family members who have undertaken to study the printed word for its faithfulness to the tone and detail of their speech, I am enduringly grateful.

I am also grateful for the friendship of Stan Myers, with whom I corresponded steadily on the subject of Maritimers in Boston from our first meeting in Holbrook, Massachusetts, in 1981 until his death in 1988.

I pause to remember others. Evelyn Allison arranged a number of these conversations in the Hagersville area of Ontario; she passed away in 1987. Lillian Prosser, my grandmother, put me in touch with several family members who had moved away before I was born; she died in 1988. Kaye Murray, who passed away in March

1989, researched many of the explanatory notes that appear at the bottom of these pages.

For their help at various stages of this project I wish to thank Ashley Allison, Ben Allison, Liz Bailey, Richard Baker, J.K. Bell, Helene Burns, Fred C. Burrill, Prescott Burrill, Roger Burrill, Shirley Burrill, Christine Cannon, Muriel Cooper, Edna Dobson, Elizabeth Fry-Gibson, Geneva Perrott, Louise Green, Jeff Johnson, Harold Landry, Fred Luff, Donna McDonald, Mary McKeen, Dave Palmater, Marcia Young Palmater, Donna Moran, Lorraine Perrott, Glorina Pontes, Victoria Reich, the late Anna Ring, Ken Ring, Paul Robinson, Dale Steeves, Bill Szulga, Linda Szulga, Nancy Taylor, Shirley Tillotson, Mildred Townsend, Morton Townsend, and Ivan Varga.

I am grateful to the Explorations Program of the Canada Council for their support, both in 1981 and 1984, and to the Assistance to Established Writers program of the Nova Scotia Department of Tourism and Culture for their support in 1991. I wish, too, to thank the staff of the Public Archives of Nova Scotia, particularly those in the Film and Sound division, who provide an excellent home for the recordings on which this book is based. The people at the reference desk at the Dartmouth Regional Library have been invariably helpful, and I am also grateful to the reference staff of the Killam Memorial Library at Dalhousie University and the Patrick Power Library at St Mary's University, especially Douglas Vaisey, who has been a particular help on matters pertaining to labour history.

For the attentiveness they have given this project throughout the process of publication, I wish to thank Philip Cercone and Joan McGilvray of McGill-Queen's University Press. I am particularly grateful for the thoroughness and care of Claire Gigantes, the volume's editor.

I thank my friends at *New Maritimes* for making it possible for me to complete this book. Lorraine Begley, Gregg Lambert, and Ian McKay covered for me during various absences while this work was being completed. Ian generously made available his research on the history of out-migration from the Maritimes, and he has helped to clarify my sense of the broad sweep of this story. Ken Clare has helped with the editing of the entire project; his suggestions have much improved the book's clarity and continuity. I am particularly indebted to Scott Milsom, who took over the editorship of *New Maritimes* for an extended period while this book was being completed. Scott has worked closely on this volume over a number of years, and I have relied heavily here on his sound editorial judgment.

I am extremely grateful to Audrey Burrill, my mother, for her help in transcribing many of these recordings.

I would not have undertaken or completed this book except for Debra Perrott, my wife. She has been at the centre of the whole project, from the conversations themselves, to the rough editing at the stage of transcription, to the final process of putting it all together. I, and this, are for her.

G.B.
Upper Musquodoboit,
Nova Scotia

Away

The Father's boy, his only joy,
Must bid a sad farewell;
They're parting here, no more to meet
On earth, for who can tell.
Far from the Isle, in prairies wild,
In countries now that's new,
Content they stay, and bless the day
They bid this Isle adieu.

Our daughters fair, in deep despair,
Must leave their native land;
To foreign shores they're swiftly borne,
As I do understand,
The tide it flows, they all must go
There's nothing else to do;
While parents grieve as they must leave
And bid this Isle adieu.

Through want and care and scanty fare,
The poor man drags along;
He hears a whistle loud and shrill,
The "Iron Horse" speeds on;
He throws his pack upon his back,
There's nothing left to do;
He boards the train for Bangor, Maine,
Prince Edward Isle adieu.

> From "Prince Edward Isle Adieu,"
> approximately 1880, authorship disputed

Introduction

Sensitive oral historians sometimes comment about a feeling they have of intruding in others' lives, of stepping into personal places where only those who are going to be around for longer than a taping session have any right to be. James Hornby of *The Island Magazine* in Charlottetown once spoke about this before the Atlantic Oral History Association. The "kind of exploitation I am concerned with," he said, "stems from the relationship of collector and informant." He continued:

It is a basic tenet of fieldwork that a friendly relationship is necessary, and that to a large degree, the result you will get from an interview is dependent upon establishing this relationship, however transitory. Informants, of course, usually know the score and most participate willingly nonetheless. I had a hundred-year-old man tell me after an interview, "Don't say you'll come back because you won't." He was a man of some experience of being visited. I thought at the time that I would prove him wrong: I would dearly love a return visit but so far he is right.

Hornby is listening here, in my view, to an essentially sound inner instinct. Most people do not offer the kind of contradiction-unravelling effort – often through re-experiencing painful memories – that makes for a gripping-to-read account, unless this is summoned out of them by a feeling of personal sharing, a feeling that, in the context of an "interview," does not exist in any authentic way. There is something in the presence of a tape recorder that is inherently blasphemous against what makes for real human solidarity, and this isn't changed one bit by the fact that people participate voluntarily in the process of making oral history.

But this difficulty of oral history can be partially mitigated through the ends that historical projects can serve. The "preservation of a spoken record" is not sufficient justification for the existence of oral history, nor is the addition of a "human side" to the "cold, dry facts" of documentary history. But common purpose sits a little deeper. The immediate exploitation created in the act of doing oral history can be justified, I believe, if the end product of the effort is designed to serve, in some way, the genuine interests of the community represented by the speaker – and in this case, by the "interviewer" too.

The idea of leaving home is an inseparable part of what it is to be a Maritimer. Fredericton historian Ernest Forbes says that the consciousness of the Maritimes as a distinct place was largely developed in the first place through the common experiences of people who worked away from home, then later returned, in the early years of this century.

It is a pattern with a long history.* As far back as 1880, there

---

* A wide variety of material has been published on the history of population movements from the Maritimes. Information on Maritimers in Massachusetts is included in *The Working Girls of Boston*, an 1889 study by Carroll D. Wright which was republished by Arno Press and the New York Times in 1969; and in Albert Kennedy's "The Provincials," a study from the 1920s which was published in the Spring 1975 edition of *Acadiensis: Journal of the History of the Atlantic Region*. Alan A. Brookes has written widely on the subject. His "Out-Migration from the Maritime Provinces, 1860–1900: Some Preliminary Considerations" was published in the Spring 1976 *Acadiensis*; his "Islanders in the Boston States, 1850–1900" appeared in the Spring-Summer edition of *The Island Magazine* in 1977; and his "The Golden Age and the Exodus: The Case of Canning, Kings County," which appeared in *Acadiensis* in Autumn 1981, is an excellent case study. A superb case study of the impact of out-migration on the working-class movement in the Maritimes is contained in chapter 3 ("The New Unionism and Economic Crisis: 1912–1926") of Ian McKay's *The Craft Transformed: An Essay on the Carpenters of Halifax, 1885–1985*, published by Holdfast in 1985. Material for an overview of the subject can be found in Kari Levitt's 1960 study for the Atlantic Provinces Economic Council, *Population Movements in the Atlantic Provinces*, in Patricia A. Thornton's "The Problem of Out-Migration from Atlantic Canada, 1871–1921: A New Look," which was published in the Autumn 1985 edition of *Acadiensis*, and in Henry Veltmeyer's "The Capitalist Underdevelopment of Atlantic Canada," in a volume edited by Robert J. Brym and R. James Sacouman and published by New Hogtown in 1979, *Underdevelopment and Social Movements in Atlantic Canada*.

were already more Nova Scotians in Boston than in Yarmouth, Sydney, and Pictou combined. In the following decade, 11,900 people moved away from Prince Edward Island. In the 1890s, 93,000 people left the Maritimes. The Shelburne *Budget* reported in 1899 that "this ever-increasing exodus has drained the South Shore of Nova Scotia of many of its best young men. Let the traveller go into the homes of people in towns and country, and he will see in nine homes out of ten the photograph of an absent boy, who is prospering under the Stars and Stripes." The twentieth century brought no respite from this unrelenting erosion of the population. New Brunswick historian Arthur Doyle says in his book *Front Benches and Back Rooms* that during World War I the large number of eligible young men who were working outside the region was a major obstacle to recruitment in the province. And the 1920s?* These years can be described, without exaggeration, as a decade of demographic disaster for the Maritimes. In 1921, the *Cambridge History of the British Empire* records that "at least 325,000 former Maritime residents were living elsewhere, about three-quarters of them in the United States." They soon had lots of company: in the course of the decade 147,000 people left the region. The population of Amherst, Nova Scotia, fell by twenty-five percent. "The Exodus Continues," "Exodus of Young People From Dartmouth," "Exodus is Still On," "And Still They Go," trumpeted headlines of the Halifax weekly *Citizen* in 1923 and 1924. The *Yarmouth Herald* summed up the local effects of the population drain in its edition of 7 December 1927: "On this side of Pubnico Harbour, from the head of the harbor to Pubnico Beach, about one-fifth of the dwelling houses are closed up ... Look over the Argyles, Eel Brook, Amirault Hill, Wedgeport ... and you will find a large percentage of the homes vacant, and should you ask a neighbour as to their whereabouts, they will reply 'Gone to the States.' "

More recent times are not much different. In her 1960 report *Population Movements in the Atlantic Provinces*, economist Kari Levitt showed that during the 1940s every New Brunswick county (except Albert and Westmorland) lost more people than it gained, and that by 1951 there were already more than 32,000 New Brunswickers living in Ontario. In Nova Scotia, Cumberland and Pictou Counties lost 2,700 people apiece between 1951 and 1956. In PEI, a quarter of the young men between the ages of fifteen and nineteen in 1951 had

---

* The decadal figures I am using actually refer to census decades: hence the years 1891–1901 are referred to, for ease of explanation, as "the 1890s," 1921–31 are "the 1920s," etc.

left the Island just five years later, in 1956. In the last twenty years, the Maritime economy has changed tremendously as the federal government has become the main financial presence in the region, but this has had little overall effect on the exodus from the area. In her *Input-output Study of the Atlantic Provinces*, done in 1975, Kari Levitt estimated that 150,000 people left the region between 1961 and 1969. In the following decade, the destination of choice was increasingly western Canada. Canadian Press reported on 17 June 1978 that 130 workers from eastern Canada were thronging to Alberta every day.

If post-Confederation Maritime economic history were written as a symphony, it would surely be one of the modern variety, full of disjoints, discords, and atonalities. Here, there is a great percussive crash, as a shipping economy collapses or a nascent industrialism declines. There, we hear a brief, light flute solo, diminishing into the cynical pianissimos of the economic-development programs of the 1960s and 1970s. Unsuccessful retunings grate on the ear following the intermissions of war. Pensions and grants ignore the conductor altogether and begin a symphony of their own. And through it all the theme of exile sounds as steadily as a string bass bowed in slow, consistent arcs, sustaining still the sad refrain: steadily they leave, from home we go, away, and away, and away.

Why this population drain persists is a complicated matter, but it is one of those complex issues at the base of which lie some very simple truths. The first of these is that the Maritimes has spent its entire history as a region at the wrong end of a core-periphery relationship, and its development since 1867 has been thwarted by policies designed to promote the interests of the region at the other end of that relationship, Central Canada. The second such truth is that the economy of Canada is of the private-enterprise, or capitalist, variety. And the third is that peripheral regions within capitalist economies throughout the western world – whether in Gascony or the Gaspé, Catalonia or Cape Breton – all tend to have the same problem, and this is due to elementary economics. Capitalist economies have these two features: people who have money make decisions about where to invest on the basis of where profits are expected to be highest; and, in order to meet their bills, a large number of people need to sell their labour to those who make the investment decisions. These two features are connected. The more investors have to pay for labour, the less is their profit on any particular venture; conversely, the lower the wages relative to the value of the product being produced, the more attractive the investment opportunity. The key, therefore, to ensuring profitability is to control the price of labour, and for this investors have a very efficient mechanism – unemployment. When there are more workers than jobs – when the supply of labouring people exceeds the demand – long-term, across-the-board profitability is far more likely. This suggests why, despite the efforts of highly trained policy makers, analysts, and economists around the world, it is almost impossible to find capitalist economies operating without significant levels of unemployment accompanied by severe regional inequalities.

Karl Marx called them the "light infantry of capital" – those migrant, sometimes-employed workers from underdeveloped regions who serve the needs of investment capital twice over: while still at home and unemployed, they act as a drag on the demands of labour in the centre area, which knows they can easily be replaced; and when the business cycle turns upward, they are summoned by the trumpets of expansion to work in the centre for comparatively little in relation to the value of what they produce. Unemployment in general, and migration from depressed regions in particular, are necessary to the smooth functioning of any national economy whose health depends upon enhancing its attractiveness to profit-seeking investment.

It is therefore not an accident that so many government programs and business-economists' prescriptions over the years have recommended facilitating the flow of people out of the Maritimes as the most effective way for the region to participate in Canada's national economy. The late Walter Gordon, in the 1957 *Preliminary Report* of the Royal Commission on Canada's Economic Problems, wrote, "If it should turn out that there is not the necessary combination of resources in sufficient quantities to permit a substantial rise in living standards in the Atlantic region, generous assistance should be given to those people who might wish to move to other parts of Canada." The Economic Council of Canada echoed this sentiment twenty years later when, in its 1977 volume *Living Together: A Study of Regional Disparities*, it expressed the view that while many "provincial officials are disturbed by out-migration ... it can be very good for the individuals concerned. Migrants who do not return – and there must be many of them if such concern about out-migration exists – are presumably better off than if they had not moved." Economist Thomas Courchene, whose thinking deeply influenced what the MacDonald Commission on the Economic Union and Development Prospects for Canada had to say about the Maritimes in 1985, came very close in a study he once authored, "Migration from the Maritimes," to calling for a policy of outright regional depopulation.

We in the Maritimes have been taught an upside-down way of thinking about the position of our economy relative to the rest of North America. The prosperity in different periods of areas like Massachusetts, southern Ontario, and Alberta has a lot to do with the availability of a work force that has had just enough of unemployment to be glad of the chance to go to work for comparatively little in relation to the value of what they produce. It is just such a work force that the Maritimes, on the periphery of North American capitalism, has been supplying to a succession of core areas for over a hundred years. And so the *real* subsidy in the relationship between Central Canada and the Maritimes consists not of the equalization and transfer payments that come east from the taxation coffers in Ottawa. The splitting up of Maritime families, homes, and communities over generations is a big part of what has made possible so many of the economic expansions of "away," and this is a currency in which it is impossible to repay.

It is a commonplace among those who study colonialism in the Third World that whenever one place is dominated by another, the relationship between the two is reinforced by the subtle and gradual process by which their culture and traditions come to be denigrated in the eyes of the colonized people themselves. Something of this has taken place over the years in the Maritimes. The Italian writer Giuseppe Galasso calls it the "psychological laceration" of the young – the idea, embedded in a culture which has sent off generations of exiles, that everything interesting, important, or worthy of engagement belongs exclusively to the world of "away." It is an idea that breeds a sense of regional inferiority, which in turn suffocates the dream that the future of the region, unlike its past and present, ought to be made in keeping with the magnificent potential of its people.

An understanding of the depth and pattern of exile in the Maritimes is essential if we in the region are ever to rise up against the structures that have scattered our people, so often against their will, all over the globe. This sense – of the need to turn things upside-down if we are to prevent the further disintegration of our families and communities by poverty and unemployment – is echoed repeatedly in the remembrances and reflections of the people who have participated in the building of this book. *Away: Maritimers in Massachusetts, Ontario and Alberta* is offered as a small contribution in that essential, that someday undeniable, direction.

PART ONE

Massachusetts

When Donald get to Boston,
He buy a suit of clothes,
He throw away his homespuns
Likewise his crooked brogues;
He buy a pair of gaiters
I think t'was size sixteen,
For Donald like the Yankee girl
What bake the Boston Bean.

> From "Donald from Bras d'Or,"
> 185th Overseas Battalion,
> Canadian Expeditionary Forces,
> Cape Breton Highlanders

The Maillets from Mavillette

Leo and Louis Maillet and the rest of their brothers and sisters – Richard, Alfreda and Genevieve – all live in the Boston area. The family had moved to Boston before the 1930s, but came back to the farm in Mavillette with the onset of the Great Depression.

LEO MAILLET – Mavillette, Digby County, Nova Scotia

A three-decker house on the busy corner of Broadway and Washington in Somerville. "Everyone that hears me knows that I don't come from Boston." Leo speaks with an inimicable combination of French Shore Acadian and Boston American accents. He is a member of the Franco-American Social Club of Everett, an organization of Canadian expatriates.

He has worked for over twenty years for the retail grocery chain, Stop and Shop. "They've got a hundred and fifty stores, from here to New Jersey. I work in the manufacturing part of it, in the bakery. They do all of their own stuff. All their own bakery, all their own cannery, all their own dairy. They've got their own potato-chip place. They do it all, they make it themselves. Like in Hyde Park ... They've got a place up there almost as big as Nova Scotia."

His conversation is punctuated with a hearty kind of staccato laughter. He is in his late fifties.

I was born over here. In Dorchester. Well, when things got tough in 1929 or '30, when the depression came, the old man took us by the ears and took us down there. He had a house built there and everything. He had a farm. And over here, a lot of people, they were on bread lines, soup lines, in 1930. Down there at least you had potatoes to eat, and herring, and salt pork, and a few turnips. It didn't taste too bad.

I went up to grade ten in Mavillette. There were two sides to the school, one from grade one to five, one from grade six to eleven. Everybody used to drop out in the fourth grade, the fifth grade, because their parents were not interested. They couldn't speak English. The books – like geometry, geography, history – were in English. So a guy like me, in Mavillette, say – a guy that goes as far as grade ten, grade eleven – he had to take a provincial exam at the College. Well, there was no way in hell he could pass it. No way in hell he could pass that provincial exam, not coming out of a school like Mavillette. The teacher, she didn't have time to mess around with you – let's say you're grade ten – 'cause she had grades five, six, seven, and eight there too. So I went as far as grade ten.

And you know how you are, you're eighteen years old and you get the itch to get the hell out of there, naturally. Everybody does. The old man was working in Halifax at the time. He was a carpenter. I think I was getting about five bucks a week for running the farm. It was during the war, and there were about two young guys, me and another guy, in Mavillette. Everybody else was gone out either to Halifax or Debert or somewhere, to Ontario, to work. Well I mean there was nothin' to do in Mavillette. You had to leave eventually. So you say, "What the hell am I doing here," right? "I can go to the States. I'm an American citizen all my life." What else are you going to think when you're back in Mavillette there with the old oxen and the plow? Up and down with those things, all day long. You've got a lot of time to think: "What am I, plowin' around with the old oxen there all day long?"

I packed my gear and went to Park Square. But you don't know what the hell you're going to meet when you come up here. If you don't know anybody, it's not easy. What do you do, not speaking English even? Well, when I was six years old I couldn't speak a word of French. All English. Then down there with all the Frenchmen, you pick that up fast, especially when you're a kid and you speak French in the house and everything else. So when I was eighteen I couldn't speak any more English. All French. They'd talk to me. "Huh?" "Huh?" [Shrugs in non-comprehension.] And not even enough money to go back. Maybe thirty, forty bucks in my pocket. So what'd I do? I had to get off the pot, right? I tell my kids that once in a while. I started working for this tree company – cutting trees down and all that stuff. What else could I do? What the hell – I was making about thirty-five cents an hour, which was the average wage in 1944. Couldn't speak English. The boss came over to my cousin once and he said, "What's the matter with that guy? Every time I talk to him he says 'Huh? Huh? Huh?'" You know, I was a damn good donkey! Whenever he'd get tired, just throw him another bushel of oats and away he went for another four hours. You know people from around there, they're good donkeys, that's about all. Work, work, work. And that's the only thing they knew how to do. I could take that axe and swing that thing all day long.

So, I came over here, I worked over here one year and I got hurt. We were taking a tree down, and the sonofagun, the tree fell and hit me right here. [He indicates where five breaks were caused by the accident.] A whole year in the hospital – St Elizabeth's in Brighton [Massachusetts]. That year, I had to get off the pot on learning English. That was the fastest way for me of picking it up. There was no choice.

So I was laid up three or four years after that. But then I figure I didn't do too bad. I got out of there, got on the ball, started working again. Got married. Five boys. I own the house. I got a car. Few bucks in the bank. Figure I didn't do too bad.

LOUIS MAILLET – Mavillette, Digby County, Nova Scotia

He is a few years younger than his brother Leo. We spoke one night after work at his home in Somerville.

In 1948, my father came to the USA on vacation. My brother was up here, so my father came up for a week. And he met this carpenter, this old-timer from Maine, who was living in this six-story house on the other side from my cousin ... They had big houses because they were carpenters. So my father, when he came home, he said, "Go to the USA and I'll get you fixed up with a job doin' carpentry." I'd been born in the States, so I had to be back before I was twenty-one to keep my papers.

Well, I got up here, and I couldn't speak English too much, first of all, because Mavillette, that was mostly French, right? You got a little bit of English in school, but after you came out of school, it was over. I didn't know the difference between a plank and a board, because in French a plank *is* a board.* So there we were. We started out, this old-timer and me. We built a couple of houses. We were workin' pretty good, but then come September the work got quiet. I worked all that summer, but there're no jobs to be given in the winter. And of course, me, I can't go to the carpenters' union because I don't know my stuff that much.

He wasn't giving me too much – maybe two bucks, two bucks and a half an hour. I saved a little, but then comes December. The little money that I'd made, that's going out the door, paying fifteen dollars a week for rent – plus I have to eat, and you have to go out a little bit. My brother Leo gave me ten bucks here, twenty bucks there. Soon I didn't have enough money to go back to Nova Scotia because I owed my brother too much.

---

* *Planche*, in French, means both "plank" and "board."

So this guy that I knew, he says, "Come on over to this truckin' outfit, and they'll put you on." My right hand to God, for ten weeks, twice a week I used to go there. So finally the dispatcher says to me, "You come in at six o'clock tonight." Now I had no car. I had no transportation. And I said, "Six o'clock tonight, that's getting me out at two in the morning, half past two in the morning, right? How do I go home then?" He says, "You wanna job or don't ya?" Now I've got no choice. I've got to take the job. So I took the job. I was working there five years without being sure. One day a week, two days, sometimes three days. At least it brought me up to where I was surviving – but I still couldn't repay my debt. I owed three or four hundred dollars. I finally paid it off.

Anyhow, I was a pretty good worker. Sometimes I probably worked too much, I don't know. But the dispatcher we had over there got through and went to work for this company I work for now. So one night he says to me, "You want a steady job?" I says, "Yeah." I came home and I says to the wife, "I think I'm gonna take that job." So I took the job. You know, I have never gone to work later than seven o'clock in the morning, and I have never lost a day since. That was one of the best things I ever did. But until then, it was not all roses. After that, it wasn't too bad.

After I started there, that was it. I worked hard. I don't mind working, but it's like the old story, "If you have a horse that will work, you work him." Now for instance, what they'll do, at one o'clock, the day-dispatcher goes home, so he'll say to me, "You strip this truck, you load that steel, you take steel off of here ..." The steel, it comes on vans, and it's got to be taken off the vans and put on flatbeds. You're all alone there. So you take ten thousand pounds of steel that came on the van, off of the truck, because you don't have enough steel coming for a flatbed. You have to wait till you can make a load out of them. So you may have three trailers there with steel, pipe, aluminum, whatever, and then you combine that all up for the day. Then after I'm through that work, I'm supposed to fuel all the tractors that go on the road for that night. I check all the trailers for flat tires. You check the oil. You check the water. So half past two these guys come in – we could go home at half past two, because from six to half past two is our eight hours, half hour for lunch – so I says to the dispatcher, "I've got an awful lot of work to do, another two or three hours. How about havin' these guys stay?"

"Oh, no, no, no, no." So this is what happens all day long. Why? Because you work and they don't. And if you want to go home, you're going to work a little faster so you'll go home sometime tonight. If you are like you should be, when half past two comes or five o'clock comes, you'll say, "If I'm not done, it'll be done tomorrow." But I don't do that. I make sure that it's all done before I go home. My right hand to God, when I go on vacation, they put three guys in my place till I come back. And they brag about it.

Maybe it's because I'm in a truckin' business, because truckin' was always push, push, push, push. I don't think carpenters push that much. Your carpenters work about eight hours, or your bricklayers work eight hours. You can only lay so many bricks, and all the mortar and all the stuff is brought to them. But when you get a truck with 40,000 pounds on it, and you go up in the morning to one of these grocery stores, and you unload it yourself, piece by piece, and you put it on pallets for them, and you lug it to the back of the truck; and after that, the same day at noon, or one, two o'clock in the afternoon, they'll send you out to three or four different stops to pick up probably 10,000 pounds here or 20,000 pounds there ... You've worked, if you've done 80,000 pounds in the course of the day plus stripping trucks in the morning. You've worked.

Now today, we had one load of steel that had been already refused two or three times because it was late getting there. So we had an appointment for eleven o'clock. Now at half past ten the dispatcher says to me, "Do you want to take your half-hour lunch, and then go and deliver that load?" If I had've taken my half-hour lunch, then went and delivered that load, I would have been three-quarters of an hour late, and they probably would have refused it again. So now you get rid of that, you run down to this other load, then you run back to the garage, you fuel all your trucks and you get everything ready, and you try to do the best you can so you can get the heck home. Tomorrow morning at five o'clock the alarm's going to go off – zing, up again, to work for six o'clock and try like hell to be back again by seven o'clock at night.

This guy next door, he came to my door one night and he says, "You know who I am?" I says, "Geez, no." He says, "I'm your next-door neighbour." Now he was living there then five years and so was I. We had never met. I worked at six o'clock in the morning. I came home at six, seven, eight o'clock at night. Never saw him.

I've got a six-year-old Ford that I've just got 30,000 miles on. I don't have time to drive it. By the time I come back at six, seven at night, where am I going to go? The biggest mileage I ever put on that car is going home to Nova Scotia. I put more mileage on that car in four weeks down in Canada, down Novey, than I do here. I don't mind working, but I've thought sometimes, you know [pauses] enough is enough.

But you take a good job over here ... MBTA* is a good job – you don't work too hard. The state's a good job – you know, where you see them all resting on their shovels there. [Laughs.] But us guys couldn't do that. We couldn't take that kind of work. Because we were always built up to work, to work. Oh, no, we'd go crazy working for the state. When we were small, my father used to work in the shipyard, the Meteghan shipyard, during the war. He was a carpenter. And there was my oldest brother, my youngest brother, and I. Now, we'd get up at four o'clock in the morning. We'd do chores in the morning, then we'd go to school at nine o'clock. He'd come home at four-thirty or five o'clock, we'd do barn chores, then back out in the fields until eight or nine o'clock at night. When the weeds came out, you'd be out there weeding. Or we used to go out with a bucket and pick up potato bugs. Go out in the rows after supper, with each a can, pickin' up potato bugs. After school in the wintertime, chopping the wood for firewood for the next year. One year, all the hardwood, the bugs got in them. Some worms got in them. They got big nests and killed all the oak and white ash and that stuff. And we had to cut those trees because they were all going bad. Within a couple of years they would have been no good anyway. And if you don't think we were tired! I was twelve years old. I wasn't very big. That's how you get paws like this. [He shows me his hands; they're big.] Everything you did, you did it with these hands. You pitchforked with them, you chopped wood with them, you picked up stones in the field in the spring. I don't know where those stones came from! Sometimes I really wondered if they weren't growing, because you'd pick them all up, and the next spring, when that frost came through, some more came up again.

The worst job that we had down there was when we went in that seaweed. When the tide would come in, it would bring the seaweed, or a big windstorm would bring the seaweed. So you'd go there in the morning and pick up as much as you could, and you'd put it in a big pile. When there was no more, you'd haul it to the house. You'd throw that under the barn, and you'd mix that up with your cow manure. This would be on a good rainy day, water up to your hips, with rubber boots, and one pushin' it so far, and you pushin' it and trying' to spread it all around, so it would all rot together. It was cheaper than fertilizer. But it was hard work. Your eyeglasses

---

*   The Massachusetts Bay Transport Authority runs the subways and buses in Boston.

would steam up and you wouldn't see out of them for the rest of the day. It wasn't too healthy.

Like I say, I don't mind working. And I've made good money. I'm putting the kids through college. I went down home in '69 and I bought my mother a house. I modelled it up, I straightened it out, and I made a nice house for her. I took all the shingles off, I did all the inside, I put in a new well, I put in a new cesspool, bathroom, I did all the upstairs. Every time I went home, that's all I did, the whole month. It was no vacation, but my mother enjoyed it. And when I finished working on that house, I says to the good ol' Lord – the Lord and I talk once in a while – I says, "If she can stay in this house five years, I'll be happy." When I bought it, my mother was seventy-five. When she died, she was eighty-seven years old. She was living there like a queen, honest to God. So it's not too bad. I've got that house there, and this house here in Somerville is not too bad either. And you know, anyway, that you have to produce. With the truckin' business, thirty years ago when you got a ten-cent raise they told you they were going out of business so you'd have to produce. Today they're doing the same thing. You *have* to produce, there's no question about it. If I'm going to work for you, and you're going to give me ninety cents, I have to give you a dollar, right? So we know that you have to produce.

From the Harvest

The Harvest Excursions, which operated from 1890 until 1928, brought tens of thousands of labourers from eastern Canada to work for short, intense periods on the farms of the West. Railways offered special excursion fares (usually around twenty-eight dollars return) as far as Winnipeg, or sometimes to Moose Jaw, and rates varied from half a cent to a cent and a half for every mile west, or on a branch line, after that. Conditions were sparse. Harvesters travelled in what the Canadian Pacific Railway called "colonist cars," equipped with slatted seats that pulled out to form crude beds, as did the berths above them. Once in the West, the harvesters' work was divided into two main parts – stooking and thrashing. When the grain had been cut and tied into sheaves by binders, it was stooked, or stacked, so many sheaves to a stook. After that, the stooks were gathered and brought to the threshing machine, or separator, which would then beat the wheat from the straw.

It was by "hitting the harvest" that many young Maritimers first came to leave home in these years. From there, however, many found their way not back home but to New England. As historian A.A. MacKenzie puts it in his essay "Cape Breton and the Harvest Excursions, 1890–1928," "It is ironic that the harvest excursions, intended partly to settle the Canadian West, helped thousands to escape to Boston."

KEN RING – North Kemptville, Yarmouth County, Nova Scotia

"Work is my whole life. I like to work. I've worked about seven days a week all my life." In his early seventies, he is up at 5:00 A.M. every morning and off to work operating a punch press in a machine shop on the waterfront in Hingham – a job he took after reaching retirement with the wrecking firm he worked with most of his life. He lives in Weymouth, Massachusetts.

It was August 10, 1928, and there was Selwyn Ring, Billy Roberts, Dave Travis, and myself. We went to Saint John and picked up the train there, and it was around nine o'clock at night when we pulled out of Saint John. And somewhere along the line, the train was doubled up – there were actually two trains, eleven cars each, and it ended up with twenty-two cars. They were what they called "colonist cars" – there was very little upholstery in them.

So we got on those, and we went three or four days, I guess. And the first place that particular train ended up was in Winnipeg. In Winnipeg they had agents in the station who would come and talk to each little group of people: "So, where do you want to go?" He gave us choices. We picked a little place in Alberta called Oyen.

We worked for a guy by the name of Todd. Well, he got you up at five o'clock, and before six in the morning you were out in the field working. His wife had a helper, a girl, and her daughter to help her. She'd stoke us up with food early in the morning, and then at ten o'clock she'd come out with five gallons of coffee and sandwiches. At noon, they'd shut the separator down, and we'd jump in the car. That's where I learned to drive – an old Chevy out there in the wheat fields. I didn't tell them I couldn't drive. [Laughs.] So we'd go in and eat a big lunch. Eat! My God, could we eat. And then in the middle of the afternoon she'd come out with another five gallons of coffee and more sandwiches and stuff. And then you'd come in at six o'clock at night and you'd have a big, big supper. And by seven o'clock, you were asleep again. Sundays we used to saddle up one of the old thirty-year-old broncos, and go hunting for coyotes.

Stooking and thrashing: each operation was about two weeks, if I remember. We were there a month. First you'd stook: cut all the wheat down and then pile it up in stooks, sheaves – pile the sheaves together. The stooking by hand – it was hard work, but it got to be fun. The reapers would cut them down and leave them in wind-rows, and you'd go along and stook them. You'd grab them by the twine and slide them down over your knee, and you'd keep on building, and you'd build a big stack.

So we were about two weeks doing that. He had fourteen hundred acres in wheat. And after all the wheat was cut and stooked, he had thirty horses. Each man had a team of horses, a cart and a fork. And you'd drive your team of horses up alongside of these stacks of wheat, and you'd pitch them on till you got a half-decent load, and then you'd drive up to the threshing machine, one load on each side of the belt. This is what they called a separator – a forty-eight-inch belt. And you'd just pitch the sheaves of wheat off onto this belt, head first. Then there was a bunch of knives, whirling at high speed, used to cut the twine. And of course it would beat all the wheat off of the straw. So the wheat would go into a hopper and the chaff, the straw, would blow out.

It was fun. Of course, I'd heard about it because the other guys in the village had gone years before. But as it turned out, that was the last excursion that ever went, because the next year, these machines started [combines] that used to go right out into the field and cut the tops off the wheat and spit the straw out behind them. The wheat itself would go into a truck, and they'd both move along together. So there was none of this binder stuff.

After that I came back and got a job working in the woods in Kempt, cutting hardwood. It was being sold to the clothes-pin factory in Carleton.* I worked there until March, and then I came to Boston. March 1929.

I had a cousin over here who worked in a garage, and he kind of had the skids greased for me. I went right to work the next day after I got here, in Cambridge. So I was a grease monkey for a few years.

---

*   Carleton is approximately ten miles from Kemptville, on the road in to Yarmouth.

I've hardly missed a day since I left. I quit one job in May, and I went home for two months. I came back and I got a job the very day I got back, which happened to be Dominion Day, the first day of July. I had a lead that I followed up. I got off the boat at seven o'clock in the morning, drove to Quincy, ate my breakfast, and went down to this gas-station place where this guy had his office. He came in at nine o'clock and I got the job and went to work that night. Eleven to seven, night attendant at a gas station. Park Square, Boston. So one thing led to another, and I haven't loafed since.

But the gas station was a bare existence, and finally I put my name in at Walter Baker's – chocolate mills in Dorchester – and I got a job in there. It was the winter. That was a seasonal job. They didn't have refrigeration when I first went there, so in the cool weather we were on, but in the spring when the warm weather came, they had to shut down. But I had contacts with the gas stations, so I always had summer work.

I was on at Walter Baker's six or seven years. I worked in the cocoa department. But that was getting to be a hard job – a lot of pressure on you there. They were always at you to do more, push the machines more. And I never liked shift work. You'd work two weeks, midnight till eight in the morning. And then you'd change – two weeks eight in the morning till four in the afternoon. And then two weeks, four in the afternoon till twelve at night. You'd change every two weeks. You could never get your system acclimated. I'd get home in the morning, eat my breakfast, and go to bed. And I'd probably sleep one or two hours, good, and then I'd hear a pin drop all day long. And by nine o'clock at night – I'm telling you! And then at ten you'd have to get up and go to work. It's a wonder I ever found the place to *go* to work. I'd be dead beat.

You were supposed to feed the machines to capacity. The machines pushed *you*. The machines I ran covered three floors of the mill. There were some sixty-odd electric motors driving different parts of it. We used to make thirty tons of cocoa a day.

The cocoa beans are roasted, then they're put through a cracker, and they're cracked all up and the hulls are sucked away one way and the kernels go in through grinding machines. The grinding wheels – one wheel's going one way and the other's going the other way, and this stuff feeds in between. And it runs like a chocolate syrup out the other end. Well, that is loaded with cocoa butter. So we had big presses down in the basement of the mill. They took, I think, 2,200 pounds each of that liquid – and it's red hot. They loaded up with this hot liquid, and they'd press the butter out of it with this big twenty-two-inch piston. That machine was as long again as this room. The big piston in the end would squeeze that liquid, and the fine stuff would get filtered out. And the residue – these cakes would be about two inches thick and about the size of the piston. They'd fall down on a belt underneath the machine, then they'd go down the belt and through a round thing with some spikes on it, and they'd try to cut it up a little bit. And there was a six-inch pipe with a suction on it, and it'd be sucked up that pipe, right from the basement up six floors. That's when I'd take it over – automatically, by machinery. That cake was still hot, so it used to have to go through refrigerated tubes.

But things used to plug up. When they plugged up, you'd break something or you'd spill. And Lord God, you were just running! As I say, the machine, its different parts were on three different floors, and when you had a spill, the quicker you could get there and shut the thing off, then get it going again, the less work you had to do to clean it up. You didn't wait for the elevator – you *ran* the stairs. So, I mean, nothing ever went right. It kind of got on my nerves after a while. After six years, that's about all I could take of it.

Then World War II came along, and I had a chance to get into a machine shop. Selwyn had worked a while at Walter Baker's, too. [Selwyn Ring, though roughly of an age with him, is his nephew. He had also gone out west and come home with Ken in 1928.] Selwyn came up here two or three years after I did, in the 1930s, but he got into Baker's before I did. And he had a good job – in the end there he was a supervisor. But he had left and gone into a machine shop in the Harbour Building [on Atlantic Avenue] in Boston. I had a chance to get in there – which I thought would be nice because I liked to run machines. I'm not a machinist, but I used to run lathes. So I went in there to work.

But after that, the machine shop, why, it kind of slowed down. And this guy I happened to know was in the wrecking game. He got me a job there – which doubled my income too – and I was twenty-five, thirty years in the wreckin' racket. And it was hard work, but then the wrecking business changed from hand work to machines. I was lucky. I had a job as a foreman. I sat in the car all day with a two-way radio, keeping my finger on what was going on. So I did alright. It was a good job.

Selwyn Ring moved back to Yarmouth County in the 1940s. Ken visits home every other year in his immaculate 1967 Cadillac, but he says he never seriously thought of moving back for good.

"I guess my memory roots are down there," he says. "But what would I do down there? I'd go crazy."

And what about missing home when he was a younger man — I press him a little — when he was not especially enjoying working in the chocolate mill in the 1930s?

"Oh, I missed it, yes. I missed the kids I had grown up with. But after all, I couldn't see going home and living off my folks when they couldn't hardly make a go of it themselves. Uhh! [Shivers.] My father, all he ever lived on was guiding American sports — as we used to call them — fishermen. They'd come down for trout fishing. He probably made five or six hundred dollars a year off them. And then we raised our own vegetables, and our own beef and poultry and eggs. And we existed. So I figured I was going to make a go of it on my own or else."

OWEN CALDWELL – Arlington, Kings County, Nova Scotia

A well-appointed home in Boston's Jamaica Plain. An antique Ford with 1957 Nova Scotia plates sits in the garage. An antique piano from Amherst is the centrepiece of the living-room where we talk. A huge "Vote Reagan" poster dominates the kitchen. Irene, his Italian American wife, is an ardent member of the conservative caucus of the Republican Party. A small, wiry man, Owen is a carpenter and building contractor in his late seventies.

I come from a large family. We were very close in the sense that what one had, we all had. We worked together. But we all realized very young in years that we'd have to get out and get scratchin' in order to survive. I would say that I left school between thirteen and fourteen, and went to work for a farmer in the Valley, Henry Blanchard, in Woodside. That was a place that I enjoyed workin'. I worked long hours, no Sundays off – from six o'clock in the morning till some nights ten or eleven o'clock at night. Pickin' apples and potatoes, and general farming. The first day I went to work for him, I picked up forty-three barrels ["burls," he says] of potatoes, after I dug them out by machine. And then I put them up in the cellar, with the windlass, through the shuttle there. I wasn't very big and I wasn't very strong, so I'd roll them onto the old wagon. Then I would bring the cows up and milk them. He had thirteen cows. I had to go down and get the cows on horseback because the old bull chased me. I stayed with Henry two years, two seasons.

I took one fall off and went out to the Canadian West. That was a big deal for boys in their teens, to go west. I and my three brothers went out in 1921. That particular fall, the Nova Scotia government wouldn't give us a cheap fare out of the province, so the boys of the Canning area – there were six of us, two other boys, myself, and my three brothers – we went to Saint John, paid the full fare to there, and then we got a half a cent a mile from there on. We went to Hamiota,* that's near Saskatchewan, and then went on a side train to a place called Brandon, which cost us, I think it was two-something extra. And we were hired there by farmers. Each farmer took two – there were six of us – and I was one of the youngest of the six, so I went with my oldest brother. At that time we got $7.50 a day for stooking, and nine dollars for thrashing.

Where did you all get the idea to head out there?

In those days all the boys were going west. It was the custom. The year that I went, the farmers in the West came in with tears in their eyes, looking for men to do their stookin' and their thrashin'. That fall there were between three and four thousand went out. There were three or four train loads.

Wouldn't that have made a shortage of men for the harvest at home?

The farmers didn't like it in the Valley. When Aldershot** opened each year, and the harvest in the West, it would leave some of the farmers short for apple pickin'. But then the coloured fellas used to come in from up around Aldershot there – they came down in the Valley in a big way – and I can never remember as a young man that the farmers didn't get their apples picked.

How would the money compare to working on the harvest in the Valley?

In them days in the Valley pickin' apples, if you were good, you might make $2.40 a day – if you picked hard all day. That's what we went west for, was the money. It was a chance to get out. Some of them would stay out and go on out to Washington and go in the mills there. And they'd cross over into Oregon – that's great lumber country there. I had uncles went out there and never came back.

But it was a lot of hard work, twelve hours a day – for a little better than two months, about nine weeks. We were in the field at six o'clock, come in for dinner at eleven o'clock. And at four o'clock, we'd have a nice lunch way back in the field. The women of the house, the girls inside, would bring us a nice feed – sandwiches, tea, and coffee. And then at seven o'clock at night we had a big feed. A *big* feed. And nothing to do but just run around the haystacks, and

---

*   Hamiota, Manitoba is approximately forty miles northwest of Brandon.
** Camp Aldershot, near Kentville: a militia summer training camp.

then retiring. And of course we would be exhausted. And then every Saturday night they'd take us to town.

The area we were in was mostly Englishmen. The farmer's name was Mr Bullwell. I hadn't heard any name like that as a little boy in the country. I thought it was funny, and we used to laugh about his name. But he was a typical Englishman, just came from the old country. It was maybe a few years since he'd taken up this government land. And the other Englishmen farmers, it was all land they had gone out and taken up from the government.

And now that year, a couple of the boys made more money than I did – more per day – but my brother and I were a little more fortunate in that we got a couple days they didn't get. And so I would say I had maybe between $400 and $450 when we left to travel again. We had an agreement between us, whoever got through first would pick up and follow the rest, rather than splitting up out west, because we were going on to Saskatchewan.

So we laid in the station all night, the six of us, wondering if we were going out further. But when the train came in, and it came east, we got on and went. By that time we were in Dutch with the station master for making noise, as we had promised to be quiet – and he warned us that he wasn't going to fool around any longer with us. So the train came and we all jumped on. It came into Winnipeg and we changed. We spent half a day or so in Winnipeg, and then we got an excursion for Saint John, New Brunswick. And we were about six days coming back – five or six days going out and we were five or six days coming back.

That fall, my father had about three or four acres of potatoes. As young boys, we felt we had nothin' in common with our father, and the attitude was, "You put your potatoes in, you can get them out." I was going back to Henry Blanchard's, and I was going to go to school. But my mother said, "You boys, now, you help your father. You all go and help get the potatoes out and then you can all separate, you can go back and do whatever you're going to do." And that's just what we did. We helped Dad, and in the time we weren't fightin' and arguin', we were workin', and workin' hard, gettin' the potatoes out. And then when we got the potatoes all out, I went back to Blanchard's and did chores for a while, helping him get the apples and the potatoes and the grain in and whatnot. I got fifteen dollars a week – and my books, he bought me my books. I went to school up there for the winter, and I stayed all winter. I went to school on horseback, and they were good to me.

The year that I went west was the year that my sister, Bessie, who was about nine years older than myself, had come home for a vacation from the States. She was living in Philadelphia at that time. But Bessie had gone back to the States when I came back in the fall. Most of my brothers and sisters had followed her to Philadelphia. She was married at the time – and we all went up there. So the spring that I was sixteen, I went to Philadelphia. My brother and I, we went to Philadelphia. In 1922. We left home about, I'd say, June the twenty-eighth or twenty-ninth. By the time we got in Philadelphia and got a pair of long pants – I had knickerbocker pants, in those days we had what we called short pants and long pants – it was the Fourth of July. I got my first suit in Philadelphia, a little brown suit. I think I paid twelve dollars. I had no money when I got in Philly, and I borrowed eight dollars from my brother.

I went to work out on house work, carpenter work, out in the suburbs – way eight and ten mile out of the city. In all the years I was in Philadelphia, I can only think of one time I worked within the city limits, when I didn't have a long way to go night and morning, working out on suburb homes. But one thing it did for me – it gave me experience in how to hang doors, and fit doors, and how to lay out roofs, and how to figure in gables ... I'd hire on as an apprentice – in my young years, you see – working for different builders. And then by the time I was old enough to call myself a carpenter and hire for the wage, I was with the government.

I lived in Philadelphia till I was twenty-seven year old. And when I was twenty-seven, I came up here to Boston. I'd been to Nova Scotia the year before to see my girlfriend – she was from down Blomidon way, Medford [Nova Scotia] really – and when I came waltzing in she said she was going to Massachusetts to live. I picked up and came here. I left all my brothers and sisters in Philadelphia. At that time there were five or six sisters in Philadelphia and three brothers, and nieces and everything ... I never went back to Philadelphia to live after that. When I came to Boston I liked it so well, I never wanted to live in Philadelphia again.

At that time I had a car here. I had a little convertible. I was with another fella and we were workin' out in Belmont. But that was the depression, and then there was no work for nobody. The government was taking over a lot of homes and fixing them, and myself and a boy who I had worked with, we went in to qualify to get on with the government as contractors. Remodelling houses and fixing them. I went with the HOLC.* It was all competitive bid. Any job I ever got I had to figure for. And I would be the first to tell you

* The Home Owners' Loan Corporation.

there were jobs I lost because of my education. When I figured jobs, I stayed up all night and figured them – and that was one thing. But when I figured them under competitive pressure, I didn't get them. In other words, it was all open bids, and when I figured them, and my bid and the others were so close that we had to go in an ante-room and figure them all over again, well, I wasn't as fast as the other boys. They could get out of the booth and be ready twenty minutes ahead of me – and I didn't get them. But when I could stay up all night and figure the job, when I had the time, and could draw up my little plans, I could get the job.

I had an education there equivalent to about sixth grade. Could poorly read or write. I felt so [pauses] incomplete as a human being, as an individual, to compete with what was before me. I went to night school off and on for maybe twelve years. I went to Franklin Union. I went to Boston Trade School. I took a course in estimating and drawing. I was one of the best students he had, he said. My problem was to designate, designating a piece of work ... But I went into the class late, and they'd had that before I got there, so Jesus, I was sweatin' gumdrops when the teacher would walk by me. Here I was a matured man, and with the government, and couldn't desig-nate a piece of work. Jesus, I couldn't understand that! I didn't know what to do. I didn't want to quit, 'cause I wanted to get help. After a month I got onto it, and I finished off good. I got my dip-loma. I didn't do it exactly, but my teacher said, "Caldwell, he gets the answers. He doesn't do it the way we teach here, but he gets the answers." [Laughs.]

So I stayed with the government the best part of eleven years, repairing houses. They never disqualified me. I went up the ranks on their scale as one of their reliable contractors. And meantime I got into the real-estate business. I've always been interested in property since I started. I had a good friend, an old gentleman from Maine, old J.B. Cavanagh, and he had quite a bit of real estate. He only went to second grade in grammar school, but he was one of the smartest men I ever met. And in the years when he was buyin', I always did his drawings. He'd buy an old house and I'd make up his apartments. I'd say, well, the stairs should go here and the door should be here and this should be here and whatnot. I stayed with him, and after he passed away, his widow told me that Joe had said to her, "If you don't keep this property that you have here, why, give Owen the first chance on it." So she did. And I doubled my money on that, and then some. So I had a few breaks in that sense. I had a good friend in Joe. I got along good. Of course, when you bought years ago, you bought for a song. I had forty-some apartments, and when I began to sell them is when I really cleaned up. I bought some of them for $3,000 and $4,000, sold them for $30,000. Some I bought for $10,000, sold them for $50,000. So I made some money in real estate. And in that way I always had plenty of money to buy gas and go home and do things I wanted to do. I wasn't very old before I quit working in the wintertime altogether. In the last twenty-five years, I quit every year on November 11 – pulled all my equipment in. I won't take a job after November 11. So ... I don't feel bad at all. I've worked hard and I've enjoyed every bit of it. I've got a lot of property, I've made a lot of money, and I feel I've been rewarded for all my efforts. I have that feeling.

I always said I love America. I love America because it's a country you can get down in and you can make out. They have a saying here: "You can make it in Massachusetts." And I say, "You can make it here in America." I think this is a great country. I can say with great honesty, just as if I was born here: I love America.

A different kind of love than you have for Nova Scotia?

[A long pause.] I've asked myself that. An old man said to me one time, "Owen, don't be ashamed of a place," he says. "You know, you can love one place and not hate another place." Sure, I love Nova Scotia. Nova Scotia is my birth place. But as much as I have loved Nova Scotia, as a child and as a man, I love America for what America stands for, and I think I know what America does stand for. Now, in Canada – as much as I wouldn't want anybody else saying anything about Canada or Nova Scotia – but in Canada, it's patterned off of England a lot. Unless you're born into a higher ... say, unless your father was in the bank, or your father was this or that, it's awful hard to get off the ground. *Awful* hard, back in them days. In this country it was different. In other words, when I filled out an application blank and they asked me my qualifications to become a contractor for the government, they asked me, "How much money you got? Who will recommend you? Can you do the job? Give us, on paper, where you did these jobs." I did it. I qualified. Now in Nova Scotia, it wouldn't have been like that. They wouldn't give you an application blank, if your father, or your uncle ... If you weren't a man of some importance you would never get an application blank. Say Canning. I was brought up on the North Mountain. If I went down in Canning, and I put "Caldwell from the North Mountain ..." [He screws his face up in mock scorn.] "Why should I bother with this Caldwell guy? The hell with him. Give it to Dickie here. Give it to Bigelow – Bigelow does all the big work around here." When I was a boy, when I was going over to Henry

Blanchard's and going to school, it was the Blanchards, it was the Dickies, it was the Kinsmans, it was the Bigelows, that built the ships there in Canning, the three-masters. And Chase's gang. Chase was a big dealer. And that fella that got killed on the railroad crossing.* It was these guys, it was these fellas, that did the work. You couldn't get in beyond the circle – no way possible. Not usin' the language that I was usin', that hadn't any further than sixth grade in grammar school, hardly able to read and write.

In this country, they didn't ask me where I was born, who my father was, where my father worked. They said, "What can *you* do? How much money have *you* got? Who will recommend *you*?" Well, I thought of the big companies around here. I went to a big company – I was buying lumber off of them. He wrote me a letter: "To whom it may concern ..." That was one. I went to a woman I did a job for over on the Arborway.** She wrote me another. "To whom it may concern," that I was trustworthy. I got three of them. And I had a little money, because I was savin' ten dollars a month, every month. Even when I was living with my sister in Philadelphia, every month I put away ten dollars. So it wasn't very long and I had $2,000 in the Building Loan Association in Philadelphia. So I had that money to buy stock. And I had some land. I had a brother that had come to the States, who was eleven years older than myself, and had returned back to Canada and went into business, and this was G.L. Caldwell. He went into business making apple barrels for the Valley. He had a shop in Delhaven [Kings County, Nova Scotia]. He had about eleven men working for him. And at that time he was buying a lot of cattle and having a big auction every year, and buying farms, farm land, and timber lots. So after we came to this country, both my brother and I – another brother, a year and a half older than myself – we used to give him the little money we would make and we'd buy these farms ... And I had these people recommend me, saying, "He is trustworthy, he is qualified to do this job." And I was accepted. I was in the good graces. And that's all that was necessary. But I couldn't have got that in Canada. Who would have given me a job of any importance? I hate to say that, but I know damn well it's true.

---

* Charles Wright, a building contractor and business associate of Hantsport industrialist R.A. Jodrey, died in an automobile-train collision just outside Falmouth, Nova Scotia, in 1929.
** A street in Jamaica Plain.

And you never thought of moving back?

My older brother and I, we got out of work in Philadelphia one winter, and he wanted to go home. My other brother, he only had the money to get as far as Boston, so we paid his way. That was my first time home after we were up here, you see, and we wanted to go home bad. I guess we were homesick to see Mom and Dad that winter. And then when spring came, around April or so, we came back to the States and went to work again. We got that out of our system.

But I can't say that I ever had any inclination to go back and work. When I went back there it was all pleasure. It was all going down there and pickin' berries, catchin' trout down in the stream – there are four or five brooks there where you can catch speckled trout – and hangin' around with the young crowd, with my sport models. I had a Cadillac, sport model – red top, white with red upholstery. There were two or three single girls around, you know ... and I had beautiful teeth in those days, and curly hair, and wore right down to a frazzle, skinny ... And I always used to enjoy the girls. And I'd stay about five weeks and then I'd come back – back to work. Back 'n' at it. And I would say, "I don't give a damn how hard I have to work now for the next twelve months, so long as I'm going home now next August."

I remember my sister saying, "Owen, you're going back tomorrow. How do you feel about going back?" And I said, "Maggie, Maggie, now that my time is up, I'm just as anxious to go back as I was to come." See, I was a young man, and I more or less ... felt this would be [struggles for the right words] – that here's where the money was, in my business. The money was all in this country – and all the excitement for us. The family, as a family, they spent their lives all in Philadelphia, and died in Philadelphia, and are buried in Philadelphia. There were thirteen lived, and there were eleven in Philadelphia and two that stayed home in the Valley. The rest all came to Philadelphia. We couldn't stay there and work on the farm ten, twelve hours a day for two or three dollars, when there was a better opportunity for us boys ... And the girls all married Philadelphia boys. So all the attraction was Philadelphia.

But after I came away there was never a payday I didn't have five dollars for Ma, and sometimes ten. And I'd collect it off Lee and Bob also – those are my brothers – and I'd send Mother and Dad anywhere from twenty to thirty dollars every week. I always helped my mother. And my father too. When I'd go home, my biggest thing, I'd buy Dad two or three bottles of liquor. He liked brandy and stuff like that. He had a little desk in front of his table – he had it filled with liquor bottles. He drank heavy before he had a large family, and while the family was growing, he never drank. And when he retired, he started drinkin'. He had a few hundred dollars, and he spent that on heavy liquor. Then after, my two brothers in Philadelphia, we got together every week and made up a little pot for Mother and Dad. And we did that for two or three years, and then Dad passed away, and when he did, Mother came up here to Philadelphia to be with the gang, and went on to Los Angeles. She had two sisters out in Los Angeles. One of them had an embalming business. A very wealthy woman. And she went out there and spent two years with her sisters, my aunts, and then my sister went out and brought her back to Philadelphia. And then I went down and had her back in Boston here. And she was up in Concord. She had a brother in Concord. Her brother had died, but she was up with the old lady.

She took a shock, a stroke. And then two or three of them came up from Philadelphia and took her back to Philadelphia and got her a wheelchair, and she lived nine months. And then instead of taking her back to Nova Scotia, the family got together and she was laid away in Philadelphia. They all wanted her there, and they'd asked her previous to this ... We knew she was passing on. So she was laid away in Philadelphia.

But as a family, we never forgot Nova Scotia, and every one of them, within the twelve-month period, they'd spend their vacation in Nova Scotia. Every year. The old home, I've seen it when there'd be six cars go down all at once, and they'd be sleeping all over the place – on the floors, in the kitchen, even in the barn. And we'd have, I'd say, a hell of a time. My one sister was in Ohio, we'd meet in Philadelphia, and then we'd all beat it for Nova Scotia. And we'd go up on the North Mountain and that old house in the Arlington Road there, and we'd park out there. I bought the old house from my brother, but in recent years I sold it to my nephew down there. It's got nine rooms, with a nice bathroom in it ... back in off the old country road ... spruce trees in back there, and the piazza runs all around the house. To me, that's one of the most beautiful spots on earth.

And I go up to the North Mountain, up to where I was born, and I sleep in the same room that I slept in when I was a boy. And I'll tell you, it was the happiest moment of my life, when I went to bed in that room, and my boy, when he was five year old, when he was alongside of me, and I looked out that window, and that moon was coming up in the same place it did when I was his age. I wouldn't put anything above that in the highlights of my life. That was the precipice of my time.

DONALD "DANNY" CAMERON –
Antigonish, Nova Scotia

Malden, Massachusetts. He is the Antigonish Donald Cameron who, following his mother's death, was raised by Duncan McRae and his sister.

My mother left home in 1892. And my father left home, Cape Breton Island, about the same time. They were married here. I was born in 1898, in Boston here, but I was only five months old when they shipped me to Canada. Mother wasn't well and she died shortly after. I was only four years old when she died. And I stayed there. Made a couple of trips out west on the harvest excursion.

I went out west in '23. Manitoba, the Carberry Plains. The fella that I was with – there were four of us with him – he had five milk cows. So we milked the cows for him in the morning and then we started just about daylight, and we would work there until just darkness. But the food was so good, and you were fed so good. It wasn't three meals a day, it would be four big meals you would have. And the money. You were getting nine dollars a day and your board, and that was big money them days. There was no such thing as income tax, and a dollar was a dollar. And the food! Breakfast, dinner, and supper was like a wedding. I never saw such food in my life, and all the boys and all the men that ever went out there will tell you the same thing. I'll tell you, at four o'clock in the evening you'd see the woman of the house, she'd have a big Mc-Laughlin Buick, they called it in them days, to move those great big baskets of sandwiches, cakes, and coffee and tea. And "Boys, let us sit down." Then you'd have a little smoke, you know.

Did you know when you went out that you were going to this spot in Carberry?

Oh no. We landed there in Winnipeg at eleven o'clock at night. And there were three guys – one from Manitoba, Saskatchewan, and Alberta. And you would talk to them, you know, and this fella would say, "Well, such and such a place to go to," and all that. That's how they hired you. And then the next day we went on the train. You see, your ticket from down east was only $27. And from Winnipeg on west, wherever you were going, it was half a cent a mile they charged. Well, we went 135 miles, I think, to Carberry. We got out there, and there was an employment office, and the fella, the farmer, would come in and hire you. And we were there till we finished.

Did that daylight-to-dark routine pretty well do you in?

Well, we were used to it. It wasn't so hard. I drove a team on the harvest. I drove four horses on the binder. And stookin', well, that took about three weeks. Then they'd start with the thrashin' after that. And we were there till we finished and then we went out to Swift Current, Saskatchewan. We worked there for a fella by the name of Rogers. He was a very fine man, too. We finished out there, then, later. Oh, I'll tell you, it was a lovely place. Not too far from the American border. The West is a beautiful place.

But I didn't come here from the harvest. I went back home to Nova Scotia. Working in different places. Working in the lumber woods, and here and there. I worked in the car works in New Glasgow, and I had a pretty damn good job. It was called the Hamilton Car Works them days. There was one summer they had a big job there for the Russian Railroad, for making refrigerators. That was $72 a week, and that was good money, them days. But it went just as fast as I could spend it [laughs], like every other foolish man.

I remember one time, I wasn't working at the time, but I happened to be in New Glasgow. I remember a delegation that came from Detroit – Ford. Ford wanted to build an automobile plant in New Glasgow, where the car works is today – or near there, Trenton. They shooed them out. They wouldn't allow them to come in. You see, in Ontario, there's a big plant there, the Ford plant. They've got two or three plants in Ontario, the Ford. And Ford wanted to come to Nova Scotia, to New Glasgow. He saw good prospects there. They wouldn't let him in.

That's one thing about the Maritimes. The western part of Canada, they were the dog, and we were the tail. They wagged us. The Maritimes got the shitty end of it, while Ontario and the West got the cream. They've always been doing that; they've always been doing it. Now I remember myself, when you couldn't get a dime in Nova Scotia, even when there were good times in the other parts. Now here's an example. The young teachers, a few years ago, would teach – you know, they'd start in September and they'd teach until the last of June – for $175 a year. All they'd have to pay of course was maybe $2.75 a week for board, unless they were boarding at home. They'd have nothing left, only a $90 grant they'd get from the government. I know – they went out with me on the harvest. The girls that went out on the harvest train, searching, the first year that those girls were there, they got $1,000 a year. They were giving them

$1,000 a year to teach in their little schools out there in the West. That's why all the girls left down east to go out west at that time.

I came to Boston from Timmins, Ontario. Things were bad, you know, '34, '35. You couldn't buy a job at home. I went to Timmins and thought I'd get in the mines, but I couldn't. I was hired, but I didn't pass for it. They were afraid ... In 1918 I had what they called the Spanish Influenza, and I had pneumonia with it, and it left a scar. And once you had a scar, they wouldn't allow you in the rock mines, on account of this what they called "silicosis." And the fella told me, the doctor told me, "You might never get it, and perhaps you'll be only six months when you'll get it." I've seen people that have died with that silicosis, and it's an awful thing. So I couldn't pass for the mines. And I couldn't get anything to do in the wintertime. I worked in the summertime there for the Canadian Oil Company, White Rose. So these two MacGillivary brothers, Ronnie and Jim, and I, we came in January to Boston. We came in by Toronto and Buffalo. And that was the first time, 1937, from the time I was shipped out as a baby, that was the first time I was back. And I had my birth certificate. It was hard to get in then – you know, hard times, depression. It was bad in the United States then. I know the other two fellas that were with me, Jimmy and Ronnie, they only got one month to stay and visit their brothers. They looked at my birth certificate and "Well," he says, "you go. You're OK. If you can get a job, take it."

Of course, you'd go down to the employment office here in the morning in them days, and you'd see a string as long's from here down to Maplewood Square.* Couldn't get a job. And then of course the war broke out shortly after that. You have to give Hitler the preference there, you know, that he started the ball rolling. Though he was a devil. It's a funny thing to me that they've got to have trouble, they've got to have war, to have industry and to have work. Now you take the depression of the thirties. My God Almighty! It was home in the Maritimes. It was here. It was every place. You couldn't get a job. You couldn't sell a damn thing. You couldn't get *nothing*. The minute Hitler took over Poland, why, the government took the purse strings off, they opened them up, and all kinds of work and money ... Of course, if there was no profit in war you'd never see one. If it wasn't for the profit that's in it for the big financiers and the big companies, there'd never be such a thing as war. Look at the money some of these big companies make. They don't care who's killed or what destruction is done. It's awful.

---

*   A central landmark in Malden.

I worked at the General Electric Company for years. I didn't get in there until 1940. It wasn't easy to get in there. Then of course when the war broke out, they'd hire anybody. There were 10,000 women in the plant during the war. There were 33,000 altogether then in the plant. See, the company didn't have to pay them. It was the government that was paying them. And after the war was over, oh, they let an awful lot of them go.

But that's one of the best companies you ever worked with, the General Electric down here in Lynn. They'd pay you good wages, and they'd even ... I never saw a place in my life that they'd come and ask you – I know I was asked two or three times – "Do you like your job?" They said, "We're gonna get you a better one." Right down here in Lynn. But we had a great union. One union. The UE. But they started: "There's nothing but communists in that." Even they were thinking that myself was one. You know what happened at the last of it? We had five different unions in the plant, and I left the union altogether. You see, one bunch would go out and the rest wouldn't go out at all. With one union ... we went out once, after the war, and we got what we were looking for. The UE was a damn good union, but then the IUE came in, and they split the thing up, and it's not worth a darn today.* They ruined it, especially the heads of the unions, the big shots. What I mean is, it's the great-

---

*   The UE, the United Electrical and Radio Workers of America, has always been noted for its rank-and-file militancy and socialist leadership, and Local 201, at the Lynn works of General Electric, is no exception. The Lynn plant was the first of GE's ever to be organized, which it was in 1933 under the leadership of Alfred Coulthard, who was also education director of the Socialist Party on the north shore of Massachusetts.

The 1950s were difficult times for the union. A major struggle emerged between the IUE (the International Union of Electrical, Radio and Machine Workers), a more conservative union with the backing of the Congress of Industrial Organizations, and the UE. The IUE won the day – barely – in a 1950 vote in the Lynn works, after which the GE workers there came increasingly to be represented by a whole series of unions, none of which was capable of leading a unified strike like the UE's long and successful battle against GE in 1946.

A core of UE activists remained in the GE plants, including the one in Lynn, despite the repression carried out against them in the 1950s under what was known as the "Cordiner doctrine," named after GE president Ralph Cordiner. In response to Senator Hubert Humphrey's 1952 congressional hearings against communist influence in the union movement, the electrical manufacturers adopted a policy in 1953 of firing employees who admitted to being communists, or who failed to clear themselves of charges of communist affiliation levelled by witnesses before congressional committees. Twenty-eight GE employees were fired under the Cordiner doctrine.

est thing in the world for the working man, organized labour. But how can any plant be organized when there's five different unions in the one building? The members of the union, they're the ones that are keeping the union up, but the big shots are getting the benefit. That's what's ruining it.

ANGUS CROWDIS – Big Baddeck, Victoria County, Nova Scotia

In his late eighties, his back is as straight as an arrow, his frame as thin as a rail. His native Gaelic has a pronounced presence in his speech, although it has been seventy years since he spoke it regularly.

A retired carpenter, he built the family house in suburban Belmont. There were so many carpenters from Nova Scotia in Boston when he came there in the 1920s, he says, laughing, that when "the boats were hauling in, you'd see them up on deck filin' the saws." He worked at the George Lawley and Son shipyard in Dorchester in the late 1920s, doing inside work on luxury yachts. "Oh, they were intricate yachts. Beautiful work. Everything balsa wood, mahogany ..." Later, he was a carpenter at the Hingham Shipyard, where destroyer escorts for Britain were produced during the Second World War.

When he returned from France after World War I, and before he left Cape Breton once more, Angus worked for a time in the carpentry department at the steel plant in Sydney.

From there we went to Detroit, in the year 1922. There were nine of us. Some of them didn't get across. In them days, if you were under eighteen, they wouldn't let you go. So one, his brother had to go over and stay by himself. We kept going to Detroit. We were there for two weeks. Couldn't get anything to do. Then we went to Buffalo, New York. We were there for a week. Then we came to Welland, Ontario. Got a job there. Welland is a nice place to work. A very nice town. We stayed there and worked all winter.

So we thought we'd come out to Massachusetts, another fella and I. A friend of mine was married to an American up here who was a foreman over in Everett, so I got a job where he was. I was only making five dollars a day. And I was supposed to work two weeks, days; and two weeks, nights; and so on – and here I was kept on the same job, nights, for four weeks. Of course, I was losing out on the parties – at that time I was still pretty young. So I was promised to go on days the next week. When I came in the morning, Monday, "No, come back when it's the next shift." I turned the thing over and I says, "No." I says, "I was promised to go on days, so I'm through." That ended my work there.

So I didn't get a job right away, nothing steady. Things weren't going too well at the time. I got along anyway. I went into the shipyard, carpenter work, building boats. But the depression came along in '29, '30, '31, and '32. There was *nothin'* doin'. Well I'll tell you, work was very hard to find. There was hardly anything in the shipyard. I had to go to work – just to pick up anything to do in the line of carpenter work – for 50¢ an hour. So I did two weeks. I said to myself, if I've got to work for 50¢ an hour, I'll go on welfare. And the funny part of it, the next day I went walking around – walking, of course, there was no other way to travel – and I saw a fella working, building a house, that I worked for in 1928. He hired me. I worked for him for six years steady after that. And then I took over the work and was doing it myself, and I didn't work in the shipyards anymore.

Yes, things were pretty tough then. People who were buying a house, they may have been paying on a mortgage for years and couldn't pay it, couldn't keep up the mortgage – they just threw them out. Fifty thousand in Massachusetts lost their homes that time, in three years. There were several that I knew myself.

People that had steady work for thirty years – *they* had nothing to do. Anybody that had a family, they could go in and they'd put them to work at something, two days a week, and the government would pay the full amount, whatever the wage would be. That's how it was at that time. I never applied for it. I could have, I s'pose – the unemployment, too.

My uncle, he was involved with the New England Telephone, and of course, there were many for the work to be done, so he was laid off for a while. His wife's father's cousin, or near 'round to it, he was a Representative in Quincy, I believe. So of course, he got in through him on the unemployment, on his regular job, two days a week where he had been. So, see, if you have a little drag with a politician, you're all set. But I don't know ... I hated to ever think that I had to go and beg for a job.

He had already been working away from home before going to the States, on a harvest excursion out west just after World War I ...

I left in July and came back in October. I worked for a farmer out there, in Saskatchewan. The man we worked for, he had two or three sections*, and he had his own outfit for thrashin'. Believe me, we weren't doing too bad at all. Six dollars a day and board. There

---

* Land area in western Canada is measured in sections. One section equals 640 acres, or a square mile.

were about ten or twelve of us, counting them who were running the outfit, and the drivers – there'd have been four horses, coming in one after the other and they thrashed about twelve hundred bushels a day. Going all day long, because they were in a hurry to get as much as possible in town first, because the price would be high.

I could have had a quarter section for nothing. All the veterans were given a quarter section. And the next section, you'd pay a dollar for each acre. Imagine! I suppose they'd give you the whole of Saskatchewan to make you stay there. [Laughs.] But I didn't like it at all. There was nothing much going on, just workin' on farms. And the air was so dry. No rain. All the time we were there I didn't see a drop of rain. And the horses, sometimes they'd be breaking their legs. The ground, it breaks, you know, it splits. I didn't like it at all. And the houses were so far apart. You'd be about a quarter of a, sometimes a mile apart, from your neighbour.

According, at least, to popular legend, the harvest trains that went out from Cape Breton were by far the roughest. His experiences lend some credence to the myth ...

That part of the train we were on was all Cape Bretoners. There were three boys with a certain talent for, when the train would stop to take on water, breaking into different places and getting all the liquor they wanted. Then they'd be drunk and raise Cain, and then the next stop again, they'd jump out, get all kinds of stuff – women's skirts and women's dresses, women's hats and shoes, men's suits and everything – and they'd take them into the rear car. Then they'd go all through the cars selling this stuff. But when they got out to Winnipeg, the leader and the boys were arrested.

I remember one time we went into a station, and there was a place run by a Chinese, and he was selling beer. Well, of course, the poor Chinese didn't know what was coming. The whole gang of them goes in, helps themselves, and then goes back in the car – and the poor Chinese went and hid somewheres. That was the kind of a gang that we're talking about. As you went along different parts, all the little stores and restaurants would be all boarded up. They had to. They took anything they wanted.

Aw, they were a wild gang ... It happened that the train was stopped. I don't know if it was taking in water or what it was doing – but they went and attached a long hose to another train, away maybe four or five cars from the rear. And when our train started off, my golly, you wouldn't dare hang your head out the window – that hose would've knocked your head off.

And then they went into a field and attached the hay rack, the hay wagon. It was somewhere near the road and they went and pulled it on the track and attached it to the rear. And oh boy, when that started to go ...

There was actually damage to the train we were on. Firing bullets ... Way down in between the seats, we watched bullets going over our heads. That was through New Brunswick. One fella was killed on our train. A father and son, they were going out west – the young fella was going to be a teacher, and the older man went out with him. It happened in the general station. He was out on the platform and he was killed. He was shot. He never knew what happened ... But after that the Mounties were taking care of it. The next year there were Mounties aboard the train from Cape Breton, watching what was happening.

LOUIS BANNISTER – Elgin, Albert County, New Brunswick

He lives in the upstairs flat of a house he bought from a fellow from Nova Scotia. The downstairs of the house he rents to a family from New Brunswick.

The Mt Vernon and Pearl area of East Somerville looks as though its aspiringly upwardly mobile days of urban middle Americana are mostly in the past. Many of the buildings look the worse for wear; kids stand around on the streets. Standing in front of his home, neatly dressed, tall and straight, he looks almost out of place here, despite the fact that he has lived in this neighbourhood for over half a century.

He was brought up one of eleven children on a farm in Elgin: "Wearin' the skin off our fingers pickin' the stones off the land." Pearl, his late wife, was from Harvey, New Brunswick. He is in his middle eighties.

I served in the Canadian army in World War I, for about a year – in Saint John and Sussex, around there. Four of us brothers were in the service at one time. Three, the older brothers, went overseas. I was the youngest. I never did get over. The war was done before they shipped me over. Then a while after we got out, my brother and I – he had been over in France for years – we went out west on the harvest excursion. I think it was 1920. We went from Saint John to Winnipeg, CPR. And when we got to Winnipeg, we talked to some people that had come back from a place that they told us about in Alberta, called Oyen. The people had good crops and they were hoping they would get some help. So we shipped from Winnipeg right across Saskatchewan into Alberta and into this little town of Oyen.

We got there – it was just a small village up on the prairie there – and we went over to the hotel and got some rooms. There were three of us – my brother and I and a friend. And we just got up in our room, and hardly got a chance to wash up when this farmer came in looking to hire us. So he hired all three of us. We said we wanted to stay there that night and have a good night's sleep – you know, take baths ... "Well," he said, "All right. I'll come out tomorrow and get you." He was a Scotchman. John Black was his name. He owned at least three-quarters of a section of land there, maybe even a section. He came out and got the whole three of us and we stayed there and did the whole harvest of stooking and thrashing. We stayed right there till he got all his crop done.

And he paid us off, and we went to Calgary. In Calgary we went down to the employment office to see whether they wanted men for the lumber camp in Crow's Nest, BC. So we all signed up and went to Crow's Nest.

I stayed there three years, in British Columbia. My brother and I, we'd get through in the lumber camp after the winter ... The logs would come down river in the spring, then the mill would start up and we'd work in the lumber yard. We'd summer there until all the lumber was cut, then go downtown for a while and whoop it up, and then we'd go back up in the woods in the lumber camps.

Then I came home one spring, intending to go out the following fall, on the harvest train again. But I never went out. Seems like I met a girl after I came back to New Brunswick – and I never went back out there.

Before World War I, I had worked in Saint John in longshore work. I worked some there after World War I, too, but then when I went out west, I let my union card run out. So I went down there and I renewed my union card, and I was working in Saint John doing longshore work for two winters after I came back. I met this girl that I married. I decided I wouldn't be going back, so I wrote to my brother and told him.

But there was nothing to do in the summer there – the ships were all up in Montreal. I spent one summer just hanging around, just fishing out of the harbour there – doin' nothin', just using up what money I had made from the winter before. I wanted to stay, on account of I was engaged to be married then. But you've got to get something steady ...

Well, I'll tell you, I had seen an ad in the Saint John paper for a man in a warehouse, something to do with candling eggs.* It was

---

* Candling is a means by which eggs can be tested for blood clots, staleness, and so on, by holding them up between the eye and a light.

right after the boats had stopped coming, and the port had shut down after the winter. So I went over to that place, and I went into the employment office and I talked to the fella, told him I was lookin' for a job. And he asked me, "What line of work have you been doing?" I said, "I'm a longshoreman. I've been working handling freight on the docks." "Well," he said, "you haven't had any experience in this kind of work?" "No," I said, "I haven't any." "Well," he said, "We don't want you. We want somebody that's had experience."

So I was pretty disgusted then. I was mad. Real mad. So I said, "All right, I'm leavin' this country. This is not for me." I came out and went to the United States Immigration Office and applied for a visa to come up here.

I came up to Boston with this friend that I had worked in the winter port with, sort of a relative – distant, through marriage. And I went just right down here [he points in the direction of down the street] to Hood's Milk, and put in an application for a job. Now here, when he asked what kind of work I did, and I told him, "Longshoreman, freight handler," he said, "Well, that's good heavy work. That's the kind of men we're looking for." [Laughs.] That's what he said! And my God, it was only about two days and they called me to come into work. He gave me a call and said, "Come on over. Be here at eight o'clock in the morning." I wasn't here a week when I had a job.

See, I made out all right after I got to the United States.

But anyway, Pearl, when I left for the States, she had said, "You go up and get a job and come back next fall and work in the port and then we'll both start out in the spring." But when I got a steady job, I wrote back, and I said I wasn't going back to the port. "I got a job here, I'm staying," I said. "You come up now or in the spring, whichever you like. But," I says, "it's good to hang onto this job while I've got it."

And I was there forty years in the milk business. Twenty-eight dollars a week – that's what I was getting. That was pretty good money then, very good money – and I think I lost one week's pay during the whole depression.

So anyway, Pearl came up in May that year or something like that, spent the summer down in Scituate* with her sister, and come August we got married – the last day of August. We got married in Roxbury. And then we moved here to Somerville. I took a little

---

*   A town on the coast, approximately half way between Boston and Plymouth.

apartment over on the next street, called Pinckney Street. We lived there about a year, didn't like it, so we moved over down to the foot of the hill there on Mt Vernon. We stayed in that flat for twenty-two years, and at the end of that time, I bought this house, and we moved up here.

I think I've been pretty successful in the United States. I've always kept my bills paid, and we paid for a house. No problem paying for a house. I've been very thankful. I've got a good home and a good life here. And [a long pause] ... and I felt that I owed this country something. Because when I was looking for something, they furnished me with a job.

Dances, Dancers, and Fiddlers

If there is one central symbol for the lives of Maritimers in Boston – in the 1920s, 1930s, and after – it is the great Saturday-night dances which brought them together. The Dudley Street area of Roxbury was best known for this, although there were many other dances as well.

Central, too, is the legendary figure of Cape Breton fiddler Alex Gillis, whose group, The Inverness Serenaders, both through dances and a regular Saturday-night radio program on Boston's WHDH, became the best-known practitioners of Maritime fiddling in Massachusetts.

RALPH MacGILLIVRAY – Antigonish, Nova Scotia

He ran dances in all of Dudley Street's great halls. Some of Boston's – and the Maritimes' – finest musicians played at his dances. Alex Gillis and the Inverness Serenaders were regulars with MacGillivray in the years before Gillis started up his own Dudley Street dances. Most of the fiddlers at MacGillivray's events came from the Maritimes, as did most of the dancers.

Many young men from the region, including Ralph himself, met the women they would eventually marry at his dances. People used to tell him, he laughs, that he was "running a marriage bureau down there."

"You'd get four or five or six hundred girls – they'd come in in groups. They'd be ready when the first dance was on, and they'd stay till the last. And they'd be nice girls, too."

Americans also came. "There were some that went into my dance," he explains, "didn't have anything to do with down home at all. They used to

*come along, some of them, Irish Americans, born here – they liked the
down-east girls. So I'd get a bunch of them, too."*

*After running down-east dances for over a decade, he sold out in 1934
and moved back home. Back in Antigonish, he continued to run dances –
on an outside platform he billed as "The Casino by the Sea." "But I got
tired of it there," he says, "and came back here. It was harder to make
money there than here." He is a carpenter by trade. "The building business
picked up some so I came back. And stayed."*

*He is in his eighties. We spoke at his home, not so very far from Dudley
Street, in nearby Dorchester.*

I always liked dancing. I attended dances when I was a kid before I
ever left home. When I came up here in 1913, I continued going. I
used to go to all the larger dance halls and ballrooms in the state. At
that time dancing was going very good here and they'd have some
very fine orchestras at times.

I joined the army when the United States got into the war –
joined the army and went to France. I stayed there and was fighting
over there. Then when I came back I used to go to the dances. I
used to prompt for them. And I helped a fellow run a dance in the
South End. I didn't help him very long. I had six months with him.
He drew a big crowd, but he didn't treat them very well, and he
drove them all away.

I started running dances myself about 1920. And I ran them till I
went to Nova Scotia about 1934. I played a run in Rose Croix Hall,
and a run in Intercolonial Hall, and a run in Hibernian Hall and a
run at Winslow Hall, right in that square of Dudley and Warren
Street. There was good transportation there. There were people from
different parts – from Malden, Cambridge, Somerville, and everywhere.

I generally conducted those dances on Saturday nights and
holiday nights, either before the holiday or the holiday night,
whatever suited me. I used to get a big crowd. I used to get eight or
nine hundred or a thousand.

Somehow or other I always felt, and the crowd told me, that my
dance was the best dance in Roxbury.

So what did it take to run a successful dance?

You had to hire a band and hire a hall and then get your advertising out. Advertise in advance, and if there was anything special that
you could think of that they'd be interested in – like if there was
some fella that was a very good step dancer, to do a step dance –
those things brought them. And once you brought them, the thing

was, make it interesting for them so they'll come back again. You want to get the best music you can get for them and have good order and don't let any crowd come in off the sidewalk and start trouble or something like that. I used to watch a dance from the time it started until I got the last person out, so that there'd be no trouble. I never had any troubles. Because generally I'd get rid of these guys. If some fella was inclined to be boisterous tonight, well, he wouldn't get in next Saturday night. I'd keep him out. I took care of that and that's why the same crowd would come in every Saturday or Sunday night.

There were only two of us that ran in opposition to each other, running the same type of dances. The other fellow, Joe Martin, was from Prince Edward Island. He used to get a big crowd, a Prince Edward Island crowd, and I got a lot of the others. Cape Breton, and Antigonish and Pictou County, and New Brunswick – I'd get them. Joe Martin ran a good time too and he kept good order. You'd have to, or the first thing they'd throw some extra police on you and if anybody turned around they'd get thrown out, and that didn't go over too well.

There was this one fella here used to attend the Prince Edward Island dance. He'd get full, and he'd get arrested. He got arrested so often that finally the judge said to him, "Look, next time you come in front of me on this charge, I'm going to deport ya." So this fella, he quit going to that dance and he started coming to my dance halls. Well, he got drunk at my dance, but I knew him pretty well. He never was a lot of trouble, for all that. There was a room upstairs that I used to use when I'd have an extra crowd, and I'd put Earl in there. His name was Earl Cochrane. I'd set him up in an old chair up there and I'd leave him. Sometimes the old chair wasn't very clean and he'd come out later covered with dust – he was a guy that dressed very well. He was a nice guy, too, and he had some very nice friends. His friends would go to the other dance, but they'd come in at the last of it and take him home. Earl never got pitched when it came to my dance. Otherwise, if he got arrested, that was it – 'cause the judge wasn't fooling around.

He had a sister that used to come in too, and she brought some of her friends from Prince Edward Island. And Earl, he wouldn't go to the other place at all. There's a lot of things you have to do if you're dealing with the public and you're going to be successful. I kept good order, and I tried to treat guys good.

ELIZABETH AND DONALD "DANNY" CAMERON – Black River, Inverness County, Nova Scotia and Antigonish, Nova Scotia

A piano, a music stand, and a fiddle dominate the living-room of their Malden home. The same Donald Cameron who went out west on the 1923 harvest excursion is also a fiddler. Elizabeth's sister, Catherine Mac-Pherson, lives with them. Elizabeth and Catherine are two of the twenty-two children of John and Mary Ann (Gillis) MacPherson. Elizabeth speaks first.

We came up in '22. My father died and the boys didn't want to stay on the farm. My mother came at that time. Oh, I'm telling you, it was lovely when I came up. It was really lovely. You could go out today and find a nice job. The United Drug was the first place I took when I came up here. That was down on Huntington Avenue, if I remember right. I went there and my God, look, I stayed there for a couple years, and I was a nut to leave it. I had the loveliest boss that anybody could ever have. Another girl, she was from New Hampshire, we were sitting at a table, and all we had to do was – medicine, like pills, any kind of pills, we had to sort them out – and if there was a spot on one, or a broken one or anything like that, we'd have to throw it away. His name was Mr Hyde. I never forgot him. And he wanted me to take care of the books on his floor. So he asked me, "Do you want to take care of the books on my floor? The girl is leavin'." "Oh," I said to him, "Mr Hyde, what would you do if I made mistakes," I said, "in the work?" He says, "You'd never have to be worried about that." He says, "I'll watch. Anything you can't do, come to me and I'll do it for you." I could do it. It was just the courage that I needed. When you're young you haven't got half the sense that you should have anyway. I didn't know enough to try it. All I had to do was try it. Oh, when I think of him ... And the day I was leaving, I sat on the chair and I cried. I really did. He was so nice to us. You know what I left it for? Catherine worked for a doctor in Chestnut Hill,* and my cousin was out there too. My cousin was leaving for down east, and Catherine was going to be alone, and they got after me to go out there. When I think of it today, I should have my brain examined.

---

*   A wealthy area, in Brookline.

You didn't find it hard adjusting to living in Boston?

Oh, I liked it. I'll tell you why. Half of the people that could ride came up here. Neighbours, girls and boys, they came up at that time. And I'm not telling you a word of a lie, we used to set the table three times on a Sunday, we'd have so many coming. Nieces and nephews of ours would come, and cousins, and oh, half of the neighbours came up by the time we'd eat. Young fellows, they used to come. We were never a day lonesome. And we had two diners, and working all the time ...

We lived in Roxbury the first years we were up, and there was a crowd there ... We used to have an awful lot of fun.

DONALD   The dances that went on in Dudley Street ... There were five halls going there strong.

ELIZABETH   They used to be lovely dances. Lovely dances, there. Oh, I love dancing. That's the only hobby in my life that I loved to go to. I didn't care for shows, movies, or anything, but where there was a dance hall, I'd be there. My God, the crowds that used to go! There was a bunch around then, so many down our way from, you know, down east. We knew everybody. You'd know half the people – more than half the people – that were in the hall. I'd be heart-broken if I ever missed a Saturday. I remember making three nights in the one week. And I was working! One night, I was working, and my hair wasn't ready at all. In them days you put the curlers on the fire in the gas stove – you know, curlers to curl your hair. And we were in such a hurry. This girl, she says, "I'll curl your hair," and she stuck the curlers in the stove. She made them too hot. Well, she took a hunk of hair this big [she makes a clump with her fingers] off my head, and I didn't think anything of it. It was a big joke to us. We combed it over. Then on her anniversary I wrapped the curlers – she got married after that, and an anniversary that she had, we were asked there – and I put a ribbon around them and gave them back for a present. She got an awful kick out of it.

We used to have such fun there. Those MacPhersons down in Framingham, there was a car-load of them used to come out, and nearly every night they'd drive us home – and that was the go-ahead with us. And this poor Mrs MacIntyre – we used to have enough of her. Her boys were living on the same street as we were, and there was one of them full of the devil. We used to talk – you know, just talk. We'd sit in the car talking for a little while. She thought, "This waste of time!" She didn't want us out any longer than coming home from the dance, you know. And she used to have a stick in her hand at the top of the stairway. And this night, Bart, one of her boys, was with us. And here the poor old soul, she was at the top of the stairs waiting – her with the stick in her hand, she was going to give it to us. So Bart caught me and threw me on his back and went upstairs that way. He didn't pay any attention to her. They were so full of the devil.

We had three brothers, lovely step dancers. There was a contest one night. That fellow over there [points to a picture], that's one of my brothers. And we went to a dance one night, they had a contest, you know, for step dancing, and there were forty altogether against him, step dancing. And he won the cup.

CATHERINE He was one of the best step dancers going. And then we had another brother, he was just as good, only that he was a little heavier on the floor. And my oldest brother danced awfully well too. My father was a wonderful dancer.

ELIZABETH He went to dancing school, my father. Of course, there were good step dancers them days. A good step dancer is lovely to watch. But it wasn't nearly as nice at our dances as the people from Scotland. I used to go to their dances too. They had them on Dudley Street, and I couldn't wait to get there. But their music was different. They had every old piece of music, you know, playing at the dances, and they danced so much nicer than our crowd did. We were dancing quadrilles, but they were dancing the schottische* and, oh, I just can't remember the names of the different dances they had. And they were a lovely, lovely crowd. I used to love to go there.

DONALD It was a meeting place, you know. Those two big halls right on Dudley Street there – the Intercolonial building and the Hibernian building. The Intercolonial Hall was a Canadian building, but the Hibernian Hall was Irish. Then just around the corner there was another called the Rose Croix Hall – it's a French name, from the Knights of Columbus. It was upstairs, and a very nice hall. Then down on Wirtle Street there was another hall there, and on Warren Street there was the Irish Hall.

ELIZABETH They were just in a circle.

DONALD You could walk from one to the other. And bar-rooms ... There was a bar-room every second door. And the people that were

---

* A round dance similar to a polka, but somewhat slower.

there. Good night! I'm telling you, it was just that you'd be waiting for it to be Saturday night.

And there was another place over in Brighton, they called it the Oak Square Bungalow. There was a fella there, he was from Antigonish. His name was MacLellan. He was running it for years over there. There was another one – a fella from Pictou, Jack MacCullum, he ran a big dance over in Circle Hall here in Somerville for a long time. At the same time there was another one over in Dudley Street – he'd get a big crowd.

The Inverness Serenaders, they played for fifteen minutes over WHDH from the Hotel Touraine, then they ran the dance Saturday night in O'Connell Hall on Dudley Street. It was in the Hibernian building. God bless us, the place would be packed. Alex Gillis, Alcide Aucoin, and Charlie MacKinnon. And sometimes there'd be another fella – a visitor might be playing with them. I played over WHDH with The Inverness Serenaders – a couple of times they asked me. I played alone, just two or three times in the fifteen-minute spot with Alex Gillis.

There were others that used to be on the radio, too. A fella name of Graham, Rannie Graham – he was from Judique, Cape Breton. He played at the Rose Croix Hall on Dudley Street there. He was on a few times, advertising the dance. There was another fella, he was more of a classical player. His name was Dave MacNeil. He was a down-easter, but I don't know where he came from. I think he was probably from down Iona, Cape Breton, down in that section. A beautiful waltz player. Oh, one of the best.

He checks the tuning on the violin. "I remember a waltz ..." He touches the bow across the strings. "Dave MacNeil would play this one." He plays a waltz.

"The Inverness Serenaders, when they used to be on the radio, used to start off with a jig, you know ..." He plays a short jig. "They generally played jigs and hornpipes and reels – anything that'd get them going."

The talk stops as he plays a few jigs for this small but appreciative audience, then finishes up with the Scottish piece, "The Battle of Killiecrankie."

"I started playing the fiddle when I was about ten years old. A little three-quarter fiddle. I played by ear then, but I took up reading the music so I'd get everything right ..."

"Were Gillis and the others note readers as well?" I ask.

"Gillis read, and Alcide Aucoin did. But MacKinnon didn't. He had a great ear and could pick it up."

"Was it the county of Inverness the Serenaders were named for, or the town?"

Inverness County. Gillis was from down Margaree. He was a first-class carpenter. And he was a foreman, too. He was a darn good one. And Aucoin was an electric welder. He was from Cheticamp. He's dead. Big Charlie MacKinnon – Tall Charlie MacKinnon, they called him – all he ever did was drink beer. He died here a few years ago. He was from Lake Ainslie. East Lake. He never had a job. Just a few odd jobs here and there, just to keep him in cigarettes. He played in different places. He'd get a few dollars here and there. Angus Chisholm* was that way. Angus Chisholm, he wasn't with them when I was there. It was before I came here that Angus Chisholm was involved, but I met Angus Chisholm afterwards here in Boston. He died here a couple of years ago. Angus Chisholm could have had good jobs because Angus Chisholm had good schooling. He was a graduate from the Normal College in Truro. But the bottle got the best of him, poor man. Awful fine man, but he couldn't leave the old hootch. He taught school down home three or four times. He gave that up. And then he was a fire ranger on the Cabot Trail for a couple of years. And he had jobs at the banks here. But he couldn't hold a job. He played a lot around here. Made good money, too. He'd play in the different bar-rooms, one thing and another. But then he'd go on a hell of a bout. He might be dry for six months. He wouldn't taste it. Then he'd go on a big one.

And talking about Dudley Street, there was one man that played years ago. He was an old man, that played in the hall there, Hibernian Hall – old Scott Skinner from Scotland, the great violinist. He made a trip over here. He was over eighty then. Scott Skinner – that's his book there. [He points to a copy of *Skinner's Collection* on the piano.] He was over here, and Alex Gillis's father was on the stage with him – Malcolm Gillis. He was up at the time. And he played for Skinner.**

I used to listen to them down east, you know, the Inverness Serenaders. We used to get them down east. We didn't have a radio and I used to go across the river. They had a radio. Saturday nights. You'd tune in to the hotel here at I think it was quarter of seven,

---

*   Angus Chisholm, a prominent fiddler from Margaree Forks, Inverness County, also played a great deal with Alex Gillis.
** Scottish composer and violinist Scott Skinner died at the age of eighty-three in 1927. Malcolm Gillis, from South West Margaree, won first place in the 1926 fiddling contest in Boston.

they used to play here, but we were an hour behind. Quarter of eight. So I got them for fifteen minutes. Well, we had the old battery radio. You could get it clearer than you can get it here. You could get it in Prince Edward Island too. Oh, we could get it as plain down in Antigonish ...

CATHERINE I'll never forget, where I was in Chestnut Hill, I used to always listen to The Serenaders. And I was dancing, step dancing away – I can't step dance, but I was having a great time all by myself – and I had something to throw out in the garbage pail, and I had it in my hand, and I got on the floor and I opened the door and who but this janitor who used to be around, Colin Campbell, and he was so shy, and he was so funny – there he was standing. I couldn't go in, and couldn't go out, because I got so scared. He was having a great time listening to me dancing, step dancing, all by myself ...

ELIZABETH Oh God, but there was a lot of fun in them days. A lot of fun ...

STAN MYERS – Martinvale, Kings County, Prince Edward Island

Holbrook, Massachusetts, just north of Brockton. In his sixties, he is a fiddler. When his father, a boilermaker, got a job in Boston in the mid-twenties, Stan moved as a boy to the States.

"We landed right in South Boston, and we despised it. There were eight boys and two girls in the family. We kept going back to PEI, because all of us hated Boston with a passion. We wanted the open spaces and the cattle and the country.

"The older brothers bought a farm back down there, and stayed down. That gave us a haven. And I couldn't wait to get back. So I talked to my father about wanting to go back with the boys. My father had to stay in Boston because of his work. So I went back and forth. I went to school in Massachusetts and I went to school in PEI – got a very good education at the school of hard knocks.

"Yes, I had a very checkered life. We all did. My brothers and I, we were back and forth, wherever we could make a dollar. We'd work in the lumber woods, we'd come up here to Boston; couldn't find a job – we'd go back down there, go fishing lobsters and salmon. We did everything but steal, cheat, and bootleg.

"Finally I went down, and I planned on staying there, actually. But a cousin of mine and I went up to Quebec, cuttin' the pulp – a dollar a cord. Just one man with a buck saw. We'd work from daylight to dark, regardless

of what time of year it was. I did that day after day. And I got sick of that. I said there's got to be an easier way of making a living than this. So I called my father. He sent me papers – I was still under twenty-one – so I came up in 1938 and went to work for the contractor that he was working for, with the Boston Edison Company."

I played fiddle all around. There were a lot of fiddlers – we used to have what we called a half-way house. Not an alcoholic half-way house, which is what most people think of. My father being a fiddler, all of these Maritimers used to come. They'd all know we came from that part of the Island and there was music at the house, so that's where they'd land. Angus Chisholm, Alex Gillis, Donald MacLeod, Chester MacDonald, A.A. Gillis, Alcide Aucoin, Colin Boyd – that's just naming a few of the more prominent ones that I can remember.

We had the guitar and mandolin and fiddle, and they'd come in and they'd practise. They used to practise more than anything else. My father didn't drink – there was never any booze in our house at all. But they'd take their own little jug – Donald MacLeod and Chester liked to drink tea a little bit and they'd spruce them up.

Donald – his brother Archie married my sister; we were from Martinvale and the next place over was Lorne Valley and that's where they came from, the MacLeods – was bound he was going to get my brother and I on the air [on WHDH]. My brother that lives in Manchester, New Hampshire, is a very good guitar player. So that's how I got to play with The Inverness Serenaders. Alex [Gillis] said to Donald, "OK, I'll put your little buddy on the air" ... Not as a regular, of course. But I was painfully shy. Because these people were experts, they were the tops. I mean, if Alex Gillis or Angus Chisholm threw their hat into the ring, that's all they'd have to do to come out with first prize in any contest. But they'd come over and watch me and my fingers would be shaking and they'd give me a slap on the wrist and say, "Loosen up, loosen up." Then I finally decided, all right, I'll go in there – and I was wishing I had some kind of a tranquilizer to kill my nerves. But once I got to the studio and saw nobody there – just the mike – it didn't scare me so bad. And this only happened a couple of times.

Donald MacLeod, now [points across the room] – he owned that fiddle right there on the wall. He played with The Serenaders. Not on a permanent basis, but Don used to play with them pretty regular.

My father played with them as a guest player the same as I did, a couple, three or four times. They tried to have one person on as near to every week as possible. They advertised it at the Inter-colonial Hall and the old Rainbow Inn, a hotel in Boston that's torn down now. Boy, I'm telling you, my father – when that radio program came on, you had better not speak while Alex was playing. And ah ... he would listen to that very intently. Very intently.

The fella that used to play the clappers with Gillis, Hugh Young, played the clappers with me several times in a place in Newton. He's quite a character, but he felt kind of lonely. He was sitting there watching me playing one time and you could almost see the tears coming out of his eyes: "You know," he says, "you play so much like Alcide Aucoin that it isn't even funny." "Well," I said, "I learned some of the tunes from Alcide." He said, "Some of the tunes you play like Alex Gillis." "Well," I said, "I've learned them from Alex and from his records." It is kind of a lonesome feeling, you know.

Besides MacLeod, have there been many top Island fiddlers around here?

Well, Chester MacDonald was from, oh, about fifteen miles from where we came from. Chester Ronnie Dan, they called him. A very fine fiddler.

Neil Cheverie was one of the best. He came up here in 1926 for the fiddling contest, the famous 1926 fiddling contest, which he came second in. He was tops. He and my father used to get together from time to time. My father was a very fine fiddler. He wasn't as well known as the other fellas, because he didn't go out. He had a big family, and he had to stay home.

Now, there was another fiddler that played for the Island championships, Jack Webster. It was his daughter Georgina that played with me over at WMBR the night they had "PEI Night," and she is tops.* She is right up there with the best of them. She's extremely good.

All Islanders, from right around our place ... An uncle of mine by the name of Ward Crane – he came to Boston and he cut some records, the old seventy-eights. I was with him in the studio when he cut them. He was a very good fiddler. He has two sons that are very good players. In fact, Jack Webster had three sons that come up here once in a while – Jackie, Carl, and Stanley – and they are extremely good players. Very good players. Stanley is a note player.

---

* WMBR (FM) in Cambridge has a regular Thursday-night program called "Downeast Ceilidh," which features a great deal of traditional Maritime music. Stan has played on the program on numerous occasions.

He knows his music inside and out. He knows music a lot better than the rest of us do.

I don't read. When I was growing up – and I had an Uncle Henry that wasn't too bad; he was a note reader – but the older fiddlers like Ward Crane, Hector MacDonald, and all these real good fiddlers said, "Don't go near reading music at all because it'll ruin your playing. You won't get your runs in. You won't get your variations and so forth. And don't start playing the slow stuff, the waltzes and fox trots and so forth. Stay with your jigs and reels."

In fact there's been a lot of fiddlers come up here. There's a Joe Cormier over here in Waltham, from Cape Breton – a very, very good Scottish player. He has three or four records out. There's another fella, a fiddler by the name of Ludger LeFort, that's very good. He's from Cape Breton, too. And then of course we've got Johnny Campbell. And Eddie Joe Boudreau – very good.

He is proud of how Islanders in Boston have stuck together – "First Presbyterian Church in Quincy is practically all P.E. Islanders," he says – and of their reputation for hard work.

"The Island people had such a good name that the contractors would go over to the Rowes Wharf where the boat used to come in from the Maritimes, from Yarmouth. They'd wait there and walk up to the people and say, 'Are you from Prince Edward Island? Come to work with us.' That's a fact.

"My brother was MC on 'PEI Night' on the [WMBR] programme one night, and he made kind of a joke about this. This actually happened too, that this contractor walked up to my father – and another fella, too – just after they got off the boat, and he said, 'Are you fellas lookin' for work?' And they said, 'How did you know?' 'Well,' he said, 'you look like you come from PEI, Canada.'

" 'How did you know that?' 'Well,' he said, 'you cross your suspenders in the front as well as the back.' That was right. That's how my father got the job. Out of that contractor's crew of forty-five men, there were forty-four from Prince Edward Island.

"And the contractor, he turned to the other fella who was with my father, C. Kimpton McGrath, and he said, 'Are you a mechanic?' And Kimpton said, 'No, I'm a McGrath – there were a lot of McGraths in Lorne Valley, you know.' [Laughs.] That was the cause of a few laughs."

"Was this contractor from the Island?" I ask.

"No. He came from Isle of Skye, Scotland. I worked with him a short time before I went into the service."

During the Second World War, Stan fought with the US Army in Africa, Italy, and France.

I got out in '45 and I played around different parties in '45 and the early part of '46, and then the Islanders got together and said, "There's no point in you fellas just playing at parties and that, why don't you start some kind of dance?" I said, "Where?" Somebody mentioned Cyprus Hall in Cambridge – Central Square, Cambridge. One of the fellas from Cambridge, from right near our hometown in PEI – I think it was him that suggested it, because he used to do a lot of drinking in the Cyrpus Gardens right below. And we went over and the owner said yes, there's nobody usin' it on Saturday nights, you can have it. So we printed a little form and sent it out, and word of mouth and telephone calls and the like. We got a pretty good following.

I did the playing and my nephew did the piano playing, and a brother played the guitar and another brother played the mandolin. There were four of us. A fella by the name of Caleb Nicholson used to call. He worked for the Carbonic Ice. And this brother of mine that plays the guitar – Vernon, that lives in Manchester, New Hampshire – he can call and play the guitar at the same time, which is quite a trick. And if he started getting tired there was a fella on the piano that could pick right up for him. So there was no problem.

Vernon had a little rack, one of those steel mechanisms that handle the harmonica, and he played the guitar and the harmonica at the same time, too. Of course, we used to goof around there a lot. I said, "Why don't you get the drums, too?" We thought this was a big joke. So we – I don't know what we got, a piano pedal or something – we hooked up the drums, and he could play the drums, the harmonica and the guitar all at the same time. And at that time I was playing the fiddle behind my back and under my leg. I'd have been a lot better player if I'd have stuck with playing instead of fooling around. But people used to get a charge out of that. My father and my uncle used to say, "You're going to ruin your playin' by doin' that," but people got a kick out of it, you know. We were showmen.

The second youngest brother – remember they had these shoes years ago with the different styles? – well, he painted some of them white with silver seal, with silver paint and the rest of them was gold – just as a comedy act. He used to call them the dancing slippers. We'd get playing the fiddle and my father or some comedian would say, "OK, Al, you go and get your dancin' slippers and come in and dance." Well, he couldn't step dance and he couldn't do any kind of a dance, but he had a little act of his own. He'd come out and put that on. People would laugh until their sides would bust. They'd roll around the floor and watch him. And two or three things like that used to draw the people in.

How many would you get on a night?

Oh, the first few nights it was discouraging. We'd get perhaps enough for three sets. That'd be I figure – what? – thirty-six people. Then it went up. Forty, fifty, sixty, and kept on growing.

All Islanders?

No, the Maritimes, but the majority were from PEI. There was a McRae fella, one fella that stands out in my mind. You've heard of the Belfast Riots in Prince Edward Island between the Protestants and the Catholics.* Well, his grandfather was the first Protestant to get killed in that riot. He was one of the outstanding characters that came to the dance there at that time.

And then we used to have guests there. This Jack Webster that I mentioned, he used to come and play with us every once in a while. And then there's a fella named Ray Anderson, from New Brunswick, that used to play. You know, anybody that wanted to could play.

But as I stop and think, there's very few of that old gang left. All the people that came to the dances – I know very few of them that are still left. I was over to Cambridge one time when my brother came down from Ontario – and as I walked through Central Square I didn't know one person, not one. There was a time when I'd walk through Central Square and I'd know every tenth person. Well, that's exaggerating a bit, one in ten, but I never went through there but what I met somebody.

Was yours pretty well the only Maritimer dance still going regularly in the late forties and fifties?

No, I played in Rose Croix Hall a couple of times after I came out of the service. The Circle Hall in Somerville was going strong, and Joe Martin's in Brookline was going strong.

Ray Anderson played for the dances that the fella ran at Circle Hall. He's a very good fiddler. A fella by the name of Jack MacCullum ran the dances and he was the permanent player.

And Bill Lamey ran a dance. He used to get a hundred and two hundred people.

---

*   On 1 March 1847, during balloting for the by-election in Belfast, PEI, fighting broke out between the supporters of the reforming Escheat Party candidates, two Irish Catholic tenants named MacDougall and Small, and Protestants who backed the Family Compact candidates, Douse and MacLean. Three people were killed and a number injured before the ensuing riot ended.

Would each of these dances have had a specific following, people from a certain part of the Maritimes?

That held true for years. It held pretty true, straight through. At Circle Hall, I would say a large majority of them, about seventy or eighty percent of them, were PEIers.

So when did that all begin to fade out?

I should imagine that it faded right out, perhaps, in the early fifties. We ran ours till I went into business in Maine in 1951. Farmington, Maine – I took a business up there, a tourist camp and a garage. That's why I quit the fiddling. I got away from all the players and everything. The group broke up and went their separate ways.

There were two guys then ran a diner here. The name was Birt – Alfred and George Birt. They were great players. They were related to Jack Webster in some way. They were from right in Cardigan, and Alfred married a girl from Iona, which is just a short piece down the road. They were right out by Monsanto Chemical, the Boston Edison – all the people used to dash in there for their meals. They had a terrific business. But I guess they decided they'd made their money – and they made good, too, for Islanders – and they decided to sell the thing before it collapsed. They sold it and then Alfred got bad and died. George moved down to Kentucky. Well, when he moved down to Kentucky, he lost all contact with the Island players.

There was a Fisher, a Jim Fisher from right near where we came from, too. He came from a poor, impoverished farm in Riverton. He came up to Hennigar, New Hampshire, and he started a dairy farm up there. And I asked him one time when I was out there, I said, "Do you ever think of going back to the Island?" He said, "No, I wouldn't move back to the Island under any circumstances." The whole family moved down to Florida. He and his wife both died down there.

It bothers my mind to think that there were so many P.E. Islanders around here at one time, and now they're gone. They've died or moved away, or lost their identity or whatever. I don't know. It's a shame. So many people have gone down south to stay. And they tend to lose contact. I know from experience, because when we moved to Maine I lost contact, with everybody. I had to start all over again.

Stan returned to Boston from Farmington when the highway was moved and his business declined. In the mid-seventies, he returned to playing old-time music for Massachusetts Maritimers. "There are about twenty, twenty-five years roughly that I was away from the fiddle altogether, that I didn't pull the bow across the strings at all. It's almost like starting to play all over again. I couldn't make the sounds – it took me quite a while to get back where I am, and I'm not back to where I was in '38, when I was at my peak."

I've played for the Grange and the senior citizens all over the area. Senior citizens in Randolph. Churches in Brockton. Concerts in Brockton, and the Scotch Club that puts on the annual Scotch concert up in the Needham Presbyterian Church.

Did you ever play at the Canadian-American Club in Watertown?

I've played there, but not as a regular. I do enjoy going over there. It's funny, I was playing at the Gaelic Club there one day, and I was up there playing and I came back down and this woman tapped me on the shoulder and she says, "You're a nice player. It's too bad you're not from Cape Breton." "Well," I says, "what's wrong with PEI?" But it was something strange – I don't think they'd ever heard it, a PEI player at the Gaelic Club. It was always Cape Bretoners. I broke the ice.

Cape Bretoners are much more clannish, I think, than Islanders, and they're a little more stand-offish until you get to know them. The first two or three times I played around with Cape Bretoners, I never knew there were so many. I knew there was a bunch up in Watertown and Waltham. But I went different places, Scituate, Newton ... That up there is all Cape Bretoners.

But anytime anybody asks me to play and if it doesn't conflict with my schedule ... and sometimes even if it does conflict with my schedule, I'll postpone something else to go. To keep the ball rolling, to get some people together.

Never Done

AGNES GILLIS AND CONSTANCE KROHA
– St Rose, Inverness County, Nova Scotia

Agnes was born in St Rose in 1887, the daughter of Donald Gillis from Broad Cove and Mary MacNeil of Mabou. Her grandfather, John Gillis, came to Cape Breton from Invernessshire, Scotland.

Her daughter, Connie, was born in Jamaica Plain, Boston, and raised by her grandparents in St Rose. In 1941 Connie married Leo Kroha, an American from Pittsburgh. He is a retired letter carrier. They live part of the year in Massachusetts and part in Florida. The four of us spoke in the Krohas' comfortable kitchen in East Weymouth, where I asked Agnes what had brought her to this country in the first place.

Let me see ... I think it was in 1905 ... I wanted to see the world; I wanted to travel. Father didn't want me to leave home at all. We had a home, a two-hundred-acre farm, plenty of everything to eat – so there was no need for me to leave home to go to work. I insisted I was going.

How did you get along when you came here?

Well, I had my ups and downs. At first I was so lonesome. I couldn't eat; I couldn't sleep. Oh, I had made up my mind I was going back. But then, the day went by, and I don't know, I changed. And I stayed.

What sort of work did you do when you got straightened around here?

I went to work like for housework. That was just about all the work you could get at that time – that's all there was. The wages weren't very much. It was [laughs] five dollars a week.

CONNIE At that time, though ... And it was the best paying work, because you had your housing.

AGNES Oh yes, you'd get your keep. That's why that's what I preferred to do.

What kind of people would you be working for?

They were quite well off. Noyes, was their name. They had a son and a daughter but they were both married. The daughter lived nearby and the son was quite a ways out, but he used to visit there once in a while.

So your job wasn't looking after children?

Oh no, no. Just cooking and cleaning the house. It was a three-story, but the rooms weren't very large. He was working – he had some high position, you know. Oh, they were lovely people, wonderful. They were so good to me. I stayed with them about a year and a half. I should have stayed with them longer, but I was so young, I didn't know what I was doing ...

When Connie was born, Agnes took her as an infant back to her parent's farm, where she grew up. But by the late 1920s, her grandfather Gillis was nearing the age of ninety. "My grandfather was getting real old and he had to go some place to be taken care of," says Connie. "Grampa went up to Uncle Joe McLellan's in Glenville. So that's when Ma decided to bring me back here." It was 1927.

CONNIE I remember my uncle lived in Needham – Emery Hatfield, a contractor from Dartmouth. Anyway, he took us all into Boston, and they had this new garage then, and you went up and around and around and around ...

LEO The Park Square Garage ...

CONNIE Well, I'll tell you, I thought, "I never in my life saw anything like that." I was terrified of it! "Oh my heavens!" I said. And I thought to my own mind, "This is not for me." When I saw all the bright lights and the buildings and everything, to me it was like one big headache.

St Rose ... We were far in the country, in the sticks and the woods.

AGNES [Protesting:] We were near the main road.

CONNIE Big deal! [Laughs.] Oh, brother, if you saw a horse and buggy go by, you'd say, "Oh my gosh, who's that? That's John Alex Beaton, goin' down after his flour." That's about the way it was.

LEO How about that fella that was always around St Rose, and one year when he got old enough he wanted to get away ...

CONNIE Angus Charlie MacKinnon ... Somebody took him up to Inverness one time. All the way from St Rose to Inverness, ten or eleven miles [gently sarcastic]. And he got up there, and he said, "Oh my God, isn't the world big!" [Laughs.]

LEO We have a friend by the name of Leahey, Jim Leahey. He's retired, and he has two sons on the Braintree police force. And this

Saturday night, Jim was on duty on Quincy Avenue. And on Saturday night, people – especially the younger ones – tend to celebrate a bit. There's a lot of traffic and everything, and Jim sees a car wheeling up and down. He pulls him over and "Where the hell are you from?" he says to the fella. "Judique," he says. [Laughs.] And he had to laugh, because Jim's mother came from Judique – so he didn't press any charges ... He'd never met anybody here who knew where Judique was.

The fiddler Alex Gillis was a distant cousin of Agnes's. Alex Gillis was one of seventeen children in a family from South West Margaree, the majority of whom lived in Boston. "That was a pretty musical family," says Connie. "There was Alex, Bernie, Jim, Jack ... And Ambrose – he lived for a while in Quincy while we were in Quincy. They used to come up to our house practically every Saturday afternoon, and we'd be making records, and Ambrose would play ... And you could always hear his foot on the floor – bang, bang – [she stomps her foot] keeping time.

"And Malcolm." *Malcolm Gillis – who was once leader of the Boston Band and who was reputed to have said of his particular musical interest that it had caused him "to be driven out of a dozen boarding houses" – was a medal-winning piper.* "He played in our house this one time – five o'clock in the morning, he was playing upstairs. And I said, 'Oh my Lord, no, the woman next door is going to have kittens.' But she said she heard it and she enjoyed it."

"Alex was in this house more than once," *Leo interjects with a measure of pride.* "We lived in Hanover before this – he was there more ... And in Quincy where we lived first, he was there ..."

"Would you believe," *asks Connie,* "from Pittsburgh, Pennsylvania, that I met Leo at Alex Gillis's dance?"

Leo tells the story. "I was living in South Boston, I was working for the Greyhound Lines at the time, and Saturday afternoons, I'd hear Alex Gillis and his Inverness Serenaders. They played over the radio for half an hour, advertising their dance more or less. 'This is W-etch-de-etch,' [WHDH] he used to say."

"Real Scotch, you see," *Connie pipes in,* "because they were all Gaelic-spoken people."

" 'Come over to Dudley Hall tonight,' " *Leo quotes Gillis,* " 'and have yourself a good time. Come over for a quadrille.'

"We liked to go to square dances in the country in Pennsylvania – so we went over. I took a couple of fellows over with me, chums from South Boston, to enjoy the evening. We always had a good time, In that same building where Alex Gillis and his Inverness Serenaders were on the second floor, on the first floor was Alice O'Leary and her Irish Minstrels. She *played the accordion – she was good. On the third floor was the Swedish dance – all blondes, too. First, second, or third floor, you could take your choice. Lively, good music."*

"There was this one family home," says Connie, "that I knew the daughter. She was about my age, and we'd see each other, like maybe at a dance, or at church, or something like that. The Beatons, the Archie Beatons, from Dunvegan. And so when I came up here, they were already established in Somerville, and that was the place that I used to go to visit all the time. And I started going to dances with them, and that's where I met Leo."

Like her mother, Connie also did housekeeping work when she came to Boston.

The majority of people, that's all they did. That was the only place there was any money for the girls. I was housekeeping for this man and his children. His wife was sick when I first went there, and I used to take care of her. And then she passed away and I still stayed there. But then I decided I would like to get a little more money. As a housekeeper there, I had a very full responsible job, but the pay wasn't very good. I was getting ten dollars a week – that was big money, supposedly. So I decided to answer this ad in the paper. The ad was for sixteen dollars a week – those then were the best wages going – and it was for a parlourmaid waitress, which I didn't know anything about, but I said I'd find out. So anyway, I went over to interview Mrs Faye – their last name was Faye; he was a professor of communications at MIT, but that was just his job, not where his money came from – and, I don't know, she just kind of fell in love with me. "Well," I said, "I don't know anything about the work." "Oh," she says, "don't worry. I know you can do it." So, "OK," I said. "All right." So she hired me and I went to work for her, and I was there until I got married.

What did the parlourmaid waitress have to do?

Parlourmaid waitress duties were to take care of the dining-room table, the silver and the waiting on table, and the dishes afterwards, and in and out of the dining-room, serving and all that kind of thing. Answer the door, answer the telephone. And I used to drive them sometimes, take care of their daughters' kids and all that.

I was the cook there when I got married. She came to me and she

* The Massachusetts Institute of Technology.

said, "I'd like you to take over the cooking." Well, cooking was four or five dollars a week more. But I was scared, I was terrified. So I said, "Mrs Faye, I'm no cook." "Oh," she says again, "I know you're capable." You couldn't believe the cooking in those places. You had your afternoon tea, and your quarter-of-seven cocktails, and then the announcement for dinner, and so on.

That was good experience, I'll tell you. It taught me a lot. Pots! When you made stock for a soup – all soups are made from the same basic stock – a pot this big and this high [she gestures expansively] would be on the stove for two days. And the stove was as big as this counter here.

And there were fourteen rooms in that house – not counting hallways and stuff like that. It was a huge house. Godsakes, the sitting-room was as big as this whole floor of the house here.

It was a nice job. They were good to work for. But there was this one time that I was left completely alone. The cook – the cook had died. She was an old Irish lady, and anyway, she died. There were three girls – cook, parlourmaid waitress, and chamber girl – and the others were all gone. I was the only one there. So anyway, this one day, I was waiting and waiting for the Fayes to come downstairs. They didn't come down, and they didn't come down. So I said, "I've got so darn much to do, I'll have to go down and take care of the maid's work in the basement." So I went down and I started to iron. First thing, they went to the dining-room and pressed the bell on the floor – that's how they called you to let you know they were there and wanted something. I didn't hear the bell. And she came to the end of the stairs and she called me by name. "Oh," I said, "Yes, Mrs Faye," and up I came. And she said, "Well, where in the world were you?" She was real snark about it. She was cross. Well, I spoke right up and I said, "I'm sorry, Mrs Faye, but," I said, "I'm one person here, and," I says, "I'm doing all the work of three people." I said, "You don't expect I'm going to be answering every bell ..." Well, you know, after breakfast was over, she came right out to me and she apologized. She sure did.

Towards the end of her stay in Cambridge with the Fayes, when she was cook, Connie was able to get her mother taken on in her previous position, parlour-maid waitress. The year was 1940. "I loved it there," says Agnes. They both worked for the Fayes for roughly a year, before leaving together after Connie and Leo's wedding in 1941.

LEO Connie got Mary MacDonald on there, too ...

CONNIE She was a friend of mine, a school teacher from Margaree. Mary Gillis. She married Angus MacDonald after that. She worked with me after Helen Francis – Helen was Irish, right from Ireland – after Helen got married ... Mrs Faye, if she liked you she liked you ...

AGNES Mrs Faye was always nice to me. She would always speak respectable and I think she liked me. She liked you and she liked me.

CONNIE And you know, much to my amazement, she came to our wedding, which is unusual for society people. They were high-society people and they belonged to the blue book ...* There was not one girl I knew of, that the people they worked for went to their weddings. Nobody. I was really surprised. In fact, I was so embarrassed when I saw them there, I pretty near fainted. I didn't expect it, you know. And of course I only had a very small wedding ... It was in a church. And she gave me a lovely gift, a hundred-dollar gift. So that was A-plus for me.

POSTSCRIPT *Near the conclusion of our conversation, Agnes, herself a fiddler, shows me the lyrics to two songs she has written, one in particular, "In a Home by the Sea," on the theme of living your life so far from home.*

IN A HOME BY THE SEA
By C. Agnes Gillis

In a home by the sea,
There's a voice calling me,
The voice of a mother so dear.
She's calling today, from a home far away,
I'm returning to bring her some cheer.

Chorus:
She is missing the love I deny her,
As she waits every day just for me.
With a tear and a sigh, I'll again say goodbye,
When her dear face again will I see?

In my dream at night – a vision so bright –
Her beautiful face I would see.
When I would awake, my heart it would break,
Just to know it was only a dream.

Chorus (Repeat).

ANN HYDE – Reserve Mines, Cape Breton County, Nova Scotia

Ann and her husband Joe live in Watertown, where he was born and where they settled after marrying in 1939. They retired in the mid-sixties, she from nursing, he from his position as Supervisor of Public Welfare for the town. His accent is all Massachusetts; hers is all Cape Breton.

My name is Ann Hyde now, but it *was* Annie Lovett MacDonald, and I trained at the General Hospital in Glace Bay. I came up here in 1928. I went into the hospital in '25, and I came right up here after, because my parents and sisters and brother came up in '26. I stayed and finished my training and then came up here. I went to the Mass. General,** and I was there for eleven years before I got married. Then I went to work again when Joanne [her daughter] was five years old, and I worked off and on for nineteen years after that.

We lived in a place called Dominion No. 4 – it's now called Passchendaele. My father was a mine manager. I was born in Reserve, and then we lived in a place called Bridgeport, which is a small area of Glace Bay, and then my father went down to this No. 4 as an underground manager, and then from that he went as manager out to Birch Grove, No. 21. From there we went back again to No. 4, and from there again to Reserve, and that's the last place we lived, Reserve Mines – then we moved up here.

I remember the big strike.*** They were burning down the company stores, as you know. And next door to us there lived a man,

---

* The term "blue book' – originally applied in the US to the *Biennial Register,* a publication of the names, residences, and salaries of government employees – means for Americans any listing of socially prominent individuals. There is no one such book.

** The Massachusetts General Hospital in Boston.

*** In March of 1925, the members of District 26 of the United Mine Workers of America in Cape Breton stopped work. The strike was precipitated by a proposed ten percent wage reduction by the British Empire Steel and Coal Company (BESCO), and by the company's cutting off of credit at its stores and providing no work to the members of the more militant locals of the union. It turned into one of the most vicious and bloody conflicts between a union and a company in the history of the Maritimes.

In May 1925, BESCO (which owned the town's power plant) moved to cut the supply of power to New Waterford, including the hospital. In June, a group of miners marched to the plant to confront the BESCO police who were his name was Donald MacNeil. He was the stableman,* and he worked – "scabbed," as they called it – during the strike. They set his house on fire. They protected our house, to see that it wasn't burning. But the times were pretty tough.

My mother always said that she was never going to let my brother go down in the mines. So we came here – and he never did.

My mother worked up here for fourteen years before she was married. She took care of children, and when she went home and got married, she always wanted to come back up here, but my father never wanted to come. But after they came they never thought to go back.

What did they do when they got here?

My father did painting, something he never did home – he always had somebody else do it. But he did painting over on St Botolph Street in Boston. My sisters were all school age, but then two of them worked in Jordan Marsh,** another worked at Gillette's, and another did housework and then became an LPN.*** My brother went to work at Woven Hose, Boston Woven Hose.

JOE It was a rubber place, they made all types of rubber.

ANN Then he worked for Chase and Sanborn, and then he moved out to Northboro and worked for Norton Grind, a precision grinding company in Worcester. He worked there until he was sixty-five years old.

How did you find it when you came here yourself?

[Laughs.] I'll let you tell it, Joe. Go ahead.

JOE Well, of course, she came up on the train, and when she went into North Station, she looked all around and she said, "Oh, I didn't know Boston had a roof over it!"

---

holding it. The police opened fire and killed a man, Bill Davis. It was June 11, now known as Davis Day in industrial Cape Breton, where Davis's death is commemorated every year with a holiday.

With Davis's death, the miners' patience evaporated. For days after, the company stores and mine-surface buildings were razed and emptied. The government and BESCO countered by sending in the troops – 1,600 were sent to New Waterford alone. A settlement was not reached, and the troops did not leave Cape Breton, until August.

* Stablemen were in charge of looking after the mine horses, which until the early 1960s were used in Glace Bay to haul coal and timber underground.

** A large retail department-store chain in the US.

*** Licensed Practical Nurse.

ANN   Of course there's no truth in it, that's just what he's always said. But I did, when I got to the North Station, I did get on a subway train, and I thought, "My Lord, this thing goes fast." To me it was terrible, it went so fast. Then after you get used to it, you don't think it goes fast enough.

No, I came up from a very small hospital, as you know, and you didn't know much of anything. I walked right out of that situation into the Mass. General Hospital, and I had to have my courage with me. But I loved it and I worked, and I really enjoyed it. I really did.

But the place was full of Nova Scotians. They had a good reputation for working like horses. Good workers. Conscientious. There was Christine Scott, she was the night supervisor – she was from Caledonia Mines. And then the girl I lived with, Christine Grand, was also from Caledonia. There were so many of them I can't think of them all off hand. [An aside, smiling at Joe:] All of these things that amount to anything are run by Nova Scotians, right?

JOE   And of course, unfortunately, they came up here just prior to the depression. Things weren't very good. So they did well to do what they did.

In the 1930s, Joe was a Watertown administrator for the Civilian Conservation Corps and the Works Progress Administration. The "CCC" and the "WPA," as everyone called them, were centrepieces of President Roosevelt's make-work depression-relief scheme. "We had a lot of those WPA programs," he says.* *"We'd develop projects so that we could hire people and pay them out of the federal program. They improved a lot of things in the town: we had them cleaning the schools and painting and a lot of food would come in, and we'd have to be the distributors. We'd get that going, distribution, then we'd get money from the WPA to run it. It made more work. And they had the women sewing and making things, you know – a salary of twelve to fifteen bucks a week was tops."*

There were plenty of Maritimers on such schemes in Watertown during the depression, he says. When the town collected statistics on which nationalities were receiving the majority of relief work, the results were surprising. "Because of language, I suppose, people were saying, 'It's the Italians, it's the Armenians.' But no, it was the Nova Scotians. It's a fact."

---

*   The WPA got underway in Boston in late 1935. Ninety percent of the workers on its various projects came from off the municipal welfare rolls. WPA workers in Boston built twenty-five miles of sewers, repaired a hundred miles of streets, constructed underpasses, and did a great deal more.

And there were some hard feelings. "They were calling them chisellers and everything else. But then we got out committees around the town in a supervisory capacity – prominent men, you know – so that we could explain to them what was happening, so that we'd have their backing. Then it kind of eased off."

Joe felt that Nova Scotians were generally anxious to get jobs and get off the rolls as soon as possible. "We didn't have any trouble," he says. Many Nova Scotians worked in the area for years after. "They worked around Waltham and Watertown because of the Waltham-West watch factory. They liked the work up there. An awful lot of them worked on the Edison Company, the telephone company – the wires and things. They were good workers. Bosses and foremen would go and bring these people in.

"This country prospered by the people coming in from a lot of these other countries. We got wealthy from a lot of these people. [A long pause.] They stole their labour."

The conversation turns back to nursing. "You got your nursing license here in Massachusetts just by reciprocity by what you took in Canada, didn't you?' Joe asks. Not quite, Ann explains – they had to send to Glace Bay for her marks before she could be accepted. Her marks were accepted, and on that basis she became an RN in Massachusetts. I remark that it seems a far cry from the state boards nurses have to write today in order to go to work in the States, and Ann agrees. Her daughter holds a Master's degree in nursing science as well as a Master's in education, and taught for ten years at the Mass. General.

"To get anything in nursing today you have to have degrees," she says. "And yet in all [she pronounces this introductory phrase as though it were one word], a nurse that's been working for a long time, like a head nurse on a floor, you know, eighteen or nineteen years, and has all the experience in the world and can go ahead and do everything, much better than some of the ones that come in with degrees – she can't hold that job because she doesn't have a degree ..."

" 'And yet in all,' " I interject, running the words together also. "That sounds more like Reserve than Watertown."

"And yet in all ...": she savours the sound. "Well, I was sitting at the desk one night in the hospital, and this young house doctor was sitting there. So I was talking to another doctor on the phone and he apparently told me to give the patient some medication. And I said to him, 'Agus! [hock] That won't hold him.' The minute I hung up the receiver, the doctor said to me, 'I know where you come from.' And I said, 'What do you mean, you know where I come from?' 'Agus,' he said. 'You came from somewhere in Canada, didn't you?'

"It's from Gaelic. Agus bha'n talamh: the beginning of the Book of Genesis."

I used to be able to read the first chapter of Genesis in Gaelic. My father taught me. My mother and father would speak Gaelic. They spoke it mostly when they didn't want us kids to know what they were saying. My mother's people came from Boularderie.* The name was Morrison. My mother's father was born in Scotland. My father was born in Rocky Boston – that's out there somewhere by Louisbourg. I'm Scotch all the way back, as far as I can count.

To tell you the truth, I really enjoyed growing up. Everybody laughs at me, but I did. I thoroughly enjoyed it. I'm glad I was born and brought up there. I certainly am.

There was somebody visiting here one time, from Nova Scotia, and he said something about how he didn't like to tell people where he was born or something. And I said, "Why? Are you ashamed of it?" I mean, you ask some Canadians where did they come from ... they may say, "Nova Scotia." "What part of Nova Scotia?" "Cape Breton." "What part of Cape Breton?" "Oh, you'd never know it ..." They act as though they're ashamed to tell where they come from. Nobody should be ashamed of where they were born.

Where is the big mining here, Pennsylvania? I have a friend who graduated from my hospital, and we lived together for eleven years before we were married – I was married one week and she was married the next – and her husband is an American citizen also. So he'd been down to Glace Bay, and he said, if you want to see poverty and what you think is run down, downtrodden, and all the rest of it, just go to Pennsylvania and see the coal mines. You've seen nothing in Glace Bay compared to Pennsylvania. So Glace Bay isn't the worst place in the world. I'd stick up for home.

GLADYS McCOY – Lockeport,
Shelburne County, Nova Scotia

Brentwood, New Hampshire, just over the state line from Haverhill, Massachusetts.

"Nova Scotia?" Gladys hollers out from her verandah lawnchair.

I nod and get out of the car.

---

*   Boularderie Island lies, going along the Trans-Canada Highway approaching North Sydney from Baddeck, between the foot of Kelly's Mountain at the Seal Island bridge, and the bridge going into the village of Bras d'Or.

"Glad to know ya." She shakes my hand and takes me inside the little country home where she has lived since 1939, and alone from the time of her husband's death in 1962. The house, which is as friendly as she is, hasn't many crannies or corners without pictures of family members of one sort or another: she has three sons, a daughter, and numerous grandchildren.

Originally an Ennis from Lockeport, Gladys is in her seventies.

The last year in Lockeport High School there were four of us in the class – Don Laing, Lindsay Doleman, Carl Hayden, and I. Don didn't finish the year – he went to Halifax Business College instead. Lindsay left to open a business, an appliance store, on Main Street in Lockeport. And Carl and I finished out the year. There were only the two of us. He lives in West Roxbury.

I didn't really intend to leave – it was just the way things worked out for me, that's all. I went to the summer school at the Teachers' College there in Truro, and I got a permit to teach. I taught just one year at West Head, outside of Lockeport, and then I came over here. It was 1927. I just came over to visit – and I stayed; I didn't go back.

I came when my father was away, or he never would have let me come. He used to go fishing, with Angus Walters,* I guess it was, out of Lunenburg, and he didn't know I was gone till he came home off his trip. He didn't like it. And when I did go back later to visit, he said, "You'd have never got away if I'd been home." That's what he said. And every time I went home, he always said, "You'd have done just as well if you'd have stayed home and taught your school." But I don't know – maybe not ...

So how did you find it when you first came to Boston?

Church was coming out. [Laughs.] It was the old *Prince George*, from Yarmouth. It used to come right into downtown Boston, right down to Rowes Wharf. And you know, down home, you only see a crowd when church comes out, so one fella said when he got to Boston, that church must have been coming out, 'cause there was such a crowd around the wharf. [Laughs.]

Well, I stayed with Eddie Allen's folks first [the people from Lockeport she had come to visit], at their summer place in Lunen-

---

*   Angus J. Walters, one of Nova Scotia's most famous seafarers, was captain of the *Bluenose*. Launched in 1921 and immortalized on the Canadian dime, the *Bluenose* under Walters, in addition to its many racing triumphs, also set the record for the largest catch ever brought into Lunenburg.

burg, Mass., for about six weeks. Eddie's stepfather was an interior man, woodwork, and he worked down in Somerville. They had an apartment in Somerville where they stayed through the week, and then they had a country home up in Lunenburg, Mass. Driving between one place and the other, they used to stop in this little store to get a paper. And one day Mrs Allen was talking to the owner, and he said, "I'm lookin' for a girl to work in the store." And she said right off, "I know – I have a girl at home, she's lookin' for a job." So she got me this job there. Their name was Allan, too, A-l-l-*a*-n. And these Allans, they took me in their home. They lived in West Medford, Pitcher Avenue in West Medford ... a beautiful home.

Once she was no longer living with the friends from home, the Allens (with an "e") she had originally come to visit, she began to put an effort into looking up people from home ...

I met my father's cousin, Harry Cook, when I was in Medford. He came over here from Lockeport and went into the Sunshine Biscuit Company as a stock boy, and he ended up as credit manager. And it's funny, one of my husband's uncles, Scott McCoy, worked for him as a salesman, a biscuit salesman.

And there were the Frederickses there from Jordan – they lived in Brockton. And the West boys from Shelburne. And the Lewises. Edna and Myrtle Lewis – Mrs Ray Treat – from Lockeport. And Fred Walls and his wife, and Abbie Seaboyer, they came over, and they lived in Brookline for a long time. And Isabel Rawlings, her mother came over – and she got me into the Canadian-American Club of Boston. There was a Shelburne County Club in Roxbury, too. Some of the people from Shelburne and Jordan Falls and around there organized it. I went to some of the dances they used to have – over to Roxbury, on Saturday night. But I didn't go very often. I wasn't much of a dancer.

Saturday mornings I helped Mrs Allan around the house. The rest of the week I worked in the store. And the pay was so that I paid eight dollars a week for my room and board – but it wasn't all in money, it was in work.

And I went to school, too, to Fisher's – it was a private school there in Somerville. I took the shorthand and typing. I didn't have to take the English and the math and the bookkeeping, because I had them in school. I went to Fisher's from eight o'clock till twelve, then I came to the store, worked till six o'clock, and then I did my homework and corrected papers in the evening. They trusted me to correct the papers because I had taught school, and they took so much off my tuition for correcting them. I had five dollars a week for myself, and after I paid whatever else of my tuition there was, I had a dollar or so left – for carfare. It worked out that way.

Nineteen twenty-eight, I graduated – with all these students. First in the class. Oh, the teacher used to say, "Here's Miss Ennis, she's workin' three jobs and she's the star pupil." And they got me a job when I got through – with the Prevention of Cruelty to Children, in Boston, the Massachusetts Society for the Prevention of Cruelty to Children. It was really a very dignified job and really nice. I was there five years – till I was married and expecting my first child.

But the Allans were very put out when I got through at Fisher's and left them. Mrs Allan said [she mimics the accusing tone]: "I *thought* this was just going to be a convenience job for you till you got through school." She didn't like the idea of me leaving, because they had a good thing.

Local 67

How can carpenters in the United States be paid $1.10 an hour while in Halifax the union rate is only 57¢ an hour?
Halifax *Citizen*, 10 April 1925

HERBERT G. VICKERSON – Hermitage, Queens County, Prince Edward Island

A well-kept house on a well-kept street in Milton, a suburban area to the south of Boston. In his eighties, he has done a great deal of travelling in his retirement – to Africa and to the Yukon, among other places. We spoke in his dining-room, a room dominated by a huge inflated globe, which he refers to often in the course of conversation.

Throughout his life in the States, he has returned every year, sometimes twice a year, to the Island, although he has had no immediate family there since he and his mother left Hermitage after World War I. The wall of his upstairs study is full of family pictures, and the top drawer of his dining-room bureau is stuffed full of charts, letters, and photographs pertaining to his genealogical studies of the Vickersons.

I started farming when I was fourteen, when the war started. During the war and after the war for a year or so, prices were good, and you could make a good living. Then prices seemed to drop. One year, it cost more to buy the extra feed – what I didn't grow – to feed the stock than I got for them when I sold them. In the spring I got 247/8¢ [a pound], and that fall I got 8¢. After I came to the USA, I remember my uncle selling a hundred bushels of potatoes for $14, and it cost him that to buy a pair of glasses. So I decided to get out of farming and look for another job. I sold off all my machinery and sold the farm.

At home we always did our own carpentry work. It seemed to run in the family to do it. My father had built several houses around the community and so forth. And so this friend of my relatives in Boston was a contractor, and I went to work for him. I actually worked at carpentry less than six months when I got the union scale. Not that you could win at every turn, but the people that I worked for, because I was willing to work, wanted to keep me. And I went to night school, took up courses in different things like architectural drawing, and carpentry, and bookkeeping. And everything went well. I met my wife – she was from Prince Edward Island, but I never knew her there – and we were married, and anyway, I couldn't have been better off.

And then – 1930 – the depression started in earnest in Boston. Work became scarce, and it was hard to make a livin'. I was, I suppose, average fortunate in getting work – but there were a great many people out of work. And at about this time, I would say that ninety percent of the carpenters were from the Maritime Provinces. The natives didn't like these people particularly, from Nova Scotia coming up here and working. Many of them worked all summer – made enough money to live down there – and went home for the winter. And there were hard feelings – people talk about it yet.

How did you feel yourself about carpenters from home that only lived here part of the year? Did you approve of it?

No. But I could see it was a necessity. After all, life can't be sustained without something to eat.

But I might say that when I saw I was going to stay here, I took out citizenship papers and became a citizen. The only thing I remember about that is the few words the judge said. He said – and it kind of tickled me, because some people didn't feel as I felt – he said, "You must remember that we don't want people comin' to be citizens of our country with malice and hatred in their hearts against their own country, for such people make good citizens of no country." I remember that well.

Was the resentment against the men from home because they were taking work at less than union rates and undercutting the union? Wouldn't most of these guys have been in the union?

Oh yes, they'd all be union, 'cause they always had somebody from home to back them up to join the union. But in those days the union wasn't perhaps too strong, you know, it took a long time growing up. Probably fifty percent of the work – in the rural area, there'd be *at least* fifty percent of it – wasn't union.

But you were in it yourself?

I was in Local 67, in Roxbury. I belonged for thirty-two years.

Would there have been many Maritimers in that particular local?

Oh yes. The president at that time was a Prince Edward Island man by the name of Jim McNaught. I remember first, when I came here, he came over to the car I was sitting in, and he said, "I understand you are from PEI." And I said yes. "Well," he said, "can you tell me, is anybody down there good enough yet to marry anybody but their first cousin?"

And the other officers – I remember them all. There was Wilfred Cameron from Nova Scotia; Dan MacAskill from Cape Breton ...

Herb went into building, mainly residential carpentry jobbing, after World War II. "I would say from my observation at work," he explains, "which I've had a good deal of, having experience on both the working side and the management, that our people from the Maritime Provinces, percentage-wise, did commendable work." But he is puzzled by another conclusion from his observations of Maritimers in the carpentry trade. "If anything, carpenters from the Maritimes did a higher quality of work when in the States than they did when working home. Because you go down there – and they, to me, do not do a good job. But the same people come up here and they'll do far better. Of course, they may have better material."

"And could the wages be a little more inspiring?" I ask.

"That could be. Yes."

POSTSCRIPT Stephen MacDonald is a neighbour of Herb's. Also from PEI, he drops in as we conclude our discussion. "Where are you from on the Island?" I ask.

"I'm from almost as far west as you can go – Tignish. We left there in 1933, our family did – my father and mother and four children. I was the oldest, and I was twelve. And the reason we left was that we were farming and fishing and in theory we should have been doing very well; however,

the last year we were there, my father said if he wouldn't have planted the
potatoes he'd have been ahead, because he never recouped sufficient income
to cover the cost of planting them. So as a result the remuneration was nil.

"My father was a carpenter by trade – he had trained in the Canadian
West. He had trained some in Boston, too, so he was a real carpenter – like
Mr Vickerson ... But not as good as Mr Vickerson." We all laugh.

BILLY MacGILLIVRAY – St Andrews, Antigonish County, Nova Scotia

He and his wife Margaret live in the suburban, southern part of Boston, in
Weymouth. She is from Lake Ainslie, Cape Breton. He speaks some Gaelic.
She is in and out of the room while we talk. They are in their seventies.

We both left. She was seventeen and I was eighteen and a half. I
came here in 1925. I came to my brother's house – he'd been here
since 1911. I landed here – there were some of his wife's sisters
around and I was shy and one thing and another, and I wanted to
get away from the house. I told my brother's wife I was going to
look for a job. "Oh," she says, "you'll get lost, you don't know your
way around." "Oh," I said, "I won't go far." She started telling me,
"Now, when you get out to Warren Street, the street cars will be
coming there," she says, "and they'll take you into Dudley Station,
the terminal. And when you get there, go to such and such a place
and get the Alston car. But," she said, "you're gonna get lost." So
anyway, I went out to Warren Street from where they were living,
and I had to ask somebody out there which way was Dudley Street,
this way or that. So somebody told me, and well, when I got to
Dudley Station I didn't know whether I could get the Alston car or
not – you know, so many different landings and all of the cars pulling out of there. So anyways, I walked up to this big, dignified man,
well dressed, with a black coat on. I asked him, "I'm a stranger
here. Do you know where I can get the Alston car?" "Yes," he said.
"Where do you come from?" I said, "Well, I come from Canada."
"What part of Canada?" I said, "Nova Scotia." "What part of Nova
Scotia?" And I said, "Antigonish." "Antigonish. What part of
Antigonish?" "St Andrews." And he said to me, "*A Bheil Gaidhling
Agad?*" So I nearly dropped, you know. He was from a place called
Beech Hill in Antigonish. He directed me and told me where to get
the car. But that wasn't the end of it. I got on the Alston car, and I
wanted to go to Ray Street, so I went up and asked the motorman if
he would let me off there. "I'm a stranger," I said.

"And where do you come from?" I said, "I come from Canada."

I went through the whole thing again and then he said, "How is your father feeling now?" So I damn near dropped, and who was he but a first cousin of my father's. My father was here the year before that, working, and he got sick and had an operation for his appendix. Hughie MacDonald – my father's first cousin.

That was my first experience, meeting those two. I figured, "Oh, I'll have no trouble gettin' along here."

You were always meeting somebody from home. You'd go down to Dudley Street where the dance halls were on a Saturday night, and you'd often meet people there. There'd probably be three dances on the weekend and at least one on Thursday night, and those halls were all together in a small community. You'd go up to a dance and if you didn't know anybody, or the right crowd wasn't there or one thing or another, you'd leave it and go to another one. A lot of people met their wives at the dances. I had that luck myself.

It was a very happy place. Everybody was working. They had money and parties. Every week there'd be a party in the middle of the week – what we called a kitchen racket. Oh, there'd be probably forty or fifty at a kitchen racket. There would be a violin player there and we'd dance. Very often the police would break it up – too noisy, you know, and the people in the neighbourhood weren't accustomed to that kind of rough dancing and hooting and so on.

Margaret interjects: They used to charge fifty cents for the kitchen rackets, didn't they?

Well, sometimes. That was when it was a benefit party. In the depression there was a lot that were up against it and they'd have a kitchen racket and pass the hat around and raise a few bucks. There would be the odd one now and again for some person who had sickness or hard luck or whatever – they'd have a party in somebody's house. But there weren't too many of those. Mostly the kitchen rackets were for getting the gang together. Mostly, it was, "Oh, there's a kitchen racket at so-and-so's house," probably a young Nova Scotia couple that got married. "And there's another one over here." You could keep going all the time. And then the girls that worked at housework here, the cooks and waitresses and one thing and another, they'd usually have a big basement – a big room, big as this house, and a tile floor. We'd have a party, invite fellas and girls and we'd dance and one thing and another. Whether the owners – who were away in Europe and so on – whether they knew or not, nobody gave a damn.

But there were great get-together parties. It wouldn't even have to be a dance or music, just congregate Sunday afternoon in the house. Everybody was happy then, smiling and dancing and having a good time. I happened to have a car the second year I was here – working as a carpenter I was making pretty good money – and we used to go to parties as far away as Providence [Rhode Island].

Did you start doing carpenter work as soon as you came to Boston?

Well see, my father was a mechanic.* We had a shop, and he was the carpenter. My brother and I, when we were eleven and twelve years old we worked with my father. We had a pretty good knowledge of the trade, my brothers and myself, and we applied it here.

I got 75¢ an hour in 1925 when I started. My brother was working into Providence for a company, and he took me up there for three months. Then I came back here, and I went to work for a big company, in town. I was only nineteen and I hired on as an apprentice. Usually, a big contractor would take you on, and you'd serve four years. You'd start off with so much and they'd keep giving you a little more every year, or every six months. In my case, I had no records where I had experience and one thing and another. They had to take my word for it. But after I worked a month, between the foreman and the superintendent, they gave me two and a half years' experience. And in a year and a half's time I was given the full money – that was $1.10 an hour. I worked with them until the big crash came in 1929.

It hit the fellows from the Maritimes pretty hard here during the depression. I did anything. You'd get a little job here and there, enough to pay your board. And then people wanted their houses papered. I took up paper hangin' on the side, and painting, inside and out. That was the Nova Scotian way, you know, you'd grab anything to make a dollar.

But even when the boom was on here, you weren't working the whole year round. You would get your layoffs, and in the wintertime the building trades would slow down. You would loaf. If you were lucky and hooked up with somebody, you'd probably get part of a winter in, but a lot of them would probably loaf all winter. When I was on outside construction, I only worked half a dozen winters all through. And there were a lot of Januarys and Februarys that there'd be no work, and you'd have to provide for that – there

---

* He is using the word "mechanic" in its older, broader sense, as "craftsman."

was no welfare or unemployment insurance. You'd have to save a little money to take you over the rough spots.

I was single then. At that time, there was no help for the single people. So Roosevelt, when he went into office, he arranged to loan money to the railroads to bring them up to date, and it was people in my category who were eligible for this kind of work. So I got on the railroad, in 1934. And I worked with the New Haven–New York Railroad for twenty-five years as an interior finisher on the wood cars.

I worked on Diamond Jim Brady's car, his private car.* I worked on one of the president's of the United States old cars. They kept it up for historical reasons. And then I worked on Andrew Mellon's car.** He was a millionaire over and over again, Andrew Mellon. There were a couple more private cars that belonged to well-to-do people. And those cars, you couldn't *put* any more money in them. You'd have to throw the money away before you could spend any more on them. They were just polished, the inside of them – everything was just aimed to perfection. The light fixtures, for instance. They had a gold finish on them. Perfect. And the hardware on the doors ... And there were showers and bathrooms and bedrooms and sitting rooms. The woodwork was polished mahogany, the finest finish I ever saw.

Well, when you had to repair that, to make it appear the way it was, you would have to know what you were doing. And the foremen there, they weren't too well up on it, because in 1934 when I went there the shops had been closed for three years. A lot of the old-timers had got pensioned off and then they hired on carpenters from the outside. The handiest thing they could get to a railroad man was a carpenter.

But then the railroad that I worked for sold out to another company. The shop that we worked in wasn't used anymore – the Pennsylvania Railroad did the repair work and such in their own shop. So I went outside to work, back out to work on buildings, from 1960 till 1972.

---

*   James "Diamond Jim" Brady was a wealthy American financier and super-salesman known more for his lavish personal displays than for his business ventures, which were primarily in the area of railway equipment.

** Andrew Mellon was a wealthy American banker who was secretary of the treasury under Presidents Harding, Coolidge, and Hoover. He held the position from 1921 until 1932.

Billy joined Local 67 of the United Brotherhood of Carpenters and Joiners of America in 1925, and except for his stint with the railroad, was in the union all his working life. He recalls that in the late twenties, as many as eighty percent of Local 67's executive positions were filled by Maritimers.

"What was it," I ask, "about Maritime carpenters, in particular, that drew them to Boston?"

There was an awful lot of building, an awful lot of house work, going on here then. Houses everywhere – a lot of single, two-family houses, along with those three-decker houses.

Three-decker work was hard work. You'd have to hand the timbers up hand over hand. There'd be a fellow on the bottom floor pass them to a fellow on the second floor, and he would hand-over-hand them up to the top floor and up to the roof. That was hard work. They were all two-hundred-pounders, young fellas that could stand that hand-over-hand with the timbers. A strong fella meant more than a skilled mechanic, because three-decker work, it's kind of what you call bull work.

Carpenter work is not an easy job. You're working in the sun and they're pushing you. They want sweat and blood of you. The American people, they didn't go for those jobs so much. They were too tough for them.

And another job, line workers, they were all down-easters. A lot of them went into telephone work. That's climbing, and in the sun, and a lot of them got killed. It was fairly dangerous then, and nobody would take it.

Then the third job was on the ice trucks. You had to put a hundred-pound pack of ice on your back and probably walk up three floors with it. Nobody would take that. So the three jobs down-easters took up were carpentry, icemen, and line work.

Take carpentry work, for instance. When the boom was on here, from 1920 to '29, if you had any knowledge at all they'd hire you. Some of them were eager to learn and they caught on to the trade. Some of them were very successful. Some of them became builders.

A lot of them were very green, you know, coming out of the country and they didn't know a newspaper or a radio. There was one bunch of fellas from my home, they went up to New York and got jobs on line work, electric lights and that. And when they were getting hired on there, they had to have a physical, a doctor's examination. Those company doctors treat you just as if you're cattle. "Come on in here and take this off and go over there." It's not like going to a private doctor. Anyways, in this doctor's place there were about fifteen of them standing up there and the doctor was asking them questions, and he told the first fellow in line, "See that bottle on the shelf there?" he said. "Take that and urinate in it." So the fellow looked back and forth, back and forth. "Did you hear what I said? See that bottle? I want you to urinate in it." And he said to the doctor, "Well, what? From here?" [Laughs.]

So some of those fellows made out pretty good. That fella, I don't think he's living now. I think he died suddenly in New York. But some of them did well. They were out to get a home, get married, have a family, and live well. They turned out to be good mechanics, very good mechanics. None of them were bums. They all made a livin'. I can't think of anybody that lived on the City. They were good hard workers, they were strong, and they would last. They would last in the sun and the heat and the cold. A lot of the natives wouldn't take the job because they wouldn't last.

And another thing about the down-easters, they'll work under any conditions. They're very loyal to the boss, and there's no grumbling or complaining. There were a lot of Jewish contractors and they liked the down-easters because they were good strong workers and they would never talk union or union regulation. They made money on them.

Was there any resentment that some of the contractors preferred hiring Maritimers to Americans?

Yeah, the newspaper even came out with it. It was in the *Tribune*, an editorial about the Nova Scotians taking all the high-paying jobs. He said it was easy to tell them when they came on the job – their dirty white shirts. They weren't cleaning their clothes. They'd wear it a week, according to the *Tribune*. It went on like that.

And then, "Why the hell didn't you stay in your own country?" I got that more than once. "Taking our jobs away from us." "Well, whose jobs did *you* take away?" I'd say. "When did you people come here?"

"My people came over here two hundred years ago." "Oh," I'd say, "the Indians. You're related to the Indians."

And then, the Irish were jealous of the down-easters for some reason. They looked down on the down-easters. They thought that they were superior, so much better.

This will give you an idea. There's a fella living right across the street from my daughter in Braintree. His name is Charlie MacGil-livary. He was in the Second World War. He's from Prince Edward Island. He went in the American army and he lost an arm, and he got the Congressional Medal of Honor. So anyways, the St Patrick's Day parade here, it's usually the governor or the senator or somebody of high standing that leads the parade. One year a couple of years after the war, the governor wasn't available and there was nobody else. The handiest person they had was this Congressional Medal of Honor winner from Massachusetts, and that was Charlie MacGillivary. It came out in the papers that Charlie was going to lead the parade and the Irish put up a hell of a kick about it. Oh, they weren't going to stand for a herring choker leading the parade, the Irish parade. "St Patrick would turn over in his grave if he saw that." So what did they do? They took Charlie MacGillivary out, and put somebody else in. That'll give you an idea of what I'm talking about.

When I worked in Reedville with the railroad, there were a lot of Irish working there. They were very bitter, the ones that had been in the trouble in the South of Ireland.* They were probably ten years older than me. A Canadian was just another British subject to them. I found them that way.

But then again, the ones that came here after the war – a different class altogether. Broad-minded people, and regular fellas. I worked with them as carpenters. Good mechanics, damn good mechanics. There was no fooling around. They'd go to work and do a day's work and work hard.

But you take, now, the Irish foremen – I'm only talking about one here and there – he would take an Irish fellow ahead of somebody else, if he was qualified or not. He would probably come right out: "I want an Irish fellow." He'd probably say that to you, half in fun and full in earnest. You'd brush it off.

But on the other hand, if you got one as a committee man, a union delegate – this was in the railroad, the Railroad Brotherhood – if you had a grievance, and you went up before management with it, they would fight their heart out for you. They would never take no for an answer. They would stay right with it till they would win your case and prove that the company was wrong, no matter who it was. They were great for that. They'd never let you down there. Even if the company caught a fellow drunk on the job, asleep, they always had a way out for him. He'd get three days off and a warning – but if there was no union there, that fella would be flying right out the window.

---

*   The Irish Free State was established in the South of Ireland in 1921, five years after the Easter uprising against British rule in 1916.

When I got through on the railroad, I got a job on maintenance work over at Tufts College. It's a big college over here in Medford. Anyways, this one day I was sent up to this particular place to work. It was for the head chef of the college – in other words, he did the cooking for the well-to-do people, outside of the students, you know. He was telling me what he wanted done and one thing and another and he says, "By the way, are you a Canadian?" And I said, "Yes, I am." He says, "What part of Canada?" And I said, "Nova Scotia." So he backs up to me and says, "When did you leave there?" "Oh," I said, "I left when I was quite young, eighteen or nineteen years old." "Well," he said, "I'm from Kansas City and I've got a trailer, and the two months we're closed here, I spend all my time up there. I travel all over the province." And then he said, "I can't understand for people to leave that beautiful country." And then he went on to say about the wildflowers and the courteous people, and you'd camp out somewhere on the roadside, and people that didn't even know you, they'd come down and give you some strawberries and cream. And talking like that, he says, "Why did you leave there?" I said, "Did you ever spend a winter there?"

You can't live on beauty alone. If people could make a decent living there, I don't think you'd see so many people leaving.

The Biologist

RALPH WETMORE – Yarmouth, Nova Scotia

A biologist of international reputation, he was chairman of the Department of Botany at Harvard University from 1932 to 1934, and chairman of the Department of Biology there in 1946 and 1947. He was a Harvard professor from 1926 until 1962, and continued his research in the Bailey-Wetmore laboratory at the university until 1972. In 1953, he served as president of the American Botany Society, and in 1967 he was an editor and advisor to the Encyclopedia Britannica. The author of over 150 published scholarly articles, he has been married twice, first to Marion Silver, with whom he had two children, and then, following her death, to Olive Smith.

He graduated with a bachelor's degree in science from Acadia University in 1921, and is life president of that class, whose members he has kept quite close track of over the years. Acadia also awarded him an honourary doctorate of science in 1948.

Some of his interest in plants may have come from his mother, Josephine

Wetmore. "My mother raised dahlias and she raised sweet peas," he says. "Those were her specialties. She had a couple hundred kinds of dahlias.

"When I was a boy, I used to go down and sell them to people going to Boston. For many, many years there was a daily boat, except for Sundays, and the boat was loaded every day all summer. Fifteen cents a bunch ... good-sized bunches."

A small apartment, within a stone's throw of Harvard, in Cambridge. He is a few months from the age of ninety.

After I'd got through my grade eleven – that's where high school stopped in those days – I'd gone to work in Crowell's shoe store, down on Main Street, Alma and Main, on the corner. But the provincial government, in its great wisdom, had decided to put in a grade twelve. And thanks to Mr Kempton, who was principal of the high school, I became a member of the first class. I think there were twelve or fifteen of us, something like that. Mr Kempton had gone around to see my father where he was working [his father was a carpenter] and said, "I think it's time Ralph came back to school." And father came home at noon. I remember he said, "Will you come upstairs for a few minutes, Ralph? I want to talk to you. Mr Kempton was in to see me this morning." So I went up with him. He said, "Do you want to go back to school?" I said, "Yes, I do, but I don't think the family can stand to have four of us in school at one time, financially." My father never made over $22 a week in his life. But on Monday I went back to school. The fifth of December – and they'd been going since early September! How in God's name I ever made it, I don't know! There were nine subjects, nine provincial exams, and there were five of us passed out of the twelve or fifteen, whatever it was. And when they told me I was one of the five, I didn't believe them, that's all. I said, "This is nonsense." There were a lot better people than I was in that class. But I'll admit I didn't get to bed many nights before three o'clock or later between the fifth of December and the next June.

So at sixteen, I went to Pleasant Valley* to teach. Because Mr Kempton came around to Father again and said, "I think this boy ought to go teaching instead of going back to his other job." He said, "After all, this province is short of teachers." He said, "I'm sure that he's as good as some of the others that are teaching in the province."

---

*   Pleasant Valley, Yarmouth County. A small community on the road from Yarmouth to Weymouth, between Deerfield and Carleton.

So there I was. Twenty-six students, grades one to eleven. French and Latin to grades nine, ten, and eleven, and I had seven, damnit, in grade one! What in God's name were you supposed to do with them? You'd give them a job to do and by the time you got to the first class, they were through. You couldn't give them things to keep them busy any length of time.

A little one-room school ... I was living with my uncle and paid him a dollar and a half a week for board. I had two cousins in school under me: one in grade one, and one in grade nine. I walked two miles to school, each way ... But it was an interesting experience. And then the next year I went to Ohio* – principal of a two-department school. I was seventeen years old.

I remember one time, when the young people in Ohio were invited to Carleton by the young people up there, for a dance. I'd taken this girl from Yarmouth in a sleigh from Bain's Stable down on John Street. We got there about eleven o'clock, I guess, and we danced till sometime in the night. Then she was due to work the next morning, and I was due at school at nine o'clock the next morning, and I had to drive her to Yarmouth. There was no way of getting back up, so I walked back up, from Bain's Stable to Ohio. And I remember I lived the first house on the left over the track. A Mrs Tetford lived there then. Her daughter Susan kept house with her. And I got there about four o'clock in the morning. Blustering snow all the way up, no train to go along to clear the tracks. And my room was on the second floor. I didn't want to wake them up. I remember climbing up the water spout, and hanging on with my knees while I pushed the window up. [Laughs.] What a damn fool I was! I got in and went to bed. Well, the looks on the faces when I walked down in the morning for breakfast. The table wasn't set for me or anything. I got to school at nine o'clock.

The next year I went to Normal School. I had been teaching with a special permit, because I couldn't get in there till I was eighteen. And then I went to Milton [Queens County], Nova Scotia, and taught four years there.

I enlisted after that and got kicked out of the army. I had bad varicose veins, but they wouldn't operate on them. They sent me down to Camp Hill in Halifax to have them looked at, and he said, "We'll just have to take all the veins out of your legs, that's all. That's that." All over the backs of my legs, both legs. And they sent me back, kicked me out. I went to Truro Academy then and enlisted

* South Ohio, Yarmouth County.

again. But I didn't get overseas for the same reason. What they did was put me in Divisional Headquarters in Halifax in charge of the Records Office. They promoted me from private to sergeant. Instead of a dollar and ten cents a day I got a dollar and thirty-five cents a day. I was there until just after the armistice. That's when I got out and went to Acadia – right away. The Canadian government undertook to get those who had come out of college, or were intent on going there, out of service as fast as they could. The armistice was on November the eleventh, and I got out the twenty-eighth. On the train going home from Halifax, I stopped in Wolfville and went and saw the burser. And he said, "Sure you can get in. All you have to do is make up the work. Can you handle that?" "How soon can I come?" I remember saying. And he said, "Any day you want to." He says, "They're coming in now, some every day."

So that was the twenty-eighth of November. I went home, spent a weekend there, and Monday I came back to Acadia. By Christmas time, there were well over a hundred returned men that were back wanting to start. But college had been going since early October, and we had a lot of work to make up. After all, mid-years started about the middle of January, and that left us less than one month to make up three months' work. I remember very well, because the day before Christmas holidays, we were called in, the returned men, and asked what our plans were for Christmas holidays. We said, "We're going home and make up some work." I remember hearing that general statement being made. And two of the professors said, "Would you be interested in staying here and having us duplicate the lectures that we've given this year, highlight them?" And they did. We covered practically everything in that extra time between then and the middle of January when exams started. They divided the group up and took us home for Christmas dinner. It was really a fantastic experience. Here was this bunch of professors, probably tired anyway, taking the whole damn bunch of us back and making it up that way. Nobody ever forgot it. And those guys worked their heads off. You'd no more flunk the course one of those men had ... I don't think there was a grade below B. They didn't give anything out, either.

There were fifty of us in the class [of 1921] – the biggest class Acadia ever had, up till that time. And I don't think it would be too rough a guess to say, of those forty-nine or fifty people, somewhere between thirty-five and forty-five of them got their doctorates, either MDs or PHDs or doctorates of education or whatnot. Several of them ended up at Acadia teaching. A very, most amazing assemblage of people.

John MacNeill was from New Brunswick. John went from Acadia to Dalhousie and got his law degree. I don't know how he got to Ottawa, but he did. In any case, John got up there and he was in the Department of Justice. He was there up until he retired.*

Charlie Huggins was a Nobel Prize winner, the only one ever from Acadia.** He was in our class but he got through a year ahead of us, because he'd missed the war, being too young. He got his bachelor's degree when he was sixteen or seventeen, and came on to Harvard that year. He went to Harvard, and I think he went directly to Chicago for his intern work. Later, he was the head of the University of Chicago cancer investigation. Charlie Huggins is probably one of the outstanding medical, true scientists in North America. He became chancellor at Acadia in 1972, and was there as chancellor for a period of seven years.

Was biology your major at Acadia?

First I was going into medicine. Dr Cutten*** had gotten me a fellowship at Yale. He thought he was doing me a great favour, and he was, because it covered my tuition, my room and board, even my laundry – everything. And whether I was a damn fool or not, I don't know. I finally resigned it, and chose to come to Harvard for nothing. It wasn't Harvard against Yale at all – it was something quite different. I had decided that I wanted to go on in biology, that work in the evolutionary field was what I wanted. I didn't want to go into medicine. I had a notion that more people might die because of my services than if I went into biology.

Professor Perry at Acadia: he had been a graduate of Harvard and worked under the same man that I chose to go to Harvard to work under, mostly because of what he had said about him and what I knew he taught.

Anyway, that fall, I came to Harvard, with not a damn thing in sight. I had eight dollars in my pocket. I washed dishes at Harvard Square – the Georgian Restaurant – because the eight dollars was gone before the end of the month.

Eighty-five cents a day was what meals cost us. We had marvellous meals in Harvard, the graduate students. I remember week in

---

* John MacNeill, from Hampton, New Brunswick, went to Ottawa in 1924 as secretary to Sir Charles Fitzpatrick, chairman of the Canadian Statute Revision Commission. He became clerk of the Parliament of Canada in 1955, and continued in that position until 1968.
** Charles Huggins was awarded the Nobel Prize for Medicine and Physiology in 1966. He was born in Halifax.
*** George Cutten was president of Acadia University between 1910 and 1922.

and week out, our dinners were forty-five cents. Let's say for a sample: we had soup, roast beef, two vegetables, potatoes, a salad, bread and butter, and pie and cake. For fifty-five cents! And that's a statement of fact, because a group of us, half a dozen of us who ate together, kept track of what meals cost and then we compared notes at the end of the year. Eighty-five cents a day was what meals cost us.

And every Saturday night, Charlie Huggins and three or four more of a group that were at Acadia together would come over to my room in Conant Hall at Harvard. We'd all walk into Boston for dinner, four miles each way. And you could ride for a nickel in those days, so we weren't trying to save the nickel. We just wanted the walk. And we walked back again afterwards, some to the Medical School and some to Cambridge. It was an interesting group, there was no question about it.

I was married in 1923, and I got my doctorate in 1924, under this Dr Jeffrey with whom I had come over to work. We were down home that summer, and I taught at summer school in Truro. I got a fellowship that next year, and came here that fall. We got a place to live over on Wendell Street, put in a good year, and then I went back to Acadia as I had expected. That was '25–'26. I had agreed to go back to Acadia and teach there, because Dr Perry was getting close to retirement, and, besides being head of the Biology Department at Acadia, he had become dean of the college. And he was around seventy-two or seventy-three years old.

Along in January of 1926 I had a letter from the chairman of the Department here at Harvard, Professor Ames, asking me if I would consider coming back to Harvard on the staff. Marion and I talked it over, and we decided no, that we went down there to do a particular job, and that I had promised Dr Perry that if the governing board saw fit, that I would attempt to take his place after his retirement. It was a challenge. I knew I couldn't live up to his record, but at least I would be following a good example to do the best I could.

And unfortunately – or fortunately, perhaps, as it turned out – my wife was invited to Professor Perry's by Mrs Perry, for one of those teas that faculty wives have once in a while. She let this thing slip. And Mrs Perry, being very interested, immediately when she got home that night, told her husband, and he, next morning, told the president – "Ralph Wetmore has been offered a chance to go elsewhere." So about ten o'clock the next morning the president, Dr Patterson, called me and asked if I could come over, or whenever I'd be free he'd be glad to see me. I went over ... He was a great big angular, thin man, about six foot two. I remember the first time that he had dinner with us – there was scarcely room for *his* feet and for others' under the same table. He laughed about it. He was kind of a wag, and a marvellous human being! Anyway, he said – he was very formal – "Dr Wetmore, do I understand that you have an offer from somewhere to go elsewhere?" I said, "Yes. I don't know how *you* found out." "Well," he said, "I have ways." And he looked at me with sort of a whimsical look in his eyes. I had gotten to know him pretty well, and I thought he was teasing me a bit.

"Dr Wetmore, are you going to accept that appointment?" I said no, my wife and I had talked it over, and that we wished to stay. He said, "Well, I've only one comment to make to that. Either you accept that appointment, or I'm going to fire you." I said, "What do you mean, Dr Patterson?" "Well," he said, "I'm going to be very honest now." He said, "We've filled every place that we can fill in North America with graduate students, and we've nowhere else to send them. I have a notion," he said, "that if you got into Harvard, you might be able to see that they accepted a student in biology from Acadia. If they can't hold their own after that, that's their fault and not yours."

We talked for a while, and I had to admit, there was some truth in this. If I went there, I certainly would be interested in seeing the kind of student that I had known at Acadia get there. Anyway, when I shook hands with him, I said, "I'll go home and talk it over, and I'll let you know." And about a week later I went in to see him and said, "We've changed our minds. I've accepted, and I've received a telegram in reply saying to turn up anytime in September and that he [Professor Ames at Harvard] was mailing me the necessary papers.

So that's what happened. I stayed at Acadia the rest of the year and came back here on the staff in 1926. I've been here ever since. At one time we had three former Acadia staff members from the Maritime Provinces on the staff here at Harvard. I was the first one. Alden Dawson, from Prince Edward Island, was second, in zoology; and Keith Porter, from Yarmouth – biology.*

That next year, we had our first Acadia graduate student, as Dr Patterson had hoped we might. And I cannot think of a year from then until I retired, when we didn't have anywhere from one to four graduate students from Acadia in biology. And there've been some good ones.

---

* Keith Porter was the second chairman of the Department of Biology at Harvard to come from Yarmouth. He held the position from 1961 to 1968.

Sisters

VILLA EASTON – Hopewell Cape, Albert County, New Brunswick

The whole Dixon family – five children and their mother – moved to Boston at various points in the early decades of this century. Bertha, a sister, was the first to leave. She died in 1978. A brother, Gordon, is also deceased.

The youngest of the Dixon sisters, Villa is in her eighties. Her late husband, Millet Easton, died in the 1970s. She lives in Waltham.

Father built ships, and he was a sea captain. He went to sea all his life and then drowned at his own door, right in front of the house in Hopewell Cape, in 1910. We lived there six years after he drowned, and in 1916 Mother said she was going to move to Moncton. Gertie [her sister] was up there then, so we went up there and Mother ran a rooming house. At one time, Mother and I, we had about twelve men living there.

What was the attraction of Moncton for her in 1916?

She thought she'd do better, and she thought it would be easier work than farming. She used to grow enough vegetables and fruit for us, and then she had two cows and two pigs at all times. She'd raise one extra of each, each year, then she would have them killed in the fall – one for beef and one for pork, for ourselves, and the others she'd sell to buy sugar and flour and things that you couldn't raise. She did well that way, but she was probably getting tired of it. We kids didn't do that much. We were lazy; we'd skip out. We were kids, I guess ...

And then from Moncton they began to slip away one by one. Uncle Jack, Mother's sister's husband, he was from England. He was president of the Andrew J. Lloyd optical company here for a good many years, and he made all kinds of money. They were wealthy people. They lived in Melrose [Massachusetts], and they had a great big home there. And as fast as Uncle Jack would find a place for us in the office or whatever, he would call. He sent for Bertha, Bertha came up, and she worked for him as a secretary for a great many years there. And then Gertie came up and took a position, and they found a place for her. And then Gordon – he was the youngest, the baby. Uncle Jack sent for him to come up and take a job up here, so he came right up and took this position. And when Gordon left home, I remember Mother sitting down and crying for a week. She was broken-hearted. "I can't live without Gordon," she said. And she said, "I'm not going to stay here any longer. I'm going to sell my furniture and move out. My family are all over there, and I'm going to go too. I'm going to move to Boston."

So she went to work and put an ad in the paper to sell her furniture. Well, my land, the crowd that arrived – the load of people that arrived that night when the ad was in the paper! The house was half full with people, and everybody wanted to buy everything they could find in the house there. So anyways, it didn't take any time to sell the furniture out. And then we came. We just got aboard the train and came up here. We left home on April Fool's Day, 1925, and got here the second day of April, around four o'clock.

It sounds as though you were very lucky to have had an Uncle Jack here ...

We did have help, I must say.

Uncle Jack started a skate factory in Malden, too. He built that for his son, Stanley, and for Gordon, for them to get started and on their own. Gordon was superintendent there and Stanley, Gordon's cousin, was manager. They ran that business over there. And they made other things at that skate factory, too. They were making heavy aluminum ware, cooking utensils, things like that.

When Gordon was only twenty, he was making a hundred dollars a week. That was in 1926 – and he wasn't a college fella, either. He was right from high school. They were lucky. Uncle Jack had lots of money, and they got started like that.

How did your mother take to Boston?

She liked it – her own family was up here, practically. Uncle Charlie had come to Boston – he was in the restaurant business. My mother's sister Lillie, who married Uncle Jack, she came up here first to take a position with Uncle Charlie, as cashier in the restaurant.

Mother was brought up back in Rosevale, back in the woods there somewhere, a thousand miles from nowhere.* Her mother had fifteen children – ten boys and five girls. Her father came over from Scotland. They gave him a piece of land to build on, back in Rosevale, and he was working in Hillsborough. I can remember my Grandmother Stuart telling us about the bears that used to come to the house. They'd rap on the walls – you could hear them, she said,

---

*   Rosevale, when it existed as a distinguishable community, was in the vicinity of Hillsborough, Albert County.

rappin' on the walls – and she and the children were so frightened to death, they'd climb up into the attic and hide up there.

And when they got old enough to do anything, her sons all went. Of course, they never had any schooling in there in the woods, hardly at all. But they knew how to cut down lumber and trees and things like that. They went out to Vancouver and went into the lumber business. And Uncle Clayton and Uncle Seymour, they became millionaires out there. They worked themselves up, even without any education. She had ten boys, and four of them were out there.

Did you get a job when you got here?

I took a position, yes. I was with R.H. White's first – they were clothing stores. But I didn't like the superintendent on the floor. We had trouble – and I saw this ad in the paper, a wholesale house, and they wanted somebody in the linen department. I had been in the linen department a long time where I was, so I went down to see them and they wanted me right away. And they offered me five dollars more. So I just took the position and I was with them for about three years.

And did your mother get a job too?

No, not Mother – she was fifty-two years old when we came. She kept house, and she kept some roomers here. She had a two-story-and-a-half house in Watertown. I was with her, and Gertie was with her, and then she rented three rooms upstairs. She rented to three men – they didn't have to come into our apartment at all. They used to go up another stairway in the hall.

I was glad to come up to Boston. As I said, we had a lot of relatives and people here – and I didn't know the people in Moncton very well. I wasn't so sorry to leave because I didn't have too many friends there. I thought we'd have a better chance up here.

GERTRUDE DIXON – Hopewell Cape, Albert County, New Brunswick

She lives in Auburndale, a suburb to the west of Boston. There are three types of pictures on her piano in the sitting room where we talk: several, first, of her family, then two of former pastors of Tremont Temple Baptist Church, and finally, a colour photo of Richard Nixon with his daughter Julie.

I was born in '95, and I was about twenty when I came up here. But I wasn't quite seventeen when I left Hopewell Cape and went to

Coverdale. I lived with my uncle and I worked for the telephone company – Eaton's wasn't there then, or any of those places – right there on Church Street, not too far from Main. And I got electric shock there off the switchboard. I was on the switchboard, and they were working on the wiring and they asked me if I would test the wires. And then they said, "Now, don't touch them anymore." And I didn't, till he came around again and he said, "I wonder now if you'd test them again." Well, I picked one plug up, you see, to plug in, and then another one, one on each side, and when I plugged in the second time – the other plug – I got this electric shock. And I was going like this [she flails her arms] and trying to let go of the cords, and I couldn't. I don't know how it was, but I remember, somebody there told me, that he went back and shut the current off, or I probably would have been electrocuted. They called the ambulance, and by the time the ambulance got there I was stiff as a poker, they couldn't bend me. And Chief Rideout was there – he was the chief of police in Moncton then. And he says – this is what the girls in the telephone office told me later – he says, "What kind of death trap have you got up here anyway?" So I was that near electrocuted. I was pretty near out. I was not quite eighteen – it would have been around 1912.

I had to learn to walk all over again. I couldn't balance myself or do anything, and I had to have two people, my brother and my sister, one on each side. And there was the longest time ... You know the streets of Moncton, you walk along and then you step down to cross the street and then you've got to step up – well, I couldn't step down and step up. I couldn't raise my body that much. I was laid up a whole year with it.

And then I came up here, and I stayed a year. I went out to Framingham to my uncle's. And then I came in town with my sister [Bertha] and worked in town a while, and then I got sick and they said I had to have my appendix out. Foolish girl that I was – I was only about twenty – I said, "If I've got to have my appendix out, I'm going home to have it out." So I went down there and I went in right away. Well, I was in there about ten days and I caught typhoid fever. And from that, right on top of the operation, typhoid paralysis set in. I had it very bad. I went down to about eighty pound, and half the time I didn't know anything. I was in the Moncton Hospital ten weeks, and I was in my bed home pretty near a year.

But I intended coming back here, because this is where the money was. You could make more money up here than you could down there. There was no chance to get ahead – down there they'd pay you about thirty dollars a week; up here they'd pay you over a hundred. When I was at Raytheon* [in the 1940s and 1950s], I made a hundred and twenty-five dollars a week. You could live on twenty-five a week, and put the hundred in the bank. That's where you got ahead. I'll tell you, I went in there to Eaton's, doing secretarial work for a while after my sickness, when they first came to Moncton [in 1920] – and I didn't make twenty dollars a week. So as I say, there wasn't a chance to get ahead.

Anyways, I got better, and I said I was going to come back. And Gordon said he was going to come too. My uncle said that if Gordon wanted to come, he'd give him a job. So he went there. And Mother, she said there was no sense in her staying then, so we sold everything off down there – we owned the house at the Cape; we didn't sell that then, but we sold all our furniture and everything – and we left and came up.

Sheriff Lynds, Ernest Lynds from Hopewell Cape, he was there, and he said to my mother, "Mary, you're making a big mistake." And she said, "Well, what am I going to do? My family's all going – I've got to follow my family." So my mother brought us up – and then wherever we went, she followed.

When we first came up here we rented a furnished apartment, and then just as soon as we could get located, we got our own furniture and got started. We rented a place, for four years, and then we decided we were going to buy. So we went over to Watertown and bought a brand new house; no one had ever lived in it. My mother and my sister Myrtle – she was here then – and I, we put our money together and we made the down payment, and bought our own home right there, in four years after the time we came here. And we lived over there till my mother got sick, and we had to give it up.

But Mother never was sorry she came. Three years after we came up here, a woman that used to live at the Cape, but they didn't own their home, she wrote Mother and said they'd like to buy the house. And Mother wrote back and told her yes. Mother had her citizenship papers. She knew she wouldn't be going back.

I go to Tremont Temple Baptist Church. Bertha had been up here long enough when we first came here, and she was a member. We

---

* She retired from Raytheon, a large electronics and data-systems corporation which has its operations concentrated in Boston.

knew we were going to live here, so we just brought our church membership right up.

They used to call Tremont Temple the Canadian Church. Nova Scotia or New Brunswick people – and Prince Edward Island, too; there were a lot from Prince Edward Island – that you wouldn't know or hear of down there, you'd go in to Tremont Temple and you'd soon find them. It seemed nearly every one you spoke to there was a Canadian – and of course you got to know them all. It wouldn't take you long till you could pick them out. You'd ask them if they were strangers first, and then, if they'd say yes, then you'd ask them where they were from – and that way you'd have a chance to find out who they were.

They have a Canadian night there once a year – or they used to, usually in the wintertime. They'd ask the Canadians to stand, all those that were born of Canadian parents. And really, there wouldn't seem to be anybody sitting down. It seemed that the whole church would get up.

Would that have been a special service, or just one of the regularly scheduled services?

A regular service – they gave the call and everything. And I'm going to tell you, I have seen them there when they have given the call, and there's three balconies there, you know, and they'd start from that top balcony … and just windrows going up and up and up, to come forward. All around the whole front of the church, people had to move back to give them a chance to get up front.

Of course we've had a lot of evangelists there. Billy Sunday was there when I first came here.* Billy Sunday, believe me, he would tell them off in a hurry when he preached there. He certainly wouldn't mince matters – he would just speak it right there. I heard people say they expected to hear a shot fired, he would be so outspoken.

It's one of the most evangelical churches there are up here. And we've had some brilliant ministers. Dr Myers – he wasn't there too long after we moved here. Oh, he would certainly give that gospel out! It didn't matter who it hit – he would just tell them they were sinners right down to the bottom.

When I came to Boston, to get into Tremont Temple, members had to have a ticket, so they could get in the early door. When they

---

* Billy Sunday, 1862–1935, was the pre-eminent American preacher and evangelist of his day.

opened that front door, they just went in in mobs, *racing* in there to that church. And if you didn't have a ticket, you might find yourself out on the street, pushed to one side. And the church held three thousand people. You couldn't hardly believe it, when they'd open that door and they'd come in in flocks, just racing to get clear up to that top balcony – 'cause they knew that they'd missed the first one, since there'd been so many members there before them. I can't hardly believe it myself, when I go into Tremont Temple and think it's the same church it was in 1920. I'm telling you, that was a gospel, saving church in those days. It's a different age today.

You know, if you've got a fair education and you come up here, there's no reason for you getting these little down jobs. It's people that've got no push to them. They get into something and take the first thing they get and then they get in a rut and stay there. I wasn't that kind, and my sisters weren't either. They wanted to get something better, and they kept looking, and they got worked up to where they brought in the good money. I worked all the time, too. Never lost a day. No, sir, I never was ever fired off a job in my life. If I got tired of it, and I thought I'd like to try something else, I had no difficulty finding work. I'd get something and line it up, and go back and give my notice – and move around, try to push ahead a little bit.

When I first came here, I went into an office. At this store it was – I went on the cash and bookkeeping. I'd had that course in Campbellton. So I went and did that. Well then, I was a little while there, till I went over to a bigger place, the United Drug Company.

You worked at different jobs for quite a while, then?

Well, I was with Thompson's for ten years and I was with Raytheon for twelve. There's twenty-two years right there. Thompson's was a big restaurant opposite the *Globe* office on Washington Street. I was up on the tenth floor – that's where the office was – on the money, the cash. And the money I handled in there! I don't know how I ever did it. I used to handle thousands and thousands of dollars there in the run of a day, and I'm not exaggerating, because they took in big money. Ten floors they had there – they were all restaurants. And the cashiers who were on the counters and places, their money would be put in a bag at night and sent upstairs for us to verify the next day. And you know, I'd only just count that money once and put it in the till, and then when it came night I had to balance it. I never checked my money a second time, but I concentrated. I taught myself to concentrate, to concentrate on that cash – and I got so I could just handle money like nobody's business.

They paid good money, but they wouldn't take any fooling. When you went in there, you had to be onto your job. You knew you were supposed to work and you did. And when you got through with your work, that was the end of it – you didn't have to do somebody else's.

And Raytheon – as I say, they paid good money over there, because it was during the war. I left the office job and went over there as an inspector. We did all government work during the war, and I'm going to tell you: I was a supervisor of inspection, and you had to be pretty sure when you were dealing with the government that you sent stuff out right, that you didn't let anything go by. But they paid you for it – and I gave them a good day's work for a good day's pay.

When I went into Raytheon, they said to me, "Now if you're comin' in here, and you want a chance to work up, you'll make better money in the factory office than in the business office – they don't pay the same amount of money." So I said, "I don't know anything that I could do in a factory. I never worked in a factory in my life, and I don't think I'm handy enough for it." "You won't have to," he said. "We'll give you inspection." And he gave me that, and then after two or three years, I was the supervisor over the girls there. I just struck a good boss there, and he just pushed me ahead. Every chance he got, he'd call me down and tell me he was going to give me another raise. He took a liking to me, I guess. He said that he never went by my desk that I wasn't always there and busy.

One of the bosses – he'd done the work that we were inspecting – one time he said to me, "You just keep two people out of work," I put the work through so fast.

Half of them, you know, at Raytheon and some of these big places, they watch their chance to get a relief and then they go off to the ladies' room – and you go out there and you find them smokin', sittin' down, talkin', instead of being back out on the job where they belong. And a lot of that goes on, an awful lot. Now, I never did any smokin' anyway, so for that reason I never went out there to smoke or anything like that – and it was the last place I wanted to go anyway. They had a place for you to go for recreation if you wanted to, that I would rather have gone to, if I wanted to go somewhere – but I wouldn't go off of my job.

The desk I was on, and the girls I was training, they would be on the job and off the job. That was what the supervisor was for – to see that they weren't running outside all the time. They'd say they were going out, and they wouldn't be back for half an hour, off of the work. I would never do a thing like that. As I say, I took an interest in my work.

And I'll tell you, I think that's an instinct that's born right in the Canadians. They're good workers – I think they are. I remember when I first went over to Raytheon, I was filling my papers out – and I was still a Canadian citizen – and the foreman, the manager, he asked me where I was born. So of course I had to tell him I was born in Canada, and I was expecting he'd say, "Well, we don't want ya," but he didn't. He said, "Well, that's who we like, the Canadians, 'cause they're good workers."

I suppose you have to work harder down there – you know, they expect more of you and try and get more out of you for the money. It seems that way, compared to what they do up here. Of course I shouldn't say that, because I'm going way back to the twenties; I don't know anything about working conditions in Canada today.

But I never had any trouble anywhere I worked. I never was laid off or pushed out in my life. Any change that was ever made, I made it myself, and I never made it unless I was sure I was going to better myself.

And I don't think any the less of Canada for coming, but I can't say that I ever was sorry I came. I've done well. I've made out well. I'm on easy street now. I've got all I need, and more too, so what else could I ask for? And I earned it honest.

MYRTLE RICHARDSON – Hopewell Cape, Albert County, New Brunswick

A friendly, soft-spoken woman in her late eighties, she lives in a large, elegantly furnished home in Waltham. She is a past officer of the Rebeccas, as well as of the Eastern Star, and is treasurer of the Women's Club in Waltham, where, she says, "you can't throw a stone without hitting a Canadian."

Myrtle has lived in Waltham for over fifty years. She and her late husband – himself from Waterside, Albert County, although she met him only after moving to the States – ran a successful electrical business in the town for decades. Richardson Electric has become a multi-million-dollar business with several dozen employees, and is operated by her son and son-in-law. Several of her grandchildren also work there.

When I was a child growing up, Hopewell Cape was a pretty thriving little place. There was fishing, and there was great lumbering down there then. It wasn't anything for three big lumber boats to be up at Cape Harbour. And there was shipbuilding – my father built three four-masted schooners. He built a large tug boat that was bigger than the *Wilfred C*.*

But there're very few families now in Hopewell Cape that were there then. I could drive right through Hopewell Cape and not know a soul. I *have*. The Ayers went over to Nova Scotia – they had a monument business there. And the Hoars: Beryl is in Hillsborough, and Charlie was a teacher – he went to Calgary; so did Blair, and Hazel; Arlington went to British Columbia; and Marion is in Moncton – the youngest girl is in Moncton. That's only two of a family of six. And then the next family up [her hand follows an imaginary road up through the Cape], the Burnses, they're in Halifax. They're cousins of mine. Then the Dixons, they're also cousins. Before I went or just about the time I went away to school, they all went out to British Columbia. Then I come up to the Steeves – I think some of them are in Moncton. And the Jamiesons – they all went away. One boy came up here, and the others are in Montreal. And then the Newcombes – I don't believe there's one Newcombe there now. And the Bennetts – that family was brought up two doors down from my house. They all ... Evelyn went to Vancouver; Mildred, she married and was up in Ottawa; and Dick Bennett, Richard Bennett, was prime minister of Canada. And then the Pecks – the Pecks all went west, the whole family. Those were the people I grew up with. All of Hopewell Cape ... I don't know anybody there now.

There were a lot of people at the Cape at that time – I haven't mentioned a quarter of them. Geneva Bennett's family – those girls were nurses. They all worked up here all their lives. The Crockers – they came to Providence. The Pyes – he was a captain, and his boys went out west, I think out to Chicago, that area out there. The Hamiltons came up here. The Beaumonts, they came – they had a big family, there were seven or eight of them. And the Taylors, they all went away, and there were eight of them.

And our family all left. We haven't any relatives down there now. We had an aunt in Riverside. We had another uncle in Hopewell Hill, and an aunt in Albert Mines – but they all migrated to British Columbia when I was in school.

I left home when I was seventeen. I went to school and I never was home much after. I went to school in Fredericton, and then I taught school out west. I was out in Winnipeg for six years, and in

*   The *Wilfred C* ran regularly from Hopewell Cape to Moncton. It was owned by Capt. Arlington Dixon, her uncle.

the meantime my family had all come here. I wasn't so happy out west, so I took a leave of absence for one year and came home. I taught school in Hillsborough, and then I went back and finished out another year. But after I went back I was never too satisfied. I'd get kind of homesick, and some of my friends were gone. So then I resigned and came here and taught school in Needham. I was in Needham three years before I got married.

And we had nothing to start with. Nothing. I had a small amount of money, not very much – you don't get rich teaching school in Canada. And we borrowed about $250, and that's what we started our business on. It was a lot of hard work. There were twelve years there, we never had a vacation. I sometimes wonder, now that I'm older, how I ever did it. I had three children, and I always took care of my home; I did a lot of things on the outside, and I took care of all the books in the business for thirty-five years.

But I think the Canadian people as a whole are good workers. Because I know families that have practically no, perhaps fifth grade, education, that have come up here and done very well. And I know several that came up here and eventually got into a big business and the whole family did well.

I remember when my brother [Gordon] was living, he was super-intendent of an aluminum factory. A lot of it was piecework, and there were quite a few Hopewell Cape boys that came up. They came up, and they all worked on piecework, Gordon always said, and they'd put out. They did well.

I know that I didn't even have to write an exam or anything when I came up here to teach. I had a New Brunswick certificate, and I had to take a course and write an exam when I was in Manitoba, but I didn't up here. They just accepted my Canadian license. I just registered at the Board of Education, and that was all there was to it. And there were four or five other Canadian girls on staff there at that time in Needham – they were all from Nova Scotia. I was surprised, so I spoke to the principal about it one day; and he said, well, he would take a Canadian teacher anytime because they were more conscientious workers. So I thought that was quite a compliment.

Members

The congregation of the United Presbyterian Church, now in Newton, Massachusetts, was first organized in 1846 by a homesick Scot yearning to hear "Scottish preaching." Donald McKay, the great naval architect and shipbuilder from Jordan Falls, Nova Scotia, was one of the early pillars of that first congregation. McKay's famous East Boston shipyard operated in the 1840s and 1850s, and the memories have been passed on of how he, his family, and his company's fifty-nine employees, filed each Sunday into the pews of "the UP," as it is known to many of its members.

In the last decades of the nineteenth century, the church established itself as a home away from home for Cape Bretoners in Boston. Its pastors from 1895 to 1919 were all Cape Bretoners, and the church was known at the turn of the century for the fine Gaelic sermons preached in its frequent Gaelic services.

But it was during the 1920s that "the UP" was virtually taken over by working people from Cape Breton. At the time, the church was located in the South End of Boston, on the corner of Warren and Brookline Streets (later, in 1946, the congregation moved out of the inner city when it purchased a former Unitarian Church building in Newton), and Cape Bretoners came from across the Boston area to meet there each Sunday. One block over from Warren and Brookline during the same years was the Scotch Presbyterian Church, now also moved out of the inner city, to Needham. It, too, was predominantly Scottish in heritage and its congregation primarily Nova Scotian. The area in between these two buildings where people used to gather after church on Sunday evenings was known as "Scotch Corner," after the Gaelic prominently spoken there.

The Ladies Philathea Bible Class of the United Presbyterian congregation was made up probably more of Cape Bretoners than any other group in the church in the 1920s and 1930s. The Class sponsored from the late twenties on what were called "Silver Teas," for which the group was divided into the four counties of Cape Breton, each county with a "Captain," and each attempting to best the others in the largest number of visitors attracted to the evening and the largest amounts received in a free-will offering. (The "silver" refers to the silver services, not to the denominations of currency taken up in the offering.)

ALTA HOLMES – Hopewell, Pictou County, Nova Scotia

She and her husband Bill live in Watertown, having moved there after her retirement from operating a nursing home for twenty-five years. He is from Loch Lomond, Richmond County, Cape Breton. During their years in Newton, they lived very close to Newton United Presbyterian Church, where they were married and which they have been attending for over fifty years. She was a Cameron. She is in her seventies.

My father was from Antigonish County – Lochaber Lake – and he was only seventeen when he came down here. He was a wheelwright and he worked here for quite a spell, from the time he was seventeen until he got married. He got married in Boston – my mother was from Massachusetts. My sister and I were born here, but we were quite young when we moved back to Nova Scotia. My father didn't like it here. He wanted to get back to Nova Scotia.

I used to work in the post office in Trenton, Nova Scotia, and there was a time I used to know everybody there. I liked that job, too, because I liked meeting the people. There were a lot I got to know – it was right opposite the steel works, which at that time was going pretty good. But I decided I was going to go in training. There was no way there of getting any kind of work outside of that post-office job, and there wasn't much money in it, so I came down here – in 1927. I went and worked with the Hood Rubber Company, and I did pretty well. They were paying very good wages at that time. Then I got my papers out to the Mass. General and I went home on vacation. And, oh, I was so lonesome. I thought, "I'll never go through three years down there all alone." So I got my papers for the Aberdeen Hospital in New Glasgow, and I went in training there. I was in there for two years, but I had to give it up. I had trouble with my feet – you know, those floors ... So then I came down here and took another course, in practical nursing. So that's what I did – and I loved it. I opened up a nursing home on my own, taking care of older people.

The church was in Boston then, near Columbus Avenue. I used to go to the Congregational Church in Watertown, and then I would go to the Presbyterian Church in town at night. The other churches didn't have evening services, and some friends of mine that used to go there asked me to go in one night. I went in and I met Bill, and then it was a few years after that we were married there.

Did you find it particularly friendly there?

Oh yes, I did, because they were more like my own people at home. I think that the Cape Breton people and the Pictou County people are a lot alike, because they have a Scottish background. The people from down east, they seem to enjoy people, and they're so very friendly when they meet them.

I'll tell you what we used to do: we used to have what they call a Silver Tea every year, and they had the four counties of Cape Breton – Victoria, Inverness, Cape Breton, and Richmond – and each group had a table. People in the group that belonged to any of those counties, they'd invite people. And they used to come – Canadians, you know – from all over the place. My, we used to have an awful crowd. They'd have an entertainment and a lunch after. They used to put on a skit, and singers and different things – a variety concert. They used to do pretty well. Cape Breton County would get the most – and it was the smallest, as far as people in the church went – because there was a man from there that had a lot of money who went to the church, and of course he used to put in quite a sizeable amount. They used to win every time.

ANGUS CROWDIS – Big Baddeck, Victoria County, Nova Scotia

The same Angus Crowdis who went to Detroit in 1922. He lives with his daughter, Dorothy, her husband, Don Smith, and their family. He introduces me to his son-in-law: "He was born in Boston but his mother was Scottish the same as myself. This man's been playing pipes since he was that tall." Don's pipe band has played numerous times for the Highland Games in Scotland. Don and Dorothy's son Bradford, Angus's grandson, also plays the pipes. It is a rather Scottish household. Don's mother's family came originally from Lake Ainslie, Cape Breton, and our evening's conversation is peppered with references to such books as The Highland Heart in Nova Scotia, *MacDougall's* History of Inverness County, *and other histories of the Scots in Nova Scotia. Copies of* Cape Breton's Magazine *are on the table in Angus's part of the house. When he was younger he belonged to the Gaelic Club and the Gaelic Choir of the Needham Presbyterian Church. He has been a member of the United Presbyterian Church for over thirty-five years.*

All the Cape Bretoners that I knew and all my friends were going there. I knew all the elders there anyway, and became a deacon myself. So they made us a real home ...

The minister of course has a whole lot to do with it. And we had a wonderful man. Dr Murray,* he was for over twenty years our minister, and I miss him a lot, because he was a really fine man ...

The leaders in the church have an awful lot to do with it, too. We've had fine people. We've had a wonderful Sunday School there. That was Neil MacLennan. He was the superintendent of the Sunday School for forty years.

DON He was a fella who came up from down east. He was superintendent of a small branch post office on top of Mass. Avenue right in Boston. And he was head of the Sunday School. In fact, the new wing that's built on the church was named after him – the MacLennan Building, for the Sunday School.

And John Carey, he was an elder of the church and teacher of the Brotherhood Men's [Bible] Class, I think it was, for forty or fifty years.

Angus had belonged to the Brotherhood for many years. "Where was John Carey from?" Don asks his father-in-law.

ANGUS New Campbellton.**

DON My children were brought up in that church. That's the fourth generation of our family that's gone to the church. The old church was located down in the South End of Boston. I only lived two blocks from there.

ANGUS And the funny part, there was just one street running between our church and the Scotch church. The Scotch church, there's an awful lot of down-easters down there. Most of the Cape Bretoners in that church are from Richmond County. A lot of them from Cape Breton County came to our church, from Sydney and surrounding towns ... and Victoria and Inverness. And every Sunday evening, the two churches would go down about, oh, twelve hundred yards, down to the corner there. The cops would be putting them out, off the sidewalk, and no sooner the police'd be gone, they'd be back in ... Well, as far as I was concerned, our church and the Scotch Church, we both had the same nature, the same people.

---

*   Dr George Murray was minister at the church from 1935 to 1956.
** In Victoria County.

CHRISTINE MacKAY CARMICHAEL –
Groves Point, Cape Breton County, Nova Scotia

Her speech has not lost any of its rural Cape Breton inflection, despite her forty-plus years in Massachusetts. In 1939 in Boston she met her future husband, D.J. Carmichael, formerly of St Ann's, Cape Breton. Their family consists of two girls and a boy: Emily, Donald, and Ruth.

I was born in Groves Point, Cape Breton, in 1915, the oldest of four children. I'd always dreamed of going to Boston. I'd heard so many stories from my father and mother, who were here when they got married. My father, Alexander MacKay from Baddeck, Cape Breton, and my mother, Annie MacPherson from Cardigan, Prince Edward Island, met in Boston where they both had come to work. My father had been a fireman in Wellesley Hills for fifteen years, but after they were married they went back to Cape Breton for a new life on the farm.

One of the things I remember from the little one-room school-house there was the stories told by visitors who had been invited by the teacher to tell about where they had been – the big city of Boston. I thought, "Now, maybe when I go to Boston, I'll be able to come home and do that too!" [Laughs.] I never did get to go back to that school room to tell my stories. Of course, maybe I wouldn't have, even if I'd had the chance.

My cousins, too, would come home to visit from Boston wearing their pretty clothes and talking with their American accents. And ladies like Letha Gray and Anna Flemming would drive home to Cape Breton "in their own car"! Daydreaming, I used to think, "Oh, isn't that great. If I had a car ..." To go to Boston and come home driving a car – that would have been the living end.

In 1938, after my nurse's training, I headed to Provincetown, Mass., where my mother's twin sister lived. They were opening summer cottages. Since I didn't have a real passport and couldn't work outside the family, I spent the summer working at the cottages with my cousin, Mary Beers from Prince Edward Island. One of the guests that summer was a rich lady from Park Avenue, New York. She invited me to go to New York with her that fall. Well, I couldn't see doing that – after all, I had my old boyfriend down east! [Laughs.] So I went back to Cape Breton at the end of the season.

Well ... [with exaggerated slowness]. Things began to look rather dreary. The social life was great, but there was no work. So I decided to get in touch with the lady from New York. Shortly after, she sent me a letter with papers from her lawyer so I could get my passport and go.

I went in to New York on the bus. As the bus pulled into Times Square, it was evening, the sun was setting – and all the people, all the cars and all the lights – it was beautiful! When I got to 730 Park Avenue by taxi, the doorman opened the car door, and – oh, my goodness – I was ushered into this big building, into an elevator, and up to the twelfth floor. And, well [draws in her breath] – such a place! They were having a dinner party that night, and they had extra help. A butler there looked like someone you'd see in the movies. He was all dressed up, with white gloves, and he wouldn't look left or right. There was a Swedish waitress, a Japanese cook, and then there was "Scott," a coloured man. He was the house man, and he could fill in anywhere when the others had a day off. There was also a nurse, a private secretary, and a full-time chauffeur. I didn't know what *I* was supposed to do.

I didn't do much at first. Then the lady decided to go to Arizona for the winter. She asked me if I would stay in New York and look after her husband. I stayed all winter. All I had to do was to bring him his tray in the morning with breakfast, and after he left for work, I was to make his bed. Then I was free until the next day.

It was 1939, the year of the World's Fair in New York, and after my duties, I would go off to the World's Fair, Radio City, or the Empire State Building. I sure had a good time, but I don't think I appreciated it then because I was so lonesome. I would walk up Fifth Avenue and look at people's faces, and I'd never see anyone I knew. People from home would write to me and give me the address of a sister, a brother, or a friend, and in that way I did make some friends. One girl was from Sydney. She was a parlour maid for Perle Mesta, "the hostess with the mostest."*

I stayed in New York until August. Some friends were going home to Cape Breton and I decided to go back with them. That fall, I came back to Boston. Boston was where I knew so many people – and relatives. My two uncles, Charlie MacKay and Murdoch Mac-Kay, and their families were very, very nice to me. I was very happy in Boston. My social life centred around the United Presbyterian Church, where my uncles were elders and my cousin, Hazel, played the organ.

I met my husband in church. The first time I saw him, he was ushering, and oh, I thought he was the best-looking man I ever saw! Coming from the farm, where most of the men were more or less

---

* Perle Mesta was a celebrated socialite in the 1930s and 1940s. She was co-chair of President Truman's inaugural ball in 1949, and then was an American envoy in Luxembourg from 1949 to 1953.

tanned, this man looked so refined ... well-dressed ... immaculate! So I was quite thrilled when he asked me if he could give me a ride home ...

I went down east again that summer, before he and I were married in September. My mother said one day that she sure would like to meet this man I planned to marry. D.J. told me he'd already had his vacation, but I wrote him anyway, inviting him to come down. He wrote right back and said he'd just been waiting for me to invite him. He asked his boss if he could have time off to get married. His boss told him he couldn't go because he'd already had his vacation. D.J. told him he was going anyway, and he arrived in Cape Breton in a few days. This was during the time when jobs were scarce, so I thought it was pretty romantic for him to give up his job to come.

We were married on September 7, 1940. My parents hosted a large reception for us at their home, and the one and only dance ever held at my parents' home was for that special occasion.

Almost every summer we came back to Cape Breton with our children. And I did get to have a car, but it wasn't quite the thrill I'd expected when I was a girl. Cars were more common by then.

ISABEL MORRISON – Sydney, Nova Scotia

She was introduced to me as "the first lady of Newton Presbyterian." She has much of the first lady about her, and she is also the sister of John Buchanan, premier of Nova Scotia from 1978 to 1990.

"John knows his way around here better than I do," she says. "He'll tell me how to get places – shortcuts. Of course, he's been coming here for years; Boston's one of John's favourite places." The family resemblance is most apparent around the eyes.

She lives in a block of apartments on busy Beacon Street in Brookline, roughly halfway between the suburbs of Newton and downtown Boston itself. We talked there one Sunday afternoon after church, along with her friend Ev Grew, who lives in Newton and is a member of the Newton Presbyterian session. Ev's original home is in Glenholme, Colchester County, Nova Scotia.

Isabel began attending the church when she first moved to Boston in 1945, just a year before it was moved from Scotch Corner out to Newton. She remembers the Silver Teas.

They used to have the different counties – it was great competition, you know. All the different counties would sit in different areas of the church. They were all out to make the most for their county, to see that their certain food was served for their county, and to see that they were well taken care of. And then when it came to counting the money afterwards, they'd make an announcement at the end, different counties that made so and so, and the largest amount, they'd say, is from ... They'd tell the county and of course there'd be great clapping and cheering and everything. And lots of times there'd be a husband from one county and a wife from another. There was great competition there. The husband would be sitting with Inverness and the wife with Richmond or Cape Breton or something like that; he'd give his money to one county and the wife would give hers – and that went on for years. They really were a lot of fun. They always had a lovely program – they'd have the bagpipes there and everything. They stopped having those, though, a few years ago. The last few years it sort of dwindled off, and they don't have it anymore ...

Attending the morning worship service, you can't help but wonder how Newton Presbyterian copes with the inevitable aging of the Nova Scotian heart and soul of its congregation. The church has the appearance of two separate congregations, I remark, in one sanctuary: the one, Cape Bretoners, older, dressed formally, with a preponderance of single, older women; the other, young suburban American couples and their families. Their congregation, Isabel says, has been undergoing many changes.

Thirty years ago it would have been three-quarters Nova Scotians, whereas today I doubt if there's ... well, certainly more than a quarter of them are Nova Scotians in there, probably nearer a half ...

EV   And they kept the church going, through the depression, through the war, through all kinds of problems, trials, and tribulations. They kept it going – and that's the most important thing to a lot of those people. They see it as glorifying the Lord, I'm sure, and they've really committed their lives to it.

Fifteen or twenty years ago, I ask Isabel, when the congregation was by and large from Nova Scotia, wouldn't some of the Americans have felt left out?

Well, it had the potential of going downhill very quickly unless the newer people's feelings were respected and honoured. But the responsiveness of the older people, incorporating everybody, and the younger people incorporating the older people, has been a beautiful thing to watch, really. Because there's been more than a ten percent loss every year ...

EV   There's been a substantial loss of the older members – through retirement, or sickness, or death, or moving into homes – and they're just not able to be part of the congregation's visible life. But then we've had a lot of young couples, as well as young singles, come into the congregation. And you have this tremendous integration on all the boards of the church, both the younger people and those who are part of the generational group of the Scotch church. Both have been heard from – and that's what's kept it growing, even with the attrition rate of retirement, death and so on.

Isabel's family has been intimately connected with this church for generations. Her mother, Flora Campbell Buchanan, was a first cousin of Rev. A. Gordon MacLennan, who served as the church's minister from 1919 to 1921. And in 1979, on the occasion of the celebration of the congregation's two hundred and fiftieth birthday, John Buchanan was the guest speaker. "Some of them from the church who were on that committee," she says, "thought it might be nice to have a representative from Cape Breton there. They thought of John, and they knew John, and they asked me if I thought he'd come. I said he'd be delighted, if he had the time – so they called him up and invited him, and of course he was thrilled. Because John knows a lot of people in that church, and he had the best time. He really enjoyed that so much. And people enjoyed him – there were a lot there that knew him."

Every December a huge Christmas tress is sent from Nova Scotia to Boston, set up and decorated at the Prudential Centre there, and lit at a special ceremony. The tree is officially given as a gift each year to the people of Massachusetts, in recognition of their assistance to the stricken people of Halifax following the Explosion in 1917.*

"It's a beautiful evening," says Isabel. "Thousands of people go in to that. It's a tradition. It's always presented here by the Province, and there are thousands and thousands of lights on it, and just at a certain time during the ceremony, the premier of Nova Scotia and the governor of Massachusetts push the plug on these lights and light the tree. John always brings greetings from Nova Scotia to the people of Boston, and he gets a real big hand there. Of course, in that audience, there are lots of Nova Scotians. And they do that every year. It's always one of the coldest nights of the winter, but everybody has wonderful spirit in there and they sing carols and they just have a grand time. Beautiful ..."

---

*   On 6 December 1917, the French munitions ship *Mont Blanc* collided with the Norwegian *Imo* in Halifax Harbour, and almost 3,000 tons of explosives were set off. The resulting explosion killed 1,963 people and destroyed one square mile of the city's North End. It was the most destructive man-made explosion in history until the bombing of Hiroshima in the Second World War.

Boats Down the Bay

LLOYD AND MERLE (SMITH) MERRIAM –
Port Greville, Cumberland County,
Nova Scotia

A beautiful painting of a ship built by Nova Scotian shipbuilder Donald McKay hangs on the wall of the Merriam's high-rise apartment in Quincy. Lloyd painted it himself. A former sailor who shipped out of Saint John, New Brunswick before the Second World War and served as a petty officer in the Royal Canadian Navy from 1940 to 1945, his favourite subjects are seascapes and ships.

Theirs is a second marriage. They are retired. Merle has lived in Boston since she was ten years old. "My father came here and went to work for Steadman Rubber," she says, "which is now Armstrong Linoleum, in 1924. Then we came up." Lloyd's been in Boston since 1950.

"I went to work in a chemical plant when I first came here," he says. "I went out on Mass. Ave. in Cambridge and started looking for chimneys. I knew if there was a chimney, there had to be a factory. I didn't know one end of Cambridge from another." He laughs. "I had had enough of going to sea."

There is a deliberate intensity to his way of talking that almost gives a tone of defiance to his still very Nova Scotian speech.

"All Lloyd has to do is go into a store," Merle says, "and as soon as he opens his mouth: 'What part of Nova Scotia are you from?' He doesn't talk at all like an American."

"And I never will." He smiles.

Merle became an American citizen in 1950. Lloyd became naturalized following their marriage in the 1960s. They are members of the Eastern States Command of the Royal Canadian Legion, and of the Canadian-American Club in Watertown.

LLOYD Going back a lot of years, this is where my family came to when they came from the old country. Some of them came and settled here around Boston – Lynn, Concord, different parts of Connecticut. There were Merriams connected with the British Army here. And the War of Independence came along, and it came to a showdown, so they came to various people and they said, "You have a choice now. You can either stay loyal to George III or you can join up with us. If you want to stay loyal to George III, then you must go across the border. Some of my family did just that. Others didn't. So that's how Merriams happened to settle in Nova Scotia.

My grandfather lived and worked and died here in Massachusetts. He was a pipe-organ builder. My mother was born in England and then they came and lived in Montreal, Canada. She was just six or seven years old when they came over from England to Montreal. Her father worked in the Casavants Organ Works there for a while. Then he drifted over here to Massachusetts. My grandfather built the organ in Trinity Church [Episcopalian] in Copley Square in Boston.

I guess she was around twenty when my mother came to Nova Scotia with a girlfriend on a little vacation, and that's where she met my father. To make a long story short, they got married. And she lived the rest of her life there in Port Greville. There're eight children in my family, five boys and three girls.

Did some of the others in the family come to Massachusetts?

Well, Barney, Lenore, Melba, Randall, Dorothy, Donald, and Dick ... eight of us. I'm next to the youngest. And I have an aunt over in Cambridge, my father's sister. She worked in a naval hospital in Philadelphia when she was a younger woman. Some of my family just lived here for a short time. But my oldest brother lived here from the time he was about nine years old. He came here – he had troubles with his eyes – and lived with his grandmother in Winthrop. His eyes got taken care of, and in the meantime he'd grown into a young man, and he went to work and stayed here. He lived here all his life, and then he died here a few years ago. Aged sixty-five ...

MERLE A few weeks short of retiring back to Nova Scotia ...

LLOYD He was going to Port Greville. He bought the old homestead and had it all renovated – did beautiful work, spent a lot of money on it – and was in the process of negotiating with the immigration. He was going to retire down there ... then he took a heart attack and died.

MERLE My father wanted to go back there desperately. He was from Fox River, which is the next little village to Port Greville. He talked about nothing else. People would come up here, like to Barney and Carey's Lumber Company in Dorchester. They'd come on the boat to bring up a load of lumber, and the men would come up to our place ... That was my father and mother's conversation.

My father was an only child, but he had a half-brother that lived down there, and two half-sisters, and he and my mother went down every year. When they no longer could afford the car, they went on the bus. So when my younger sister got through school, my mother said to him, "OK, this is it. If you want to go back, now I'll go." Well, he went down. But once he knew that he could, he didn't want to, because we were all here – my brother and his wife and his family, my sister and her family ...

LLOYD I've been back there practically every year for thirty years.

MERLE Some years twice. [To Lloyd:] You went down there four times in one year when your parents were sick.

LLOYD Nobody but me knows the feeling I have for Nova Scotia, and for Canada in general, although I'm a citizen of the United States. [He measures his words out slowly.] That little, insignificant place there, to me, is home ... That's the only home in this world, to me, that I know is there. I live here and everything. I'm content to live here, more or less. But *that's* my home. And always will be. That's the way I feel about it.

MERLE On a good day you can see forever [she gestures towards the window], but on a good day, you know, we see Boston Harbor. [Laughs a little.] He takes the boats in and out of the harbour, but I think he'd like to be watching the gypsum boats come down the bay.

PART TWO

Ontario

Here lies Archibald MacDonald,
of the Whycocomagh MacDonalds.

> – gravestone in Clinton, Ontario
> (from *Proceedings of the Atlantic
> Oral History Association*, 1984)

Parliament and Gerrard

BRUCE AND MOLLY GREENLAW –
Isaac's Harbour and Canso,
Guysborough County, Nova Scotia

*He works for the municipal government in St Catharines, though he'd
shipped out previously for seventeen years as a seaman on the Great Lakes.
She is a cashier at Dominion Stores. Their daughter, Juanita, is a police-
woman; their son, Bruce Jr, is a fireman. In their forties, everything about
the Greenlaws is friendly, and their conversation is laced with laughter.*

BRUCE I had to lie on my age when I first came up, 'cause I was
only fifteen or sixteen. Red McLaughlin, he was the first guy to ship
me out – now he's over in Geneva someplace. And Hal Banks, he
was the union president.* The first time I was here, we were on the
beach. Everybody was on the beach. And at that time, nobody had
too much money, and we were sleepin' down in the jungle ...**
We'd sleep down there, everybody'd be sleepin' all right around,
and then the cops would come in and raid. You had to get up and
run. And so finally I got shipped out. The *John O. MacKellar* – I got
on her. And then once you got shipped out, once you got your
permit, you were all right.

MOLLY By the time we got married, he was sailin' up here. This was
his job. He went back and forth, sort of thing. That was in '61. We
were in Halifax then. We were married a couple of months; I was
working at Dominion, and Bruce was on a dredge in Bedford Basin
when they were dredging it out. But when it tied up, and it was
April or something, and the Lakes were opening, we decided to
pack up and head for here, so he could ship out.

---

* Hal Banks was the American gangster brought in by the Canadian government in the late 1940s to smash the radical Canadian Seamen's Union.
  Banks's Seafarers International Union took over from the defeated CSU
  completely in the early 1950s. Red McLaughlin was president of the union in
  Canada following Banks's departure to the US in 1964. McLaughlin later went
  with the International Labor Organization in Geneva.
** "On the beach" is a seamen's term for unemployed. Some seamen also had
  what they called a "jungle" – a community of unemployed men, living
  outside, pooling their resources, similar to the hobo communities during the
  depression – at Thorold, near St Catharines.

BRUCE   We lived in Toronto first.

MOLLY   We lived in Toronto about a year and a half – that was plenty. Oh, that was quite the life ...

BRUCE   My geez, that was something. When we first moved up here ... well, we didn't know Toronto. I knew it, but not that well. I'd just sailed. So I brought Molly up, and the first place we got was on Seton Street.

MOLLY   I can still see it. That wasn't a bad house, really.

BRUCE   Oh, that was a good home, a nice home. But the guy! That guy was a finger man,* or he was running away from something ... Now, Toronto was bad, especially that section. But *this* guy, he had a Dobermann pinscher, and that Dobermann pinscher was trained. He wouldn't touch you. You could meet him in the hallway and he'd walk right by you, wouldn't even look at you. But that guy told every tenant, "When you come down to pay the rent or to do anything, don't put your boot toe over that threshold in our quarters." So I figured, "You know, that's funny." So I went down and knocked one day – I don't know, to pay my rent or something. Oh, gee. That thing was layin' down, and it leaped, and by the time it landed on all fours it was standing right in front of me. Jaws! You ever look in a Dobermann's jaws? Them teeth were hangin' down about that far [he gestures a set of fangs] and him just a-growlin', his ears right back. He was an attack dog. So that's when we first started putting two and two together. And all these cops in at all hours of the night ...

MOLLY   That was terrible. Three o'clock in the morning you'd hear people banging, and the cops would be running up and down the halls. Those great big boots ... Oh, it was terrible. Especially when he was sailing. I was only nineteen, and suddenly in the middle of the night there's all this banging and yelling and hollering.
    I don't know what he did. Bootleg, for one thing. Whatever it was, it wasn't legal. [To Bruce:] Remember he took you in one day? We bought an electric toaster off him or something, and he had a whole arsenal of guns up there?

BRUCE   Guns! You wouldn't believe. I mean, he couldn't sit down on any part of the furniture that there wasn't a gun underneath. He was hiding from something ...

---

*   Someone who squeals on someone else.

MOLLY We stayed there a couple months and then Bruce got off the ship and we moved down to Sackville Street. And that was a nice place, a nice lady. And then we moved to Winchester, about a half block away, and a lady was murdered next door and so we moved. We had to stay in this section, see, because when the ship did get in, Bruce could be home in twenty minutes or half an hour. If we were up in the north end of Toronto, he'd never get home, 'cause he wasn't home that long. And then we moved down to Parliament Street, and that was quite an experience.

BRUCE Parliament and Gerrard ...

MOLLY [Sarcastically:] That was a lovely place ...

BRUCE In the evening, we used to turn off the TV, turn off the lights so there was no light behind us – 'cause a sniper almost took my head off one time – lift up the blind ... and there was nothin' on TV could ever match what went on outside that window.

MOLLY Oh yes, the Gerrard Hotel ...

BRUCE We'd seen guys come through that plate-glass window on Gerrard so often, I wondered why they even put the glass back in. [Laughs.] Oh yeah, right out on the road, and all cut and bleedin', and the ambulance'd come down and cops'd be down. And then one Sunday we were sitting there – and this was in the afternoon. You didn't know what was going to be happening out there outside – you just kept an eye on it. So there was a couple at the bus stop, and they were kinda gassed up. They were more or less from just around that district. It was a skid-row district. And so the cop on the beat walked by. And he just turned his head and said something to her like, "Maybe you better get a taxi," and he kept on going. His back was to her. Well, she had her purse in her hand. It must've been yea big. [He indicates a decent-sized bag of potatoes.] And she wound up with that purse – and that purse was just like a great big bag, eh? – and she let him have it behind the back of the head. And the old hat went flyin', and he went right to his knees. And when he went to his knees, she jumped on his shoulders, and the old guy came around and started beatin' him on the front. Well, the cop got up and she was still on his shoulders. And here she was grabbin' his hair and pullin' on it ... And this was in the afternoon, on a Sunday! [Laughter.]

MOLLY Well, the streetcar stopped and the guy got out and grabbed them and helped the policeman ... Oh, it was funny. We had more laughs there, but –

BRUCE   That was a rough place ...

MOLLY   Oh yeah. There was a young couple lived upstairs. She was sixteen and he was eighteen, or something, and she had a wee baby. We had Juanita by this time. She was a few weeks old. And there was this other baby in the back. So anyway, the old landlord owned several houses, and first he wouldn't use garbage cans or something, so they fined him $10 for not using garbage cans. And he didn't pay it so they threw him in jail. So the night he's in jail, the power goes off ...

BRUCE   'Cause he never paid the electric bill ...

MOLLY   Now, we've got no electricity, and we've got babies, and there's only one gas stove in the whole place. Judy, the little one upstairs with the baby, had a gas stove. So I went up and I said to her, "Judy, could I just use your stove to heat up the baby's bottle?" And she said, "Sure, no problem. Just go in there," she said. "I never use the kitchen."

   "Oh, OK." So I went in there and she had the baby's bathtub and everything piled on top of the stove. [Laughs.] "I never cook," she says.

BRUCE   They used it for storage. She never, ever used the stove. She didn't know if it worked or not.

MOLLY   The poor kid, the only thing she ever did was scrub the floor. Scrub the floor, mop the floor ...

BRUCE   And it was the cleanest floor in town!

MOLLY   She used to mop the floor, throw the Ajax on the floor and mop it again. So she always had Ajax up to about here [her calves], right? [Laughs.] And she was in her bare feet when she was doing this, and this was one thing: her floors, you could eat off them. Always clean. Her feet weren't, but her floors were. [More laughter.] And when I was in the hospital after I had Juanita, one night this Judy arrives at the hospital. And Bruce said he saw her coming down the hall and he looked to see if she had put her shoes on and washed her feet.

BRUCE   [Still laughing:] The first thing I did was look at her ankles. I didn't want her her coming in with the Bon Ami in front of her ...

MOLLY   And when we first moved in, the first week we were there, every morning, 7:30 – bang, bang, bang on the door of the apartment. And finally you'd say, "What d'ya want?" And she'd say,

"There's no mail." And she'd walk away. But she'd bang on the door till you answered her.

BRUCE Once she'd got you up to tell you there was no mail, then she'd walk away. But she'd bang there for half an hour if you didn't answer her.

No lock on the front door. I mean, right in that district. Anybody could walk in, all hours of the night. But nobody ever came in and bothered us.

MOLLY I should have been terrified right out of my head, but for some reason I wasn't as nervous then. I guess I was younger. Because I was alone there again when he shipped out. He shipped out around May or June, I guess. And I said to him, "When you ship out I'm packing everything" – well, we had a furnished apartment, just our TV and stuff like that was ours – "and I'm putting it in storage and I'm going back east." And I said, "When you get off in the winter, you come home for the winter, and then we'll relocate someplace else." But I said, "I can't stay here all summer with the baby." And so he said, "That's fine," 'cause my brother was going east in July.

But anyway, in the meantime, the day he shipped out, he left in the afternoon. I'd taken Juanita out, and I'd taken her to the store and the bank or wherever, and I'd come back. So I had to get the girl in the back to help me get the baby buggy back up the steps, because the steps were steep and the little driveway was on a hill. I put her up the little walkway, put the brake on the carriage, and went in to get the girl in back. Well, there was a little guy lived upstairs, about three. And he had come out the front door, and I spoke to him, but I never thought anything ... And when I came out in a minute the baby carriage was laying upside down in the middle of Parliament Street! And this was rush hour. I still get cold chills ... I knew that the kid had knocked the brake out and it had rolled. And I just stood there. "My baby!" I was scared to pick the carriage up, 'cause I didn't know ... And people were standing, watching me. So I went and I got it up, and luckily, there was nothing the matter with her. And this poor fella came up the street – he was just a rag-bag type a' fella – and he helped me get her up, and he said, "Is she all right?" And I looked at her and I said, "Yeah, she's OK." You know, a car could have hit her or anything. So he says, "I'll help you." He carried the carriage up on the steps for me, and he said, "Do you want me to stay here and talk to you for a while?" And I said, "No, that's fine, I'll be OK now. I'm OK now.' And I still swear this fella must've been from down east, 'cause he was so nice to me

... So I took the baby into the house – and that little fella, I think if I'd have found him, I'd have killed him. So that was a bad scare.

My sister and brother-in-law were out in Edgar* on an air force base, so I went out there with them for a month, and then when my brother Bob was ready to go home on vacation, we went home. And then Bruce came home in the winter.

Then he came back up the next spring – to St Catharines. And I guess it was July when Juanita and I came up again.

Once we settled here, we were OK. It was a whole different story then. We like to go to Toronto now for a weekend, and walk around and see the sights and whatnot, but you wouldn't catch me back there ...

BRUCE   At that time we were just starting out.

MOLLY   Broke, broke, broke. Even with the baby, we were broke.

BRUCE   You'd save all summer, because in the wintertime you couldn't get a job anyway. If you were looking for a job and trying to get one, you'd go to a place and they'd say, "OK, what's your last occupation? Where were you workin' last?" You've got to fill out where you worked for the last five years or some stupid thing. "Seaman." So they knew darn well, just as soon as spring came, you were gone. They'd just train you, and then they'd have to train another guy. So you couldn't buy a job if you were a seaman.

MOLLY   I think at that time unemployment was $27 a week, and you got it every two weeks, or something like that. So you'd save all summer, and all winter long you'd live on it. So when spring came, you were back to square one. You know, just the last little scroungings in your bank account.

BRUCE   Just a vicious circle.

MOLLY   You had to save. You had to look forward. You couldn't just say, "Well, today's today." You'd know that winter was coming.

But we had a bunch of down-easter friends – Newfoundlanders and Cape Bretoners and whatnot. There were about fourteen of us, and every two weeks when the unemployment came we'd have a party. This Saturday night it might be at our house, and we'd have spaghetti or whatever, and they'd bring their own booze, and we'd party from eight o'clock until daylight.

---

*   A town between Barrie and Orillia, Ontario.

BRUCE All it cost you was a couple cases of beer. And we'd have a big party.

MOLLY They'd go home at daylight – and eight o'clock, nine o'clock, they were back to finish up what was left from last night. And this would go on all day Sunday. And then they'd clean up. And then the next week, or the next two weeks, we would be at maybe Millie and Dave Porter's. They'd have maybe corned beef and cabbage or whatever, and you'd take your own, and we'd go on like this. And we did that for two winters. We had a ball. We all got along well, you know, and our kids were little then. And what we used to do when we went, we'd just take the kids and put them to bed there. And when they came to our house, it was the same idea. So there was no babysitting problem. And they'd sleep right through this whole mess ...

BRUCE And the whole thing was, every two weeks you'd get your unemployment, but then somebody else would get their unemployment in between that. So it wouldn't be every two weeks, it'd be every week. A party every weekend, every Saturday night.

MOLLY And we'd have a good time. Nobody ever got drunk or rowdy or anything. A lot of them are still around – we still see them once in a while, type of thing. But some moved back down east, some split up, you know ... Now Dave and Millie, they went back and got a nice place in Glace Bay. That's where they were from originally ...

BRUCE Dave, every time I see him, he says, "Whose turn is it to clean the room?" He always used to say that. See, on the ship, there were one, two, three, four, five – six guys in one room. And they've all got bunks. So there'd be three bunks on one side, three bunks on the other side, and half the time, it was so damn small that when you'd change watches, you'd wake up one guy, and this guy would get up and get dressed, get all geared up and go out, and then the other guy, he'd get up. But the two of them couldn't get up at the same time and get dressed, 'cause there was no room. And you had to make your bunk and stuff ... Well, it wasn't like the navy or anything like that. You *could* leave it go. But you sort of had to make it up, 'cause if you didn't, Christ, there would be a mess. So everybody, there was one thing they had to do: everybody had to take their turn at cleaning up the room. If there were dirty socks or anything – didn't matter, whatever it was – just open up the porthole and heave them out. If it's not supposed to be there, heave it out. So I had my turn at it, and this other guy had his turn at it, so it was

Dave's turn. Jesus, we were out, and she was just a-wallowin', just a-blowin' a north-easter. The old ship was just a-goin' up and down. And it was warm, because we were right at the boilers. So Dave opened the porthole, and we had a back wind. A back wave came back up to the stern, just flooded the whole stern, and of course when that porthole was opened, that just came in there like a fire hose. There was everything floatin' around – boots and suitcases and everything. Then Dave opened the door to the fantail, and Jesus, the water flooded right out. [Pauses.] Dave said, "That's it. I did my turn at cleanin' 'er out," he said. [Laughter.]

Bruce recalls work on the boats without nostalgia.

Those were the old coal-firin' days. You were down in the stokehole shovellin' coal, and man, it's ... well, it's slave labour. They wouldn't do it today. You're pullin' hot fire right out at your feet, and then you put water onto it, and white ash goes up and it all comes back down on you. You're stripped to the waist. And then sometimes the grate bars used to buckle. The heat would bend the middle bar, and then she'd fall down. Now if you had four fires in a boiler, they'd keep three fires going – a guy would be out there stokin' them. And you used to crawl in there with all kinds of clothes on, and take all the grate bars out, and put the middle bar in. You'd only stay in there about two minutes, and then you'd come back out, 'cause you can't breathe. There's no oxygen, 'cause there're other fires. There'd be a fire on this side of you, and a fire on that side of you, and one in the middle. That's where the big fire is. They'd put a board in there where you'd crawl in, and it used to smoulder. And that's what you used to do. You'd crawl right in there. And they'd think nothin' of it. They'd say, "That's your job." And we didn't know any different.

How long a shift would you do that for?

Four on, eight off, unless somebody else paid off and you had to stay there. On the old coal burners, half the time when you got to the [Welland] Canal, guys would pay off in Port Colborne – guys would jump ship and what have you. And then you'd have to work six and six down through the Canal. Then half the time they couldn't get anybody, especially in the summertime, and, say, if you went down to Seven Islands or Labrador, you had to work six and six all the way down to Labrador and all the way back, till they shanghaied a guy out of here to get him on.

Shanghaied?

Oh yeah, they used to shanghai you right down here in Thorold – the union hall. You'd get a coal or hard-firin' job, and see, the phone would ring, and you wouldn't know what it would be. It could be a good job, it could be a bad job. Well, if you had a book, you could refuse three jobs. But if you had a permit ...

A book?

There's a permit and a book. Now if you're a book member of the union, you could refuse. But them years you had to have somebody know you, plus sail for three years – plus you had to pay a hundred dollars for that book. Now, if you didn't have a book, and just a permit, the phone would ring ... And you didn't know, so you'd stay there. The next thing, boy, you'd see them. One guy would go for one door, with shoulders on him about that wide [door width]. The other guy would go to the other door. The next thing they'd give a signal. Both doors'd slam shut. And that's it. They would stand there. And you can't get out. Then they'd turn around and say, "OK, all you book members ..." So the book members'd get up, and they'd go over. Now they're watchin' everybody. They know. They say, "OK, you want the job?" "No." "You want the job?" "No." [Calls out:] "OK, permits!" And then it's, "Hey guy, you take this job." "I don't want that job. I can't do it." "Gimme your permit." They take your permit and hold it like that [he demonstrates] – one thumb on one side and one thumb on the other. "Do you want this job or do you want me to tear it up and you get the hell out?"

It's your living. It's your livelihood. So what're you going to do? You're going to have to do it. So you're stuck on it. And then you *are* stuck on it. You got on a ship, you were supposed to stay on it for sixty days. And even when they shanghaied a guy, he might only be on there for a week. There's a lot of them couldn't do it. No, Jesus ... 130, 140 degrees down in the stokehole. You had to be young. It got so, shovellin' coal, that we used to go in a tavern, and you'd get your hand like that [his palm is outstretched], and you'd say, "I bet you a beer I can blot a cigarette out in the palm a' me hand." You were shovellin' coal all the time. You never used mitts, you never used nothin'. And right in here [his palm] – that was just the same as a board. And you used to get a cigarette and blow on it, turn it around, till it just came to a real fine point. A red glow. And they'd say you couldn't do it. And you'd just take the cigarette, just take it right slow, and you'd just blot it out in the middle of your hand. You couldn't feel a thing, 'cause it's just solid callous.

Jesus, that was an awful way to live.

MOLLY Finally, one day, the ship was in Thorold at the paper dock, and he said, "I'm going over today and pay off. I'm quittin' sailin' and that's gonna be it." "Yeah," I said, "Fine," you know. 'Cause I had heard this before. But there just weren't any jobs ashore, so he'd always go back sailin'. And I said, "Go ahead." The ship was going to sail at noon. It was about eleven o'clock in the morning. He said, "I *am*." I said, "OK, well fine, go ahead." So he had the old car, I guess, and he goes over and tells the captain, "Payin' off." And the captain just about threw a fit. 'Cause they're ready to sail. But Bruce argued with him enough and finally he paid him off.

BRUCE Oh geez, he was going to send my discharge book and my gear to Ottawa! You're supposed to give him forty-eight hours' notice, see. I'd only given him about an hour and a half ...

MOLLY But seventeen years, and they don't even say goodbye. We've often said, you work some place else seventeen or twenty years, you're pensioned, eh? But seventeen years ... and you just walk off with your sea bag the same as you went on.

BRUCE Discharge book and an unemployment book, and a sea bag over your shoulder, talkin' to yourself ...

It Owns You

BUD MacLEOD – Westville, Nova Scotia

In his late twenties, he sells men's wear in a mall in the Mountain area of Hamilton. "The number of Maritimers I serve ... I ran into a MacDonald family that lived eight miles from me. And there were four other couples that same day – they were all Maritimers."

I left home when I was thirteen and I went to Ontario. I washed windows in the apartment buildings on Bank Street in Ottawa. They're these big high-rise buildings, and I washed windows in them on those little ledges outside. Twenty-seven stories. I did that for two years. And then I worked in a pizza place, Cicero's Pizza. It's right on Bank Street. And then I moved back home for a year, worked on the old man's farm. And then I joined the army. I was seventeen. I was six months in Egypt, six months in Cyprus. I was all over Europe. France, Denmark, Norway, Germany. And then I got out and it was really hard to get work. Really hard. I went and applied at Michelin Tire. It's about a mile and a half from where I live. And I gave them my whole army background. They didn't hire me, and I went all over the place looking for work. They'd hire every Tom, Dick, and Harry, but they wouldn't hire me. A guy works for the government all that time, and if a war had started, would have defended the country and all that crap – and as soon as you're out, they throw you aside. But then they'll take these guys that drop out of school about grade six, never worked a day in their lives, and they still don't work – they lay around and smoke dope all day. I don't know what it is. I guess they don't want good workers or something. These guys – I'm not saying they're stupid – but some of them, I mean, they aren't bright. How did they get in to start with? Their father or their uncle got them into these things. It's like you've got to know everybody in the place, you know what I mean? Like my uncle knows everybody in our town and the surrounding towns, and he drinks at the pub with the plant manager and all that good stuff, so he's in. You can be from there, but if you're not living there ...

So that's when I came up this way. These two brothers from down home who live in Simcoe, every time they come home in the summer – which they do every summer on vacation – they take somebody back with them. I went back up with them. I lived with them for a month and a half, two months. I went to Stelco, Dofasco.* I went down to Hagersville, to Livingstone's, the box factory. I never got any calls back from Stelco or Dofasco.

I can't lie. When I go fill out an application form, I can't tell them I've got grade ten or I've got grade twelve. Well, I did lie at the [men's wear] store, but that's only because the guy that hired me told me to lie. He said, "Why don't you tell them you've got grade twelve?" This was the manager. He's a great guy. He said, "I like you. I think you can do it. You tell them you've got grade twelve." I told him, "I don't like to lie. I've only got grade eight."

"No, no, no, no." So I lied. I said I had grade twelve, and I got the job.

A guy came in today. This suit fit him, but the sleeves were too short, and it needed to be taken in at the waist. Now ordinarily,

---

* Stelco, the steel company, is Hamilton's major employer. Dofasco is a smaller steel company, also in Hamilton.

they would've sold the suit to him and told him that we could fix it up for six dollars. And I told him, I said, "Look, why don't you go down to The Third Degree [another store in the mall], and get what's called the 'athlete's cut'? It's for tall, skinny guys, and it's tapered at the waist." I got my suit there. He was built something like me. And he couldn't believe it. He looked at me as if to say, you know, "You got some kind of a thing going down with them too?" Surprisingly, my boss was pleased. That guy's going to tell three other people ... But I wasn't thinking of that. That's not my angle. A lot of people look at me kind of weird when I'm friendly in the store. They look at me as if to say, "All right, what d'ya want?" But I think of every ten people who come there, I turn three away. I say, "There's nothin' here for you." I don't force them. I don't like to.

Another guy, I sold him a blue blazer and a pair of pants and a shirt or something, and when he got it all on, it didn't really look that good. I felt sorry for him, 'cause he wasn't all that good-lookin', and he kept looking in the mirror, like, "Hey! Great! Love it!" This was going to cost him a lot of money. And I sold it to him. And really, I got right down in the dumps about that. All I could picture was this guy going to a wedding, walking around, not looking all that good, but wearing a lot of really expensive stuff. It fit him all right. He thought it looked good. But it didn't really look good on him. I really felt kind of shitty.

And this other guy comes in with these two little people, a little short man and wife – and this monstrous son. He was taller than I was. And he was a little touched in the head. Not retarded, but he was a little slow, and he was kind of afraid of his father, this little, weasely father. They brought him in 'cause they had bought a suit for him, and we'd altered it – taken up the pants, let down the sleeve and taken in the waist. So this guy came in. He was kind of excited. His father was giving orders – do this, do this, do this. So he went in and he put the suit on, and the pants kind of came out, and showed about this much [half a foot of] sock. They were too short. And the other guy in the store said, "Great. Hey, looks perfect." And I said to him, "You're not goin' to sell that suit to that guy? Lookit," I said, "that pant's gotta come down another four inches." These two people were looking at me and they were saying, "Maybe it is a bit." And I said, "Of *course* it is! Take a look." And I grabbed this great big monster by the arm and I took him over in front of the mirror and I said, "Now what do *you* think?"

The other guy comes over and grabs me by the arm and pulls me away and he says, "When I'm servin' a customer, don't you interfere." And I said, "If I see you doing something I don't like to some people, I'm going to interfere." Well, they didn't buy the suit, and of course all this got back to the owner. And I told him the whole story, and my boss told him the whole story, and I got a pat on the back for it.

But it still bugs me about that other guy – even if he feels good in it. Well, it didn't look horrible on him. But he didn't look good. I could have made him look good for probably less money. But he was set on having that. I'd like to freeze them, get them all dressed up the way I want them, and say, "OK. Now you buy that. This is gonna look good on you." But you can't do that.

I just found it a hard place to leave, old Nova Scotia. But they didn't want me – so OK, I'm happy here. I've had the urge ... I'm fightin' it. Well, I'm not fightin' it anymore. I think I'm over it. I don't really care. Being in the army I was away from it all that time. But it's like Nova Scotia draws you back. Back home, it's a totally different life-style. People. The laws. Silly little things that you have to do here. Like safety checks for cars. A little crack in your tail light. Down home they'd certify it for you and you'd give them five bucks and they'd say, "Come in and get it fixed" – and it's up to you. Here they're so ... Not just cars, anything. I'm always bitching about it. Like if you pull up to a four-way stop, they're right behind the wheel like this [he frantically clutches an imaginary wheel]. They've got to be the first one to whatever it is they're going to. I can't *stand* it.

And right now, I'm liable to be the worst driver that ever existed, 'cause I just do anything to get ahead of somebody, and I've got to be the first one off that stop light, and I hate buses in front of me. I've got to get in front of a bus. If I'm coming up the mountain, and there's a bus in front of me, I'll speed up to get ahead of him – stuff like that. That was stuff that didn't bother me before.

You look at your friends different, too, when you go home. You look at them and say, "I grew up with that guy?" You've changed, and they're in this mould ... And people look at you different when you go home. People that have never been away say, "He probably thinks that he's real good now, comin' from Ontario. Big shot." And you find yourself slipping. You find yourself saying, "Well, up in Ontario I did blah, blah, blah, blah." And you catch yourself saying these things. You know, "These people are gettin' bored hearin' me say all these things about Ontario." Like, "Who the hell is he? Why doesn't he go back to Ontario?"

In the summer I'll be sitting here, and I'll be wanting to go home so bad. In my home town, there's a garage right across from this restaurant right in the middle of town, and you can sit there at three and four in the morning – sit on the hood of your car in the summertime, and drink beer. It's a self-policing town. Only two cops. They'll come up, and they'll say, "How ya doin'? Keep the beer bottles off the pavement so the cars don't drive over them in the morning." And the people do it. They don't want to misuse this thing, so they put the bottles back in the car. They sit there, and there's nothing else for them to do. But it's fun. It's really fun. And summertime at the beach, you know. Making clam chowder right on the beach. And partyin' all night on the weekend, things like that. It's almost a scary feeling. It's scary the way Nova Scotia can have that hold on you. It's as if it owned you and just lets you out every now and then. I can't get away from it.

Up and Down the Road

JIM ORMOND – Amherst, Nova Scotia

An English teacher in Burlington. Barbara, his wife, is from Chatham, Ontario. They have three school-aged children – Sean, Catherine, and Jesse. They live in Hamilton.

I never liked it in the Maritimes very much, for me, to start with. And I remember experiences in my childhood, which I may have blown out of all proportion, but which I think were significant. We used to get the Montreal *Star* at home. My father used to bring it home. And at that time – they don't do this anymore – but at that time the sports pages during the Canadiens season used to be full of pictures that they would take in the dressing room. And they would show these guys holding the pucks up – like if Rocket Richard got a hat trick he'd hold the three pucks up. And there was something about the photography. Maybe the photography wasn't as sophisticated as it is now, so you'd get this kind of dark visage of these eyes kind of burning out of his head. That made a tremendous impression on me. I thought, there's something there which is more intense, more exciting than I could ever imagine, and I don't think I will find it here. Maybe I'm exaggerating that experience, but I remember I was most impressed and taken. And the other thing that happened – and maybe this is a result of a kind of stultifying school experience – but I used to be fanatical about the movies. I really, really liked the movies. I had a kind of built-in good taste for the movies. And I remember when I was thirteen, fourteen, seeing *On the Waterfront* – and that was like nothing I had ever seen in my whole life. And I thought, "That's it. There's something going on here, which I don't know anything about, but this is a fantastic thing." And I certainly didn't make this connection or realize this, except maybe in some part of me which I don't understand, but I said somehow, "I've got to have something to do with that." And then I went to St FX [St Francis Xavier University] because I was a good Catholic boy and my father always told me I was going to go St FX, and I thought, "Well, that must be the place for me." And at that time, people didn't really decide about what they were going to do with their lives, it seemed. People just sort of moved into things for what I would consider now to be not very good reasons. Well, an example – I didn't take arts because I didn't know what people "did" in arts. I didn't know what it would mean to study philosophy, or English, or to study history. And maybe you couldn't get a job. So I took business. And plodded through the business. And didn't like the business very much, and then, because I got a job in Toronto with the income-tax department because those people came down to interview at St FX, I went to Toronto. And then, just prior to that, we decided we were going to get married. We did, and I then thought I would like to move on to bigger and better things, so I got a job in General Motors in Oshawa. I was a cost accountant. I remember distinctly the day that I got the job. I called Barbara and I was tickled. I thought, this is it – this is the apex of something. I had a very odd notion in my head that I was going to make a lot of money, and that because I was going to make a lot of money, and because General Motors made tons and tons of money, somehow we were made for each other.

So I went to work at General Motors in an office with about a hundred other people in it. A very, very big glass-and-plastic place with rows of desks, four across and twenty-five deep. And all of us were doing the same terrible thing – pulling cards out and costing them to find out how much it was going to cost to make their Chevy II or whatever that month. And that was kind of insane. But at the time they decided, for some reason which I never understood, that they had to expand the staff by, I don't know – fifty. So every joker, me included, who walked into General Motors was plunked into this plastic and glass. They had all of these really, really bright guys – guys with sociology degrees and philosophy degrees – all sitting here doing these cards. Nobody went crazy. We'd sort of zip through this work and then we'd run back and forth between each other's desks telling all kinds of weird stories and so on. People were doing bird calls ... So that was good fun – to a point. And then it got to be really depressing. All kinds of people were ready to leave and then one guy did leave and sort of proved it could be done – like, "People can actually leave this place, they haven't got you." So lots of other people got the same idea at the same time. I was really fed up with the job, I was really fed up with General Motors, and I was really fed up with being slotted where I was being slotted. The job was totally meaningless. It had absolutely nothing to do with anything that I would consider real. It was just a stupid job.

So I was sick of that. But I wasn't sick of lots of stuff. I wasn't sick of Toronto. We used to pack lunches at five o'clock in the afternoon and roar through the traffic to Maple Leaf Gardens and run up in the stands at Maple Leaf Gardens and watch the hockey game. I wasn't sick of the movies – and the movies were alive and well at that time. There were lots of movies around. And there was really good music in downtown Toronto. We used to go to the Colonial and hear wonderful jazz for no cover charge and a dollar for a beer. And I wasn't sick of that. But I missed my family. I wouldn't see very much of them, and I was missing them. And I felt that I was missing the Maritimes, but when I think of the Maritimes as I know it now, and when I think of the Maritimes I knew that I left, I don't know what I thought I was missing. Maybe I thought that our lives were a little bit hectic, a little bit too impersonal. Even now, I think it's very impersonal and I think that it's difficult for that reason to live in Ontario. At my house on 51 Havelock Street in Amherst, the door was open. That's a cliché, but it was true. My mother didn't care who came or when they came. So after school kids would go to Jimmy's house to listen to the radio, and my brother's friends would go to the attic and my sister's friends would come. And none of that happens here. That's not an exaggeration. We have people who I would consider to be very good friends here – and that doesn't happen. So maybe that got me down. It's hard to know. So, still trying to be the business man, I wrote a series of letters to companies in the Maritimes, and said that I had a business degree and that I was working as an accountant, blah, blah, blah – you know, give me a job. I got a reply from Hawker-Siddeley in Trenton. I met the guy who was doing the hiring, and I was hired at Hawker-Siddeley. I went to work as the assistant to the comptroller. Which meant nothing. It sounded wonderful. It was a joe-job too.

Barbara interjects: I was staying in Amherst with Jim's family with the baby while he went and found us an apartment, and he went down there to live with his aunt and started to work. So he was gone for a week. He came back the first weekend – and I could tell as soon as I saw him that we had made a mistake. It was a really bad time for us. He was really depressed, and he spent the whole time looking in the Globe, *looking in the* Star *– "What am I missing?" Every Saturday: "We could be seeing this. We could be seeing that."*

I sort of feel a little bit disappointed in myself about that. I have a friend who's a priest at St FX and I said once that Antigonish was boring and that the Maritimes were boring, and he got very angry. Not just stiff – he got angry. And he said, "Anything that's worth doing you can do here. There's lots to do, there's lots to see, there are lots of interesting things and you can read whatever books here you want to read." There's a part of me that says, "Maybe I wasn't inquisitive or interested enough, or industrious enough, to make a go of it in New Glasgow." But I hated it. I used to walk downtown in New Glasgow every Friday night and go to the G.D. bookstore. Every Friday night. And find no G.D. books. Every Friday night. And I went to the record store every goddamn Friday night, and I would have the same experience. It's a terrible exaggeration to say we had nobody to talk to. We had my aunt, who I really love and who Barbara really loves and who really loves us back and who was most kind to us. And she would pour us our tea and we would have a very, very nice time. And my cousins were nice enough guys. But there was nothing happening. I wasn't really interested in the things that people were talking about and I didn't really feel any sense of my belonging there. For instance, I've been to New York twice. When I got to New York for the first time I said, "I belong here. This is me." Like, "Everything's working the right way here." And I never felt that in Nova Scotia, or in New Glasgow. We had a very bad time, actually – like together we had a very bad time. That was the only time when we were ever unhappy. We really get along. But we didn't get along there.

And so, well, I think I realized at that point that business was stupid. Business was manipulative, and business was being hungry, and business was affixing seminars to your name so that you could go and present something with more authority than you could if you didn't have them. It was just a joke. And I realized at that point that I wasn't very interested – or interested at all – in money, and that I wasn't certainly very interested in "making it" in the conventional sense. I used to have dreams about numbers going through my head. Literally, I would wake up with all these numbers rattling around and be thinking them and saying them. So this was the big element of chance in my life. My sister was at St FX at the time and occasionally I would go down and see her at Mount St Bernard.* I went down one night and I was standing in the lobby, and Father MacSween** came along. And he said hello, and I said hello, and I said, "You might not remember me, but I was in your English class a long time ago." And he said, as nicely as he could, "Yes, I do remember you." I was doing a lot of reading at the time, and I think we talked about Thomas Wolfe, and I said, "Did you ever read anything by Thomas Wolfe?" And he knows an awful lot, but he's rather condescending and he said something like, "Oh well, when you grow up you'll leave Thomas Wolfe behind you," that kind of thing. But he was very interested in the fact that I was reading. So we talked about books. And then the next time I went down to see Louise, there he was again. Accident. And we talked about books again. And he said something like, "You read a lot." And this sounds like I'd been unconscious my whole life, but that was the first time I really realized that was true, and that I cared about that being true. And I went away thinking, "Yeah, I do. I read a lot and I care about reading and maybe that means that I'm really interested in it and I could do something with my life with that." It was that big. So that was during the winter and I was going crazy with the job and crazy with New Glasgow, and I decided I was going to go to St FX and take English. I had one English course. I had no idea why I was going to St FX to take English. I didn't know. I thought that it might be a good thing to do, and Barbara was probably really glad that I was doing something other than what I was doing. We had no money and that didn't matter and everything was fine. We went down to St FX and I took my five English courses, and we were certainly happier.

I finished my five English courses, and then I started leafing through calendars finding out where else you could take English. I had pretty well exhausted St FX. And so we went to Windsor [the University of Windsor, in Ontario], and were really happy there. Really liked it and had a good time. Ended up with this masters and then said, "What do you do with a masters in English?" I don't

---

*   An affiliated college of St Francis Xavier, Mount St Bernard runs the
     women's residences there.
** Father R.J. MacSween is an English professor at St Francis Xavier and the
     founder of the literary publication, *The Antigonish Review*.

even remember how this happened. It was certainly not planned. I thought, "Maybe I should try to teach." And so I got the job in Burlington, and we haven't really thought of going back. Sometimes I think I've had enough, but I think that it's when I'm tired or angry or when this thing about the impersonal Ontario life gets me down particularly. But when I think of where I could go, that stops me short. Because I know that I couldn't live in New Glasgow, and I know that I couldn't live in Truro. And I hate to sound "Ontario," but it does seem small and provincial. And I think that in some ways I'd be more angry there. If I'm angry about things here, I would be even more angry there. I think I would be really angry about the politics there in a way that I'm not here. I mean, at least you see glimmers here, whereas what seems to happen in the Maritimes is that people get into these terrible familial ruts with politics, and they vote stupidly and mindlessly. Not that they don't here, but it seems that they have more reason to vote sanely in the Maritimes, and they don't. Maybe this is true in Ontario, too, because there is a lot of this in Ontario – but there is this other element, of politics as a kind of horse race where all the three are lined up together and they're all running at this finish line. But they never say who represents what, or why are these people Conservative – or a better question yet, "Why am *I* a Conservative?" Or, "Why am *I* a Liberal?" Or, "What's the connection, the relationship, between being a Liberal and my real life?" None of this happens. And maybe it's not so bad in Ontario that this doesn't happen, but it's bad there that it doesn't happen.

The people in the small towns – maybe I travel in the wrong circles, but it seems to me that the stories are unhappy stories. It seems to me that people have sad, dreary, not very interesting lives. Tremendous drinking and a tremendous sort of sexual tension, and tremendous sexual energy and not much to do with it. These really kind of pathetic guys wandering around in these dance halls, and they don't know what they're doing or why they're doing it or where they're going. Unemployed, or pumping gas at some corner, to get ready for whatever it is they're getting ready to do on Saturday night. And they're so silent. They're not ominous, they're not scary. But there's something sort of sad in their quietness. And they sort of hang there. They do that funny thing at weddings. The weddings are really peculiar. They start out very stiff. They all go to the church and they're all dressed up. They're clean and they're sparkly and they've got the car all shined up and the whole business. And they go to the church and everything's hunky dory. And then after the church people start to shift, people start manoeuvring.

Whether they're not comfortable with their wives or they don't know what to say to their wives at that particular moment, or they think they might have some fun with the guys or whatever, I don't know. But the ladies stand around talking about I don't know what, and the guys stand around talking about really nothing. There's a sense of anticipation about it all, and yet I don't know what they're anticipating because I don't think that anything very much happens. They're sort of waiting. And then they go to the hall. They eat their sandwiches and drink their tea and there's this funny lull. And then all the guys head out the back door. And this guy's got a quart of this, and this guy's got a quart of that, and they've got the beer in the truck, and they're all standing there, and they're not saying anything. It's like "bad boys out." They titter and giggle and shift from foot to foot and, as I said, wait. But what they're waiting for, God knows. And then the guys get half drunk, and a lot of the women get mad and they say, "I'm goin' home." And they have these little back-and-forth disagreements, and then the guy talks the woman into staying, and they go back in, and the guy's sort of staggering around – not quite, but he's pretty full – and the woman's sort of glad she's there but she's not quite sure. And then they start to dance. And then everything's all right for half an hour. So they make peace, and they dance together for half an hour. And then they start shifting around. And this guy's with this woman, and it's "Well, look what I've got," this type of thing. But they don't do anything about it. It's not real. Nothing's going to happen. They go on and on and on, and then the thing's over. And you see these guys the next day, and they're all sort of loafing around with a beer in their hands. "Boy, last night," they say. And that's that.

Probably Amherst hasn't changed all that much since I've been there, and I just don't think that Sean or Catherine or Jesse would have a good growing-up experience there. That makes it sound like it's impossible to have a good growing-up experience in Amherst. I almost myself don't want to admit that ... I don't know why ... It sounds like you're almost betraying it when you say that. But ... I don't have any sense of being a Maritimer. Maybe if I took a test, some sort of definitive test, for "the Maritimer," I would be one. But I don't feel that. Whatever pull was there, I think it's gone.

BUD AND ESSIE DAVIDSON – Ecum Secum, Guysborough County, Nova Scotia; Cape Tormentine, Westmorland County, New Brunswick

Burketon, Ontario, some twenty-five miles north of Oshawa. Their two children are Carrie and Kirk. They are in their forties.

BUD I was fifteen years old when I first moved up to Brampton. I moved up with my father and stepmother. I went to school, not too long, and then I got a job in Trans-Canada Airlines – TCA, they called it then. I started there when I was fifteen. I was an office boy. And I was seventeen or eighteen when I moved back down again. I moved down by myself and stayed with my mother and stepfather in Halifax. I worked in a few jobs there. I worked in the fish plant on Water Street, and I worked on the highways for a while – putting in creosote bridges. And then I came back up when I was about eighteen. I came back up with George Young. He worked in General Motors, and Mrs Young, his mother, used to live across the road from my mother. He came home on vacation, we got talking and he invited me to come back up and get a job up his way ... make better money. I wasn't makin' anything there, you know, to talk about. Unless you had a trade or a lot of education, there wasn't much future there.

So I came up, and I went working at the Airlines again. I was loading the planes and fuelling them for a while. And then I got into Gen-Auto Shippers. I was driving the new cars out of General Motors over to a lot and then parking the transport and loading them. That'd be back in '59. I worked there till '62. In '62 I went to General Motors, working on the line – '62 to '67.

ESSIE We were married in 1963. I was seventeen – but I had been out on my own since I was fifteen.

Had you come up with your family too?

ESSIE No. I just left and came up to get a job.

You weren't frightened to come up here alone at that age?

ESSIE I don't think I had fear in my body then. At fourteen, you could say I was twenty-five. The kids down home were different. Like my girlfriend – she got married when she was thirteen and had a baby. A lot of girls were married down there that age – so you were just a lot more grown up.

The way I looked at it, if I stayed down there, where was I going to be? It was like, "I have to get out and get a good job." Mom and Dad always said I felt I was too good for the people – but it wasn't that. It's just that I didn't want to end up married and buckled down with six kids and some man beating me up and pounding me around and telling me, "You do what I say." That's why I left home – nobody was going to pound me. And that's the way the majority of them live in these little fishing villages. Husbands beat their wives up and the women don't think for themselves. The husband says, "Get me this, get me that" – and they just jump. And even though I'm a little bit like that, I still like to be independent ... You have dreams, and you want those dreams to happen, so you just get out and go – see if you can make them happen.

My cousin was home, and he said, "Why don't you come up to Ontario?" So that's what I did. I got a job at the Ontario Hospital in Whitby, and I worked as a nurse's assistant there. That was a good-paying job. Then I got a job over Chrysler's in the trim plant. We made the car seats and stuff. That was in Ajax – and that was really good money.

But I'll tell you one thing that *did* bother me. Another cousin, now, she was up in Ontario mostly all her life, and she was more on the go, even though she was younger than I was. I'd never been to Toronto, and I wanted to go, just to have a look. I'd heard of Jarvis Street, and I wanted to go and see what it was like and whether it had all these red lights and all this. So my cousin says, "Well, I'll take you up." So we hitch-hiked ... and it frightened me so bad, the street and the place, 'cause I'd never been in a place like that before. It wasn't as bright as I thought it was going to be at night. It was dark and gloomy and people were like a bunch of strangers. All I could think of was, "I want to go home." I said, "I want to go home," to my cousin; [urgently:] "Let's go home."

So the guy that was driving the car we were in, he said [comfortingly], "That's a good girl" – like that. He says to me, "I'm a cop from Whitby." He said, "I figured you weren't from around here." So he drove us right back to our door. I never ventured again into that situation. You could get yourself killed ...

So anyway, we hadn't been married too long when Mom and Dad came up. We sent for them. They couldn't get work down home. And my sister had already come up – she was quite young too; she was looking for a job. I got them an apartment, and Dad got a job as a mechanic up here. But he didn't like Ontario – he couldn't take it. He had to go back. Supposing he never had a job or anything half the time down there – he'd get the odd job, enough to

keep him, and trade a little bit here and a little bit there. And he
went back down. They were here for two or three years.

Mom didn't want to go back – she liked being up here with both
of her daughters. See, when we came up it was good money here,
so we figured we could bring our family up and we could still all
be together – but it just didn't work out that way. Mom went back
and Dad went back – and almost everybody goes back after they've
been up here and worked for a while ... You take everybody – I
figure anybody over the forty level, like in our age group – they
think about going home. I think once your roots are there you
always think about going back. [A long pause.] Most of us, given
the chance, would be down there so quick it wouldn't be funny.

BUD It was '67 that we moved to Woodstock, New Brunswick. I
quit General Motors. I had four and a half years there – I never did
care too much for the place anyway. And I had trouble with the
cartilage in my knees from work. Following the line, twisting and
turning all the time – you know, following it steady and trying to
keep up to it. And the heat's fantastic in the summer. Workin' two
weeks, nights, two weeks, days. And always wanting to go home ...
I said I'd go and that was it – I quit GM.

We should have had our heads read, I guess, at the time. But see,
myself and another fella had been down to Woodstock on a long
weekend, and I was promised a job on construction, learning to
drive the heavy equipment. I always liked to work outdoors. To
make a long story short, we packed our stuff and moved to Woodstock, wound up in a little apartment down there, and then politics
changed hands. And you know what it's like ... One day all the
Conservative dump trucks were workin', and then the Liberals got
in and fired them all. That's just what happened – the politics
changed, they brought a lot of Frenchmen down who would work
cheaper, and out the window we went. They had us out cuttin'
brush on the highways instead of learning to drive trucks. They
were building a highway through there right then. So I went and
had it out with the guy. I told him, "Look, you promised me a job
driving heavy equipment, learning to drive it on the highways."
"Well," he said, "if you don't like it you can always quit." That was
the attitude he had then. But he'd promised me a job. So I quit. I
packed up and moved to Halifax. We moved right to Mom's. I got
work as a parts man – but there was no money in it and I couldn't
see any future into it. The guy that I was working with had been
with it for ten years and he wasn't making any money – so what
future was there for me to stay in that? It was fantastic being there,

with Mom and Ken, my stepfather. But all we wanted was to come right back.

ESSIE My sister came down for a vacation. And she came to Halifax to visit us and she said, "Essie, why don't you come back to Ontario? Come on back," she said, "and you can stay with us and you'll get your old jobs back." She didn't even have to say that once, and I thought, "Well, that's it. I'm going back."

BUD We always wanted to go home, but we went the wrong way. We had no money. If we moved home again, it would be a different thing. We could sell our home and come out of here with enough to go down and buy a place with. Plus I'd have a trade, as a tractor-trailer driver. I could probably pick up a job. But then I was workin' GM on the line, and they didn't have any GM plants or anything down there. I was soldering – the trade of soldering vehicles. But you know, there's not much of a trade for soldering any place. So I just moved foolishly, really. Moved with nothing ...

ESSIE But that was another thing – there were no relatives up here to talk to, us being young, and no relatives to tell us, "You're making a stupid mistake." We talked it over ourselves, but we didn't know what we were doing. We'd have never done it. We lost everything when we went down there.

BUD That was the centennial year, '67, so I called it my Centennial Project ... But we came back with nothing, absolutely nothing. Hardly any furniture. I think we moved our hi-fi back and a baby's crib – those were the only things we moved.

ESSIE M-hm. We had to sell all our furniture down there ...

BUD I sent Ess and Carrie back on the plane two weeks before I came. I stayed and worked another two weeks and got everything all packed up in the car and took off. And I drove the car up by myself. Ess got a job back at Chrysler, and I was lucky – here a few days and I got the job I've still got. Awful lucky. I just drove over to ICL there [International Carriers Ltd] – well, I knew some of the guys from where I'd worked in Gen-Auto Shippers before, driving cars. The manager of the place, he used to be our dispatcher – and he introduced me to a top-seniority guy. So he said, "Why don't you go with Bill there and see if you can back one of them tractor-trailers in?" So he gave me a really good chance. I went out with it, and I was all over the place backin' in, 'cause I had never backed one in before. I backed into the cement a couple of times and things like this. I finally got it in there. And we got back and he says to

Bill, "How did he do?" "Oh," Bill says, "he backed into the wall a couple of times, but he's gonna be all right." So they hired me and I went to work nights. I worked steady nights for about a year.

We had to start all over again from scratch. Just from moving down there – for what? Three months. Crazy, you know. I shouldn't have gone that way.

ESSIE He went with his heart ...

BUD And I made that mistake once and went down that way and pretty nearly lost everything – so that makes it three or four times as hard to even think about doing it again. I have a home, I have children, and I have a job. I've got quite a few years in where I'm at. I've got steady days; we've got guys that work steady nights there – all kinds of them. And I've got pretty good seniority.

But each year I go home on vacation, it's harder to come back. I'm getting older, I think. Maybe I'm getting more sentimental. Even now, I think if I could make close to what I'm making here, that I'd go home.

What kind of a job would you be thinking about? Some plant in Nova Scotia like, say, Michelin?

BUD No, non-union. I think that's definitely wrong. The union is the only way you've got a chance. If you're in a non-union plant and something goes wrong – they fire you. You haven't got a leg to stand on. Out the door you go. But if you've got a union there, the union says, "Whoa, just a minute. You've got to have just cause to fire that man." And they'll get in and fight and get your job back for you. That's what your union dues are all about. Now I complain that we pay something like $200 a year on union dues; but without that union ... Like the foreman, he has to be careful what he says to you. My manager can't come up and swear at me, 'cause I can cost him. He can get fined $30 by the union for swearin' at me – "using profane language."

We're in the Teamsters Union. Some people call it the Racketeers' Union, but I've got to say that we've had guys at our place that have had an accident and the company was going to let them go; we had the union go in and fight for them, explain to them how that man has a family, it was an accident, that they couldn't prove it was definitely his fault, and everybody's entitled to a mistake – and that man has got his job back. As far as the company went – and they had an arbitration board and everything else – the union fought and got him his job back. He's never had an accident since – he's the best worker they ever had.

ESSIE   A factory can be hard enough to work in, without having to work there without a union.

JAMES CLARKE – Three Brooks,
Pictou County, Nova Scotia

He and his wife, May, live in Brantford. She is from Pictou. Their youthful good looks make it hard to believe that their three children are all grown up and on their own. He has a marvellous head of red hair; "Red," she calls him.

He has uncles and aunts in British Columbia and Massachusetts; one of his brothers lives in Fort McMurray; another is in Crowsnest Pass, Alberta. "We're kind of roamers," he says in a way that is both mild-mannered and self-assured. "I guess we're not a close-knit family, my immediate family from home, 'cause we haven't been together now for close to thirty years. My two brothers and my sister and my mother and my father haven't sat down at a table for thirty years.

"My oldest brother," he explains to me, "is thirteen months older than I am. He was fifteen when he came, and I followed him. I was fourteen when I came up."

"Fourteen! That must have taken a lot of guts."

"No – it just took a lot of hours on my grandfather's farm."

I started workin' out, away from home, when I was ten ... in the summertime. I started with one of our neighbours and that summer he was killed in a horse-and-wagon accident. I was with him at the time. From that year on, I was workin' with my grandfather. And when you're fourteen years old, out there in the middle of a field, with the sun balin' down on you and thinnin' turnips and this kind of stuff ... Goddamn stuff – I just heaved the hoe across the field. I said, "That's it," and the next day I was on the train for up this way. This was in August of 1950.

Well, my brother and I – he had gone maybe six months prior to that – we thought when we got up here, we really had the bull by the tail. [Smiles.] Oh, I guess when you're that age and right off the farm, you figure there isn't anything you don't know. Give it a go, eh? After you get workin' out for a couple of years, you find out you've missed a lot of things. Your education, you know, and like that ...

I guess we spent about a year and a half up here that first time. I was workin' for Gunther's on Murray Street [in Brantford]. They make jewellery boxes and this type of stuff. I worked there for three months and I quit there and I went to Slingsby Manufacturing, in the woolen mills. I worked there for a year and I quit there and my brother and I went out workin' for a guy painting barns. Well, in November the painting got run off, but the guy gave us a place to live till spring. Just a room. We had to fend for ourselves. Things didn't look that rosy, so my brother, one morning he just woke me out of a sleep – this was November, six or seven inches of snow on the ground – and he said, "Do you want to go home?" And I said, "OK." That afternoon we were on our way – hitch-hiking home in a snowstorm. Four or five days later we arrived home. And the two of us ended up going and working in the woods for a local guy down there, cuttin' logs and this kind of stuff. Four dollars a day.

We lasted a year and I was headed back up here. I had started going with May then, and I just said one day, "That's it. I'm headin' back to Ontario." She was all ready to go into the VG [Victoria General] in Halifax for nursing. And she said, "Well, I'm goin' too." So that was it. May and I, we hitch-hiked back up. We were thirty-six hours coming back up, the two of us. We did real good time coming back up.

May moved into a boarding house over on Port Street, with some people from Truro. And I picked up a job right away here. But I guess we were gone [from Nova Scotia] for about a month and things got really bad here. That would be about '53. I got laid off and picked up a job on a farm down in Caledonia.* I was down there for two years and a friend of mine got me a job in Brantford in White Farm,** which was Cockshutt then. So we came back to Brantford. I worked there for about a year – got laid off. We had our holidays all planned and everything. So we just went on our holidays anyway. I figured we'd worry about it when we got back. So we had two weeks of holidays, home, and a guy offered me a job down east. So I took the job while I was down there. [Laughs.] I worked two or three weeks and I still had no job to come back to here, and the rent was paid up in Brantford and everything so we figured, "I'll work for another two or three weeks." And one thing led to another, then we decided to *move* back east. So a friend of mine lent me a truck, I raced up here and put all our furniture on, packed everything up – and back to Nova Scotia. And we stayed fifteen or sixteen months, something like that. I worked for Don MacLean's White Rose service station, outside of Pictou going out

---

*   Caledonia is approximately twenty miles from Brantford.
** White Farm's combine-harvester plant was once one of Brantford's major employers.

the Sunrise Trail. I worked for him for $35 a week, seven days a week and two nights. Seven days and two nights until eleven o'clock.

So when I got a call back from White Farm, I was gone the next day. I was still on the payroll. I was on the seniority list. And I'd left a forwarding address, so they sent out a registered letter. There was really no hesitation. It was just – bang! I was gone. I got the call in the afternoon; I phoned and made reservations; I was on the plane the next morning, and I was working that night in the plant.

We came back here and we moved back into the same house we moved out of. The apartment was available, so we moved back into the same house.

May interjects: Three times we moved into that house ...

Yes, we moved into that house; we moved out to Caledonia. We moved out of Caledonia and came back to Brantford and moved back into the same house. And we moved to Nova Scotia, came back from Nova Scotia, and moved back into that house.

But we came back up that time and we kind of settled in. I got back to work at White Farm ... But the damn job, geez, it was work a few months, laid off, work a few months, laid off. So the last time I got laid off I picked up a job in Cainsville* with France Packing. It's compressor products. They make compressor rings and packaging and stuff. I got a job there at about half the wage I had been making, but it was steady. I stayed there for about six years. And the man that was my foreman there, he started his own place in St George – that's ten miles north of here, out on the 24 Highway – so I went there with him. And I've been there since 1960.

There weren't many opportunities down in Pictou County back in the 1950s. I was out of a country school. Three Brooks. Fourteen years old. I had no trade, no nothin'. There was no one willing to take me on. No education – so what I've got, basically, is what I've grasped myself, just what I was fortunate to pick up on. People say I'm mechanically minded. I don't know how I ever became mechanically minded, because there was nothing on our farm, there was never anything mechanical there. But I came up here, worked in the various shops around. Then I got into the machine shop at White Farm. Now I've got machinist papers. And another fella and I, we're in the process of owning this shop that I work in.

---

* Just outside Brantford.

I don't think I'd ever move back. I don't have anything against the life or the lifestyle or anything like that – but it's just that I've been away from it for so long that we've made our home here, I guess, and I think this'll always be home.

BILLY KING – Springhill, Nova Scotia

"My father worked in the mines. I worked in the mines when I was ten years old. Everybody did. It's the one thing you knew ... like father and son, son and father – you had a job. My father moved up here in 1949. That was the best move he ever made, as far as I'm concerned. He lost a couple friends down the mine and he just ... 'That's it, no more.' He just packed the baggage and came here to Ontario. He had $150. He came here by himself, and then Mom brought us up."

Fortyish, with a speaking pace not far from a machine gun on fast forward, Billy and his wife, Barbara, from Halifax, live in suburban Guelph.

I went with VS Services for about eight years. It's food vending. It's the biggest diversified food service in Canada. They go into hospitals on a consulting basis. Like, they moved into the Children's Hospital in Halifax, and all they really put into the Children's Hospital, the offices, was their own office equipment – a couple typewriters and a couple adding machines. Some paper. And a manager. That's all that's invested. The rest is all hired. So when they lose a place, as a matter of fact, they can pull out in a day. Everything's there. Everything's compact. Oh, there's big money in it. We used to operate on eight and a half percent. Like, the budget for the Children's Hospital for dietary was around a million and a quarter a year. Now, eight and a half percent of that was VS Services' fee. But see, there's a catch. When you go to make a budget out – it takes about three or four weeks – you're talking company money, so you've got to be very careful. Everything's projections. You think what are going to be your key costs for a year. Like food costs, labour costs – your unemployment insurance, and taxes, and workers' compensation, blah, blah, blah. And this is what it's going to cost you a year: a million and a quarter – and that's with our eight and a half percent. Now, if it turns out to be, say, a million and a quarter, *and* $100,000, VS Services is out $100,000. So what they give you, more or less, is law. This is it. Now if there's any excess profit over the eight and a half percent, it's split fifty-fifty. Fifty percent for the hospital and fifty percent for VS Services.

It wasn't bad. The only thing I find ... big companies, I don't like 'em, because I think they're just so impersonal. You're nothin'. I went down east from Ontario. The Children's Hospital had lost money for four years and so had the Aberdeen in New Glasgow. They had a lot of problems. So they shipped me down to New Glasgow. They had a lot of problems there and I straightened them out. My first year there they made $40,000 profit. So they shipped me then through to Halifax. I was area manager and trouble-shooter. So they sent me to the Children's Hospital in Halifax.

I was so involved there, I really dug it. I thought it was great. I was happy with children. And it's such an involved hospital. Down east, the Children's Hospital is a specialist hospital, and Dr Goldbloom is one of the top pediatricians in Canada and the States.* So it was a really involved hospital. It was a *good job*, something you could put yourself into. Actually, it's the best place I ever worked in my life. And it wasn't the money. It was just that everybody was for one specific thing, and that was the kids. This is what counted. You know, you're workin' there ... and I've always been a family man, I love kids, and I can just see those kids right now. Tubes in ... So if you had to work twenty extra hours, it didn't make a great deal of difference. The effort was there, and you didn't mind putting it out. At least you knew you were appreciated. And the money was there to spend, that was the great thing. 'Cause you go someplace else, they say, "Here's your budget. Seven percent. You gotta stay within this budget. That's our money you're spending after seven percent." The Children's Hospital was different. They'd sit down: "You want a party for the kids?" It was nothing for me ... Well, for instance, Hallowe'en. I went down to one place and I bought two hundred Hallowe'en masks in a little store. And the guy's just lookin' at me ... It was nothing for something like this ... And go out and buy boxes and boxes of candy and we'd bag them all up. Oh, we used to put on some real good do's. It was nothing to throw a party for two hundred children. We had Christmas parties, and Easter. I used to hire two or three guys to dress up in rented costumes – like the Cookie Monster, stuff like that – and go all through the hospital. I've still got a lot of the pictures. They're down there [in the basement] on the wall. I really enjoyed it. I really dug it. It was really good. That's the best job I've had, when I worked for VS Services in the Children's Hospital. I thought it was the greatest thing I'd ever done.

*   Dr Richard Goldbloom was physician-in-chief at the Izaak Walton Killam Hospital for Children in Halifax from 1967 to 1985.

The deal was originally that they were having problems, and I was supposed to go down for two years. That was 1970. And I went. And what really cheesed me, I went and sold my house. And I didn't make money on it. I really didn't. And I'd put a lot of bread on it. So anyway, we moved out there and we lived out there, and it was really good. I really loved it. But then almost four years went by. I went to head office and I said to them, "You said two years. I didn't say yes to you for four years, I said yes to you for two years. How about giving me a break?" You see, I wanted to go to head office, that was the whole deal.

So back in Halifax I called the area vice-president. That was Hallett MacDonald. And after eight years with VS Services, we'd been all over hell. Do you know what that was worth to him? "We pay your wages," he said. "You'll go where we tell you."

That was Friday at two o'clock. At two-thirty I had my stuff packed, cleared my desk, and walked out. That was it. And the assistant manager was there. I said, "You better phone head office and tell them." I walked out, went home, and told Barbara. She wasn't very happy. But I thought that the man had given me his word. I gave him my word. I moved my family, my kids – and I didn't think it was fair. So that was enough for me. I said, "Well, that's it." I went home and he called me and he said, "You'll never work for food services again." I said, "I wouldn't work for you again for anything." No, food services stinks.

I started off in food services years ago here in Guelph, at the University of Guelph. VS Services used to be at the University of Guelph, but it was kicked out of there. In-house management took it over. I made a big mistake in a way. I should have stayed there. I had the choice. But I was a bit younger, and I had my sights on something better. More money, a little better prestige ... I went with the company. It was the biggest mistake I ever made in my life. But I got experience. I think I got a great insight on business, on big business. And it stinks. 'Cause the guy on the floor doesn't realize. Some guy'll say, "The management – God, they gave us a six percent raise. They really gave us a break." And they've got four fingers shoved, and the guy doesn't know it. I've sat on both sides. I was a steward in a union up here for a couple of years, and I sat on the other side of the table and negotiated a contract. And you sit there with management and you shake your head, 'cause you know how much they're rippin' you. You hear it: "We've talked this over and we've decided you guys have to have a break," and blah, blah, blah, blah – and you're sittin' there shakin' your head, 'cause you know how much garbage is coming out of them. That's the way with big business. That's the name of the game.

We sold the house down there, and I think I left fifteen hundred dollars' worth of furniture. I came back and I phoned my brother here. He said, "I think I can slip you into GE" [General Electric]. So he went up to see the foreman. And I got the dirtiest job – but I had to take it, 'cause I needed a job. I said to Barbara, "Well, the money's not that great, you know, but we'll survive on it." She wasn't workin' then. And then I got paid. Thursday. The guy says to me, "OK, here's your cheque." [He opens an imaginary envelope.] "I don't believe it!" I was makin' over five hundred dollars a week in Halifax. I left a job that was ten dollars an hour – that's the God's honest truth – and when I started with GE, I made four dollars and thirty-nine cents an hour. I brought my first pay cheque home from GE; it was five days' work; it was a hundred and eighty-two dollars. "That's it? I can't live on that." What are you going to do?

But I got it made in the shade now. I've got steady days. I'm at the regular rate, so it works out pretty good. It's a great place. They make great big transformers. Everything's custom made, so production's not a big deal. Oh, you've got to do a little bit – let's face it, everybody does. But it's not the number-one thing. The number-one thing is quality. They want it once – and they want it right. They say to a guy, "You've got a job to do. Take your time and put a little bit of pride into it." I work my forty hours a week. But when the bell rings, I don't give a damn. I'm through. Eight years in VS Services, twenty-four hours a day. It got to the point where it was interfering with my family life. If I wanted to go down to the cottage on the weekend, I had to give them the number at the hospital. It took me four hours to get down there. I'd get there Saturday afternoon, and if anything happened, I'd get a phone call and I'm on my way back. You had no privacy and no home life, period. Since the day I started workin' with VS Services, I had no home life. Now, I work eight to four – I'm done. Now, if they come to me and say, "Listen, can you work till five o'clock?" I might say, "OK, fine." Actually I could work overtime every week. But it's great to get to the point in life where *you don't have to do it*. Scratchin' and diggin' right now ... it's just not that important to me anymore. Oh, we could all use the extra bucks, let's face it. Nobody's rich. But I'm just at the point in life ... I'm in my own niche. I'm happy with the family. I'm happy with my life. I've finally found my own niche after all these years. That's the way I feel about it, anyway. I'll never die a rich man, but I'll always have three squares.

I never thought down east got a fair shake from the government. I never thought it was fair. They never had a fightin' chance. They've been puttin' it to them since day one – that's the way I feel about it. 'Cause unless you're born into money down there, or else your family's had a business for years, you cannot really get ahead. I'm not fooling myself. I've had five new houses since I've been up here, over a period of years – and I could never, ever have done it there. I'd either be renting a house or living in a small apartment. Part of me would like to live there, to live down east – but as far as the money, I can't afford it. I'm spoiled. I was acclimatized to this place when I was young, and I got used to the money and I got spoiled. It's strictly money with me. That's all it is. Things are going higher and higher. I've got to live. But choice, as far as living is concerned, I'd have never left down east. I like the people. I like the atmosphere. There's nice people up here, don't get me wrong. But there's a difference. I don't wear a watch. I can stop people on the street any place in Halifax – "Hey, got the time?" – and they don't look at you like you're screwy or something, or you're on the bum. You stop a guy on the street here, he thinks you're trying to rip him for something.

Barb's the same way. She'd move down tomorrow. Myself, the same as Barb. Our roots are down there. We feel happier there. But we can't live down there the way we'd like to live. So we both agreed on it. When both of us are sixty, that's it. Everything is paid for. Barb has a pension. I have an RRSP. I've been stickin' it in there bit by bit. And when I'm sixty years old, I'm getting out. We're set. That's the way it's going to be. We'll build a cottage down on the shore, and six months here, six months there. Six months we're going to stay up here, summer months we're gone. Those are the plans anyway.

I've always been a homebody, and I've always lived in small places. I like them. See, I wasn't born up here. I really couldn't stay here as far as roots. Some people are drawn to Ontario. My big thing is, I'm drawn back down east. To me, that's it. That's my thing.

Pulpits

The moderator of the United of Church of Canada serves a two-year term and is the church's equivalent of a chief executive officer. Since the church was formed in 1925, of the four Maritimers who have held this position, three came to it from jobs outside the region. Willard Brewing, from Sussex, New Brunswick, became moderator from a pastorate at St George's United in Toronto in 1948. Angus MacQueen, from Port

Morien, Cape Breton, was minister of First–St Andrew's
United in London, Ontario when he was elected moderator in
1958. (He also, later, was at St George's in Toronto.) Clarke
MacDonald is from Green Hill, Pictou County, Nova Scotia; he
was working with the United Church's head office in Toronto
when he became moderator in 1982. The only exception was
Clarence Nicholson, from Dominion, Cape Breton, who was
principal of Pine Hill Divinity Hall – now the Atlantic School
of Theology (AST) – in Halifax both before and after becoming
moderator in 1950.

The path of ministers from the Maritimes to Ontario was
summed up in an editorial in the Sackville, New Brunswick
publication, *The United Churchman*, on the 1958 meeting in
Ottawa of the General Council of the United Church (the
church's national ruling body), at which Angus MacQueen was
elected moderator:

While we do not wish to encourage sectional thinking within the
Church, nor emphasize the part played by one area of the church as
over against another, yet we were impressed by the places filled by
former Maritimers in preparations for the recent meeting of the
General Council.

There to meet us was the Chairman of the Local Arrangements
Committee, the Rev. Norman Coll of Parkdale United Church,
Ottawa, a native of North Sydney, a graduate of Mount Allison, and
still a Maritimer at heart ... The Secretary of the Host Presbytery [the
local level of church government], the Ottawa Presbytery, and
Chairman of the Press and Publicity Committee, was Mr James R.
MacGregor, a native of Westville ...

The next Maritimer aboard to greet us was the chairman of the
Ottawa Presbytery, the Rev. Howard Hamilton of Menotick, On-
tario, another native of Westville, graduate of Dalhousie University
and Pine Hill Divinity Hall, who served several pastorates in the
Maritimes before moving to Ontario following his service in the
Army Chaplaincy during the Second World War.

The Host Conference, the Montreal–Ottawa Conference [Confer-
ences are the church's regional governing bodies], extended its
welcome to the Council through its President, Rev. Perley C. Lewis
of Cornwall, and Belmont, NS, another graduate of Dalhousie and Pine
Hill who served his early ministry in Upper Musquodoboit, Noel and
Trenton, before moving to Ontario in the thirties.

It was no surprise to us that a General Council meeting against such a
background of preparation should elect a former Maritimer to be
Moderator.

REV. ROBERT MUMFORD – Liverpool, Nova Scotia

"I'm the third Maritimer to occupy this pulpit since 1939. Dr Willard Brewing was here. He was moderator, and he was here in the thirties on to the early fifties, and Dr MacQueen was here for sixteen years. This is a strong Maritime church."

St George's United conveys a sense of Toronto establishment. It is the city's second largest United Church congregation; only Timothy Eaton Memorial is bigger. Before becoming minister there, Rev. Mumford had been a professor in the theological college at Queen's University in Kingston, Ontario. Prior to moving to Ontario, he had served a variety of pastorates in the Maritimes – in Lorneville and Saint John, New Brunswick, Spryfield and Truro, Nova Scotia – and been president, in 1973, of the United Church's Maritime Conference. He is in his fifties.

One interesting difference here is in how you relate to your congregation. If you didn't see your people in Truro on Sunday morning, you sure saw them on the street, or at the Legion, or at the supermarket, or in the drug store. They were there. It was cohesive. There were a thousand families – so you saw most of them one way or another simply by walking around. That's not true here. That is one thing – the capacity for anonymity when you want it. But I find that the difference here is the very, very different weight that this puts on Sunday morning – what is sometimes described as "the quality of the liturgy." And that has to be, really, the primary demand. But my time is much more my own here. There is the recognition by, I guess, lay people in the congregation, that if they expect there to be some degree of fruitfulness on Sunday morning, then the person who's responsible for that has got to have some uncluttered time. That's kind of nice. And my wife was making the point, too, that there is a tendency here – at least in this congregation, but I don't think it's terribly untypical – that the minister in some ways has office hours, and his or her work and consultation and availability is in the office hours. There are very, very few phone calls at home, unless there happens to be an emergency. But there are not very many people who phone up just to chat about the day's church activity. That is "home." The manse is much more a private home, we've found it here, than we've ever found it elsewhere in the ministry. Much, much more. The other stuff about living in a city – I suspect the conveniences of Toronto are not significantly different, with the possible exception of the arts, from, say, the availability of services in Halifax, Saint John, or Moncton.

It's nice to hear the Toronto Symphony, to see the Blue Jays, to see concerts at Massey Hall – but I don't think the quality of life is significantly better than any Maritime city. But the matter of privacy ... That's important. And I must say, now, having gotten a taste of that, that would be pretty hard not to have.

Were you ever aware of any sense of feeling "pulled," inwardly, over the years of your ministry in the Maritimes, towards Toronto?

As far as coming to this particular congregation is concerned, I had never thought about being a minister in Toronto. I was fifty-four when I came here, and if you don't move into this area by the time you're in your mid-forties, then usually you're not going to. But these people invited me to come here – I didn't apply for it, it came purely out of the sky – and my wife and I discussed it a great deal and decided to come here. [Pauses.] There is a factor of wondering what it would be like to be a minister in Toronto in one of the larger congregations ... of wondering whether or not you could hack it ... There is that.

The other side of the coin is that I was always aware in Pine Hill that Maritimers occupied what used to be called "the most important pulpits in the country." And that was always pretty clear, directly and indirectly, that that was one of the reasons Pine Hill existed – not only to serve the Maritime Conference, but to serve across the country, in the big churches. There was no question that that was one of the things we took in. And I think that kind of infuriated some of the other seminaries, who've had perhaps a broader sense of ministry than Pine Hill might have had. Pine Hill, in my time, was absolutely outstanding in biblical studies. It was very high in an unconscious, indirect sense of ministry. You had never any doubt that the ministry was the queen of the professions. But I'm not exactly sure the training we had in Pine Hill was as markedly superior as we had always assumed it was ...

The thing is, there *has* been a great migration of Pine Hill graduates, but I guess that one of the less useful things is that most of the Maritime pulpits are still manned or womanned by Pine Hill or AST graduates – and that's a pity. I used to send a lot of students from Queen's to the Maritimes in the summertime, on mission fields. Some of them found it pretty disastrous. Well, it's fairly typical of here, that surface amiability that you get in this particular area – "Hi! How are ya? Nice to see ya!" – that kind of stuff. The students assumed that this represented a familiarity and a friendliness, in the Toronto area, that they weren't getting [laughs] down on the Eastern Shore ...

REV. IAN MacLEAN – Edmundston, New Brunswick

The minister at Newtonbrook United, a suburban church in the Willowdale area of Toronto, Rev. MacLean comes from a family well represented in the United Church in the Maritimes. His father, two uncles, two brothers, a brother-in-law, a cousin, and a niece, are or were ministers. He is in his forties.

"Maybe it's me that feels the pressure, the awareness that they are sort of expecting you to come back, and that to some extent if you don't it's a rebuff or something. Sometimes it's an open question and sometimes it's kind of under the surface. There's the comment that, 'Well, I suppose there's no place really you could come back to after you've been in Toronto ...' And then the other one is, 'When are you coming back?'"

When I had been nine years in St Paul's [United] in Fredericton – which is a large congregation in the Maritimes – I had thought, "OK, where do you go from here?" I had begun to say to myself, "When I go from here I want to do something different. I don't want to go to another St Paul's in another place." My wife and I had always said that Toronto was about forty-ninth on our list of places we wanted to live. No way, Toronto. And then this opportunity came up. We really came to Newtonbrook and not Toronto. We came with the typical Maritime stereotype in mind, although we had been through the city a couple of times. Toronto was just hustle, bustle, rush, and roar. People had no time for people. And then we landed in Willowdale, living on a street much quieter than York Street in Fredericton – and had our stereotype smashed all to bits. We came from a congregation which was by and large well educated, pretty sophisticated – a lot of UNB [University of New Brunswick] professors, medical doctors, the professions well represented – to a congregation here which is just a few years from being a little rural church with fields all around it. What we discovered was in part a rural congregation – very conservative compared to Fredericton. And most people just don't hear that when you say, "Toronto." They assume that Toronto is bustle, bustle, sophisticated and worldly, and that the Maritimes is backwater. And what I discovered over a period of about two years was that in some ways St Paul's and Woolastook Presbytery as a whole were more free and innovative than Newtonbrook or Toronto Presbytery. It really was a major "Ah-hah!" for me when I finally twigged to that reality. One of the ways that happened was a team ministry event that was held downtown in Toronto. I was there with Sarah Harrison, my colleague at Newtonbrook for six years. Sarah's another Maritimer, a commissioned minister.* We had a student with us who was being supervised that year. So the three of us were at this event which was designed to help teams relate and communicate. We were asked to depict in some way the congregation we served. It could be through a poem or graphics or anything. It just happened that the student was pretty good with a charcoal-pen sketch. So we talked, and as we talked she got ideas and sketched them. What she sketched was the interior of a church, with an A-frame design and figures at the front – obviously Newtonbrook, a modern, 1960s church. But right in the centre of it she drew the little brick church that used to sit on Yonge Street not too many years ago, that *was* Newtonbrook, just like any other little brick church you see as you drive north from Toronto. She stuck it up on the wall when it came our turn to talk, and I sat there and looked at it and suddenly it was like the pieces of a puzzle falling together. I said to myself, "That's what I've been trying to get a handle on. That's it! *That's* what I have come to, and it's very different from what I was in, and I haven't made that mental shift."

Kicking It Around

BRAD ELLIOT – Dartmouth, Nova Scotia

The president of the local of the United Steelworkers of America at Hamilton Foundry, he, his wife, Pearl, and their two children live some twenty miles from the city, on Highway 6, between Caledonia and Hagersville. When he left Nova Scotia in 1967, he was the first in his family to do so, although most of the others have since moved to Ontario. He has a strong, gravelly voice.

Pearl and I didn't have any children the first time we decided to come up. We didn't have any money either. I'm a tradesman, a moulder, and I had a job down there at Dartmouth Iron Foundry. That was in Woodside** at the time. But things were pretty rough down there. There was no time-and-a-half overtime, no time-and-a-

---

*   A minister with theological training, who is not ordained and whose work often lies in the area of education.
** An area in the southern section of Dartmouth.

quarter, or any overtime – you worked straight time. I decided to quit. Myself and Glen Jardine, a friend of ours. He had written to the Chamber of Commerce here and they'd sent him some literature, and through correspondence to some of the foundries in the area, Glen got assurances that he could get a job here. So I thought we'd come up and give it a shot. We came up and looked around at different foundries. But at that particular time there was not too much going on, and I sort of ran low on money. Glen had relatives up here, but I didn't. So we talked it over and he decided that he was going to stay; I went back.

So Pearl and I were back in Dartmouth for, I guess, about two and a half years. I went back to the same place again. And somebody else took over the Dartmouth Iron Foundry – a firm called Hillis & Sons in Halifax. The owners of Dartmouth Iron Foundry went to work for a firm called the Grimsby Group, an English firm, and they decided that they'd start up a new foundry. So they sold the place to Hillis & Sons, and they approached me and two older fellas to see if we would come to work with this new group. They promised us that we would get a 15¢ an hour raise at the time we left, plus another 15¢ – this was in the fall – at the beginning of the next year. So we agreed and we went over. And after we got the foundry started, they got some more people from the old place. There were twelve or fourteen of us.

So we worked there, and then at the first of the year we were supposed to get this 15¢ increase. January went by and no increase, and the middle of February. So we all got talking it over, and I went up to the front office and I told them that this increase was past due and we wanted it retroactive to January first like we were promised. And they said, oh no, at that particular time they couldn't see their way through to paying us that. So we said, "You promised it to us and we deserve it, so you better give it to us or we'll ... we'll ... wildcat." So we talked it over: "No, we're not going to settle for anything. We're just not going to work – that's all there is to it – until we get this 15¢. So the boss came down. There was no union – and naturally, he asked everybody individually: "Do you wanna work?" "Do you wanna work?" By and by they said they'd give us 7¢. So they would ask a guy, "Will you work for 7¢ an hour more?" The guy says yes.

"Will you work for 7¢?"

Yes. Yes. They came to me and I said no. "I was promised fifteen, that's the reason you got me here, so I want the fifteen." So he said, "The rest of them will take it. We can't give *you* that." I said, "OK, fine. I'm giving my notice. In two weeks' time I want my vacation pay." They said all right. Two weeks passed – it was on a Friday, the last day – and I went up to the office and I asked if they had my vacation pay ready. Freeman called me into the office – he was one of the big shots, one of the guys that had been involved with Dartmouth Iron Foundry. He called me over and he said, "Are you serious?" I said, "Yes, I'm serious." So he kept me waiting there about an hour, an hour and a half, then he came back in and said, "We'll give you ten cents more an hour." "No," I said. I was promised the fifteen," I said, "and that's what I want – the fifteen." So then he went away again and he was gone for another half hour. And he came back and he said, "On the condition that you don't say anything, we'll give it to you." And I said, "It's too late now. Give me my vacation pay." The next morning I left for Hamilton. And this was the middle of winter. I was so peeved off about this deal that I just got up and left. We had one small baby and Pearl was pregnant for another one. I just moved her in with my parents, packed bag and baggage, and I came up.

And naturally, I went to see this friend of mine, Glen Jardine, who I had come up with in 1967. He was still working at Hamilton Foundry. They didn't need anybody there. So then I went out to Grimsby, to Lake Foundry, on the Queen E.* I asked for a job there and he said, "Well, we're building on an addition and I'll need you in about three weeks' time, maybe a month at the very most. I'll hire ya," he says. He guaranteed me that he'd hire me. In the meantime I checked around some other places. I could have got a job at the McCoy Foundry [in Troy, Ontario], and there was another foundry in Guelph, but from the people I'd been talking to, they weren't very good places to work. After a week went by, my money was getting kind of low – strange place and everything. So I went out to Lake Foundry and saw him again, and I said, "Listen, you know ..." I told him, I said, "My money's getting kind of short. I was just wondering if you had a place for me until the addition is built on." And he says, "Why? Where are you from? Aren't you local?" I said, "No, I'm from Nova Scotia. I'm up here and ..." "Oh," he says. "Why didn't you say that in the first place? You start tomorrow morning." So I went out to Lake Foundry. It wasn't bad. The pay was pretty good. It paid a hell of a lot more than I was used to down there, around sixty cents more.

---

*   The Queen Elizabeth Highway. It goes from Toronto to Niagara Falls along the shore of Lake Ontario.

And about a month later, he called me into the office and he asked me where my wife and children were. And I told him. I says, "They're in Nova Scotia." He said, "What are you waiting for? Why don't you bring them up?" I says, "Well, my funds are kind of limited and it costs money. Plus the furniture and everything else – I've got that in storage and scattered with different friends all over the place." So he says, "Well, how much do you need to bring them up?" "Oh," I said, "I don't know, maybe $100, $150." He just reached in his pocket and gave me $200 cash. He says, "You get that wife and kids of yours and bring them up." This was the manager, and he was the owner, of Lake Foundry! So I brought them up.

This individual, Stan Millen, I tell you, I never met a man like him in my life. I went in the office about three or four weeks later and I told him, I said, "Stan, I keep getting my pay cheques, and you're not taking anything off from this loan that you extended me." He says, "What do you think is fair?" I says, "You better start taking ten dollars a week off my pay." He hollered over to the bookkeeper, "Take ten dollars off of Brad's pay."

So the next pay I had ten dollars taken off, and then the next pay I received after that there was no ten dollars taken off. So I didn't say anything. And then the pay after that there was no money taken off, so I went in and I said, "Stan, you know, I want to get all my bills straightened up." I said, "This thing bothers me. I want to pay it off as quick as I can so I can start bringing my furniture up." "What?" he says. "You want some more money?" "No, no," I says. "I'm working things out on that end of it. I just want to pay my obligation off to you so I don't owe you anything." And he says, "Well, do I look worried about it?" I says, "No." He says, "Then don't you worry about it." And I never did. He wouldn't take a cent.

When I brought Pearl up here it was in March, and the baby was born in June. We stayed with some friends for about two weeks, three weeks, and I found an apartment in the East End on Champlain Avenue. And then from there things just kept getting better and better. I only worked at Lake Foundry for a year and a half. Things got slack there and they called me at Hamilton Foundry. It's a beautiful place to work. It's a small place, the guys really work together. So I went to work there. Things were slack at Lake and they were thinking of going to a four-day week until they picked up. So I went in and I saw Stan. I told him that I'd been offered a job over there. So he says, "I wish you the best of luck. Hopefully things are going to get better here, but there're no guarantees. And if you can better yourself by goin' to this place – I know it's an established firm and they've got steady customers – you're better off to go there." And I did.

And you've never thought seriously about going home since?

I never would. Once I got the job ... Well, to me it was a challenge, something completely different. It was a big deal – another province and a big city. And the work was challenging. I'd seen these different jobs coming in at Lake there, and I just wanted to be able to produce something like that. And up here we seemed to have more modern techniques, a little better materials to work with, and the machinery was kept in better condition. I really got interested in what I was doing.

And I was just so mad at that system down there, and the people that I worked for – the businesses that were down there and the wages they wanted to pay. When I was working for Dartmouth Iron Foundry they bought out Dartmouth Machine Shop. And there were individuals that were sent down from there to work for Texaco, or Esso, in the Dartmouth refineries. Different times they'd need welders and they'd take them from Dartmouth Machine Shop. And they'd be working on a Christmas Day or a New Year's Day, and I'd see them – they'd come into our shop periodically and do a little bit of work, and I'd be speaking to them. And in the meantime I'm hearing stories from the big bosses, and some of the foremen, kicking it around: "We've got these individuals workin' out at the refineries, the company's grabbing fourteen or fifteen dollars an hour for them working out there" – and here they were only paying them three dollars, plus giving them time and a quarter for Christmas Day. Can you believe it?

Poor money, poor working conditions – those are some of the reasons why I left. I just couldn't see my life down there. You just lived from day to day and pay cheque to pay cheque, hoping that you never got hurt, because if you ever got hurt ... Where were the meals going to come from? How were the kids going to get fed? That was my concern.

ALLAN COOPER – Moncton, New Brunswick

A bachelor apartment near High Park in Toronto. The son of a railroad man, he is the only one of a family of four to have moved away from New Brunswick. He is nearing retirement with Stelco's lakefront operation in Toronto.

In the winter of 1941 a bunch of us came up to Montreal. We started on production work and we were getting about fifty cents an hour. That was before wages went sky-high. I started at fifty-five an hour, eight hours a day, seven days a week. And during the time I was there it got up pretty close to a dollar an hour – I think it was around ninety cents an hour or something. That wasn't bad money in those days. It was considered pretty good money.

Well, of course, toward the end of the war, things were closing down rapidly in the war industry, so to make a long story short, I came up here and lived with one of my cousins – a family actually, my uncle and aunt and a couple of my cousins.

Why Toronto and not back to Moncton?

I had a choice to make. I *could* go down home, but then I figured, "If I go down home, what will I do? I certainly don't want to go back and work for the T. Eaton Co. again." I worked for them for five years after I got out of high school. I worked for the mail order. At that time, there was no place else to go. For some reason, my father didn't seem to want me to work in the CNR. He seemed to be against it. But I don't think he realized that we had nowhere else to go. With a high-school education, the options weren't too good.

I graduated from high school in 1935 and I went to Eaton's, for which I was paid the grand stipend of seven dollars a week. Every time a raise came around, it came in a little envelope marked "Private and Confidential": "We have been pleased to increase your salary from seven dollars to eight dollars." [Laughs.] And then it came along from eight to nine – so that at the end of five years, I was making eleven dollars. There was no chance of getting anywhere. When I started working in 1935, married men in Moncton with four children were making as low as fifteen dollars a week. How they did it, I don't know. Of course, you were coming out of a depression and things were pretty grim.

I came to Toronto in the fall of '45. While I was here I had an operation on my foot – I had a problem with one of the bones in my ankle. That put me off work for about six months. Eventually I got back on my feet again, and took a couple of small jobs around the city. I worked for a paper company for a few months, and I worked out in the East End looking after supplies for a welding company. But that was just an interim job – it didn't pay very much. And then I went out to the West End and worked for a company making electric fans and things. That was another fill-in job – it was just a matter of doing something rather than sitting around waiting for something to come along.

So then I went to the steel company in 1948. At that time they only had openings for die-store staff, so I started out in the die-store department. I got my foot in. And then they were looking for a man to schedule the tool room. Of course I had no experience at all in tool-room scheduling – just my natural knowledge of that game through my machine-shop work in Montreal, and what I'd picked up in the stores department. I was given the job and more or less left to myself to pick it all up. Over a period of time you learned all the various machine operations. So I was in there doing that for a couple of years, and then I had an opportunity to learn the heat-treating for the tool steels. So I served my time up in the heat department, learning how to heat-treat tools. And eventually I ended up upstairs, in the salaried department. Up until that time I had been a member of the union, but then they changed my job and sent me upstairs out of the bargaining unit. And as time went by the job was upgraded into what they call "Process Planner." I've been at it ever since. It's strictly estimating, scheduling, making the various reports – weekly, monthly, things of that nature. Tool-room production, and some machine parts ...

Would you have gone back if you could have got a job home at the same pay?

Yes, I probably would have, if I thought there was anything there with comparative pay. Because I like the Maritimes – I like the slower lifestyle they have down there. And I don't think you really miss out on anything. Certain things, I suppose, you'd miss from up here – like symphony orchestras and operas and plays. But it's no big deal. I've been to a few symphonies, I've seen a few operas and I've seen a few plays. It would be no big deal if I never saw another one. It's never been a part of my way of life. I'd rather be out going for a walk, playing a game of golf, or just visiting somebody, than sitting on my fanny watching somebody else do something. It doesn't appeal to me.

A lot of people say you can't go back. I was talking to one fellow – he's a general foreman, he comes from a small town in New Brunswick. He says, "There's no way I can go back again, not to live. I'm in a different income bracket from what I used to be when I was down there," he says. "I had nothing when I was there, and now I've got a home, a cottage, a car, and you know, the whole works." He says, "My whole life is meshed here with life in Ontario."

But I know lots of people who have gone back. We had a chap just quit here – now he's gone down to Nova Scotia to live, him and his wife. Apparently he was from Nova Scotia somewhere. Then we've had fellows that worked in the steel company who just all of a sudden chucked it up and went back home. They figured it wasn't worth it – you know, the rat race up here. Everything in Toronto is chasing the big buck. It's very materialistic ... Several fellas quit and went back from around the Shediac area. One fella, he worked for the machine shop here in the city, for Stelco. He went back and started a little machine shop just outside Shediac, on the Shediac Road. I think he's much happier there.

It depends on the individual. Some people would miss the bright lights of Toronto, the tinsel and the glitter – which don't mean a thing to me. I couldn't care less. You can go out every night of the week here in Toronto, and always do something different. There's so much to do, there's no reason to be bored. You don't even have to go downtown for your variety, because we've got so many shopping malls all scattered over the place, and we've got a great variety of stores. But how much do you really want? You could pile the place so full that eventually you'd have to move out, there'd be no place to put it. You can only buy so much.

At one time I thought of retiring when I was fifty-five and going back home, while Mother and Dad were still around. And looking back you often wonder, "Well, should I have done it or shouldn't I have?" But you don't know what to do. You could retire at fifty-five with twenty-five years' experience – but I would only have gotten out maybe forty percent of my pension – I would have to get something else. And you know what the Maritimes were like about that time. Plants were closing up. The CNR wasn't hiring as many. Everyone was cutting back. Everything was going against you. So where I could have found work, God only knows.

I don't know what I want, really. I guess the thing is that once you get a pension, then you have lots of time to think about it. While you're working you really can't put your mind to it. But I don't think I'd have any problem relocating. I know I always figure, when I'm driving down east, that when I get into New Brunswick, I'm home. I've always felt that way, every year I've driven down. It always seemed I was coming home.

JEAN ANDREWS – Harmony Mills, Queens County, Nova Scotia

She lives with her husband Arnold, their three daughters, and her father-in-law, in an apartment in Hamilton's North End, where they have been since moving to Ontario in 1978. Mr Andrews, Sr moved up in 1980, following the death of his wife.

Bonar Packaging, where Jean works, is in Burlington. Arnold works on the tugs in Hamilton Harbour. When they were in Nova Scotia, she had worked at the nursing home in Caledonia, Queens County. Arnold and his father were contractors together in the woods.

The woods work was kind of getting petered out. The biggest and the best stands were getting cut out, so they were getting back to harder, longer hauls and everything. So that didn't help matters. And then when Bowater's mill went on strike,* that really put the kibosh on. That really wrecked the business, because when they went on strike for that long, there was just no money coming in. They had nowhere to sell to. And when you've got all those big payments to make, tree farmers and skidders** and all that ...

Well, my sister lives next door here. She happened to be home on holidays. She had an extended holiday the year we left – she was home for about a month. And they were supposed to leave on Sunday or Monday, they weren't sure. They were up for the evening, and after they left, I said to Arnold, "Well, I don't know. Maybe we should think about moving. Maybe, you know, there'd be a living for one family in the woods work, and then if it didn't work out, at least we'd be situated and we could help your mother and father. Or they could move up and we'd already be here."

So we figured, well, maybe two people could get a living out of it. But there was no way, with us and three kids. If it had been just Arnold and I, I probably wouldn't have moved, but when you've got three kids to consider ... You can't get by on nothing.

And believe it or not, we decided in ... Well that was Saturday night, and I said, "I'll wait and let you think about it overnight so you're sure that you know what you're doing," and Sunday he said, "Yeah, I think it's a good idea." So then I came and brought the kids. He stayed to tie up the loose ends. My sister and her husband, they waited an extra three or four days while I got organized. And then I followed them up. They helped me drive, 'cause I wasn't used to driving in the city that much. And all we could bring was what we could get in the car. No furniture, just bedding and towels and things I could get in.

---

*   Locals 141 and 259 of the Canadian Paperworkers Union and Local 709 of the International Brotherhood of Electrical Workers went on strike against the Bowater-Mersey pulp-and-paper mill in Liverpool, Nova Scotia on 30 October 1976. They did not return until the following February. Bowater's is the only pulp mill in western Nova Scotia.

** Heavy equipment used for hauling logs out of the woods.

I guess we got here maybe the second week of August. I think I was only up here two weeks when Arnold, he flew up. And he stayed with Marilyn and Jack till September. And that was something! Her bedroom looked just like a dormitory. Our three kids, and she's got two, and the two of us and the two of them. There were roll-away cots lined up like ...

We came up in August, and then the next May, Arnold's mother passed away and we had to go down to the funeral. We were pretty strapped for money. So we were going to take my car, but then Marilyn said she'd take hers and drive us down. So Arnold flew, because he wanted to get there fast. We couldn't all afford to fly, so Marilyn took the car, and there were the five kids, her two and my three, and my other sister went with us, so there were eight of us. And she's got a Dodge Dart – so it wasn't a big car. And we drove through. We didn't stop overnight. And I always think, "Never again will I drive through." And then the next time I decide, "Forty dollars for a motel room? I'll drive through." Even if I've got the money, leave with the money intending to spend it, then when I think about it – forty dollars for a roof over your head for one night ... So Marilyn drove till we got to Rivière du Loup, and she thought she had us on the right road, and I don't know if she did or didn't, but anyway, she pulled over and I said, "I'll drive now," because I had slept. So I started and she went to sleep. Well, I didn't know, but I was on the wrong road and I ended up ... We were almost to the Gaspé when she woke up. I had started driving about ten o'clock at night and by this time it was about three o'clock in the morning. When she first woke up, she said, "Well, you should have woke me and asked me or something!" She was savage for about an hour. And then by this time, it was three o'clock, there were no gas stations open until morning – it wasn't like on the highway where you could keep going and find one. We ended up having to sit from about 4:30 or 5:00 until 8:00 when the gas tanks opened up, before we could get back – and then we were trying to catch the boat [the Saint John-Digby ferry]. I think it was two hundred miles I took us out of the way.

And the kids ... After the first day on the road, they fell asleep and then they were just like sardines. They looked funny. You'd look in the back seat and here were all these five kids, all lined up, and one would lay their head on the side of the car, on a pillow, and the next kid would have their head there [on her shoulder], and the next kid, and the next. And then after a couple of hours of that, somebody'd get cramped and they'd stretch and they'd all lean the other way. We laughed so hard about them leaning one way and then the other, all just piled like that. [Laughs.] Nobody had to worry about falling over if they fell asleep, because they didn't have room.

Arnold, I think he really thought he was just going to come up for a holiday and then go back. In the top of his head, he had himself convinced that he was going to stay here, but I think that deep down, he didn't really want to. But meanwhile, Marilyn took me, and Jack took Arnold, just everywhere, and we'd go in and fill out an application. Either they were hiring, or they'd say, "Well, we're not hiring right now, but we do take in applications." So we'd fill them out and take them back. We kept doing that for a couple of weeks, and then we got jobs.

I got a job the first of September at Lifesavers, on Cumberland Avenue in Hamilton. But it was just making those Christmas story books for six or eight weeks. Minimum wage. And Arnold got hired down at Dohler's. Die casting. He was on a machine that made fuel pumps. And then this Bonar & Bemis called – it's just called Bonar Packaging now. I went out for the interview, and I was lucky, 'cause they pay well. When I went to work there, they said, "Oh, who'd you know? How'd you happen to get in?" Because everybody, pretty well, knew somebody that got them in. It's hard to get a good-payin' job without drag. But I just walked in off the street and picked up an application form – I didn't know what sold there!

So I started there at Bonar & Bemis in November. I was lucky. I hit it right away, pretty well. That's not long to get a good job. And then in May they went on strike. I was working in the factory then. They settled the strike on about the first of August. But I was on layoff – they called me back and then laid me off until they got the business going again. In September they called me back to work. But meanwhile, I couldn't just sit back. 'Cause in about February, Arnold had quit his job because he didn't like it. It was hot and dirty and kind of dangerous work, too. He'd never been used to working inside, either – and this was hot metal, molten. I don't know what the statistics are on it, but there are quite a few that get burned. And I couldn't draw unemployment from May till August because I was on strike. I got a job at the Yacht Club the first of July. Then in September, they called me back to Lifesavers. So meanwhile, when the strike finally ended and they laid me off at Bonar & Bemis – once the strike was settled, they had to lay you off if they couldn't use you – I still couldn't draw unemployment, because I was working at the Yacht club and you can't quit your job and then draw. I could have gotten more on unemployment than I was makin' at the Yacht Club or at Lifesavers.

But then Arnold got on with the boilermakers, and that got us through. My brother-in-law's a boilermaker, so Arnold got on as a permit man – he couldn't get in the union because it's closing up like everything else. But he got on as a permit man. He went up to Douglas Point* and worked at the hydro plant. But by September, I was working at Lifesavers on day shift and for the Yacht Club in the evenings, because by that time Arnold's job was finishing up. And the unemployment [the Unemployment Insurance Commission] is awful. He got laid off, and it was September, from July to September, before he got anything. And then he got a job at Wilkinson's, making manhole covers and stuff like that. He liked that. It was outdoor. But he was back to work there before he got a cent of unemployment.

But I did get back at Bonar & Bemis. They phoned me, and this job I got, it had been posted before, but everybody said, "Oh, you wouldn't like it, it's a terrible job, it's so much responsibility." So I didn't apply. But then when I was laid off, I thought, "I'll try anything – so I went and tried it. It's working in quality control, and I really, really like it. It's in the lab. We do all kinds of tests on plastic bags. And we have to check the machines, and the extrusion and everything, right from the resin, practically, to the finished product – just spot-checking it.

And then Arnold, last spring he went out a few trips [on the tugs]. But he was the last one hired, so the first one laid off. But they called him back and he's getting quite a bit of time now. And this is really the first steady job that he has picked up. So we're finally getting stabilized.

Did you find it hard getting used to Hamilton?

I like Hamilton. I liked it from the time I moved, really. Hamilton to me doesn't seem like a city. It just seems small to me. And the people ... Well, at least here in the North End, everybody seems almost like down-easters. They're all friendly, helpful people. For instance, when we moved here, we didn't know anybody but Marilyn. And we knew a few of the couples they knew. And down-easters, too – like a couple of the guys that Jack works with, we had

---

*   On the shores of Lake Huron between Sarnia and Owen Sound in Ontario.

met them, and friends that Marilyn had in the North End. And then one night they said, "Oh, let's go over to Joan's for a while." And it was thundering and lightning and miserable and I said, "Oh no ... I'm not going."

"Oh come on and go." Meanwhile, Arnold knew what was going on, but I didn't. And it never entered my head. They all got together and had a housewarming party for us. Everybody that Marilyn knew that had something, maybe just in their basements, they all brought it. I thought that was really something. We were complete strangers to them all. We hadn't known them more than a month. I was astonished. And we didn't *have* the money to go out and buy all the stuff to furnish an apartment.

But I guess that's where family comes in handy. I don't think I'd probably ever have got the nerve to come all by myself, not knowing the city or having a place to stay. With no job or anything, it would be pretty hard.

I've got Marilyn here, and I've still got a younger sister in Toronto, and a brother in Alliston.* I did have a brother in Toronto, but he's since moved to Manitoba. I've got family in either place. That's the reason I could settle down here. I could go to Timbuctoo and have my family. I could make a home wherever the family is. Because I don't care, when it really comes down to the cold, hard facts, you can have all the friends you want to, but when it comes to the pinch, it's the family you rely on.

GREG KAVANAGH – Wolfville, Nova Scotia

A guitar player in his twenties. Before moving to Toronto, in between stints in Halifax, he also played with bands based in Los Angeles and Detroit.

All I have to go on is that I worked a lot easier in L.A. and Detroit and Toronto than I was able to work in Halifax. I had steady work in all those places. We went to L.A. and we rehearsed for a month, then started work. We didn't work *steady* steady, but for L.A. we worked steady. We worked about two weeks a month. And then Detroit, we were there about two weeks, and we worked steady after that for about eight months. In Halifax I don't think there are any bands that keep working all the time. And the people in the

---

*   Alliston, Ontario is approximately sixty miles north of Toronto.

States were more open to different styles. In Halifax – the Maritimes, generally – it's one thing pretty much all the way around. They like rock. They like drinkin' music. Partyin' music. Maritimers party hard. They work hard, and I guess they party hard. It's sort of their outlet, so you have to supply them with that. You've got to play rock or country rock, or just something that really kicks – you know, that really boots them and lifts them off their chairs so they can get drunk and eat beer bottles. That's pretty general. Whereas in the States, especially, they're a little bit more open to all kinds of music. I think it's got a lot do with the country's sense of unity. They sort of think as a country, so anything that's done in that country, they'll give it a shot. They'll give it a chance. Canada in general lacks that. The Maritimes have more of a together sort of feel about them, but not the willingness to accept something new. They want to hear what they've heard before, the local names that grew up in their home town, that are relatively big – in the Maritimes. It's hard to compete with that if you're trying to come up with something a little different.

The funny thing is that we've gone back to Nova Scotia billed as bands from Los Angeles, and we've got about twice the amount of money as we could've had in Halifax before.

With the same group you had before you went away?

Yeah. Two were from California, and three of us were from Nova Scotia. The band was called Flying Easy. We went to Los Angeles, worked a bit there, worked some of the rooms, then called a Nova Scotia agent – the same guy I'd always dealt with before – and said we were coming up to visit. We got easily twice the money. It paid our way home and gave us $350 a week. This was '76! "Direct to you from Los Angeles, California." [Laughs.] We had a picture of the five of us standing on the Hollywood Hills sign. So no problem. Book the band? [Snaps his fingers.] Sure, take you right away. It was the most incredible thing that I'd ever seen.

Playing the same kind of music you'd been playing there before?

In fact, we weren't doing stuff as commercial as what we'd done before. We were doing much more obscure things, things that were well known in the States but hadn't as yet gotten to Canada.

Were people pretty well aware where you were really from?

We didn't keep it that hidden. We said we were from the Maritimes. We weren't ashamed of it. In fact we're proud of it. It was just a scam. It was hilarious. It's stupid, really: if you're a Maritimer and

you work in Halifax, you're not doing as well as if you're a Maritimer and you come to Halifax from Toronto, or Detroit, or L.A.

Are there a lot of players from the Maritimes in Toronto?

The best players in Toronto are from the Maritimes, oddly enough.
The ones that are doing a lot of the work, the people that you go
and hear. Anything other than rock is hard to do there, so they do
it in Toronto. Everybody down there that's not rock 'n' roll is in
Toronto. You know, you can only stay there so long. There are a
few people there who are great jazz players, but they're not making
a living playing jazz, they're making a living playing rock 'n' roll.
You know, a week playing rock 'n' roll, a week doing advertising ...

It's just a lot of hard work. You have to travel an awful lot. In the
Maritimes you've got to go all over the place. In Halifax there are
five or six clubs to play in, but like anywhere, it's the people that
have been there twelve years that do the playing. And they're
playing the same thing they've been playing for twelve years. I
guess if I wanted to do that I probably could ... Well, even then it's
hard, because the clique there is very tight and they're hangin' on
for dear life to what they have, understandably. They don't really
want to give too much. But that can quickly be changed. It's a
competitive business, and all you have to do is sell yourself ... It's
really hard to pinpoint the problem. I think the problem that I have
is that I don't really want to play three-chord rock or old Beatles
tunes. If I'm going to play an old Beatles tune I want to do something with it. I want to take a Beatle tune, take the nice melodies,
but do them the way I interpret them, add a little artistic freedom.
I'll bend. I've certainly done that before. But I'm just not content to
sit around there and blow my ears off playing rock all night long.

TED RING – North Kemptville, Yarmouth County, Nova Scotia

*A stock-room attendant at General Motors in Oshawa. "I generally pick
stock for the dealers. It's the old-age home of General Motors, they call it –
high seniority and all this bit, where you can go in sort of dressed up ..."*

*He and his wife, Faye (Wood), from Raynardton, Yarmouth County,
have three grown children.*

Things were getting tough back then after the war and in the fifties.
That's when they really came up here in large numbers – when GM
went on two shifts in the early fifties, after the war. They wanted to
build more cars, so a lot of men came here. There were a lot of

Maritimers that came to Oshawa. They were coming to the Motors because they'd put on a double shift. And then you had foreign people that came from Europe – Dutch, German, all different nationalities. We all worked together. Some kept their language and didn't speak good English. Other fellas, with European parents but who were raised in this country, they spoke English well. And some were fairly highly educated. Even with degrees, they'd be working on the assembly line – for the money and security. It's economics. They came to Ontario because they wanted work. They wanted to be able to build a home. They wanted to get married and raise their families.

I came here really young, at sixteen. I quit trade school to come up here with my parents. I was living with my parents at the time. I was the only child in the family, so we all packed up and came. We arrived here in GM Town when all the GM employees were getting out, and it just looked like a madhouse. It was a hot summer day. We stopped on the street, and my dad said he almost had an inkling to go back home to Nova Scotia. But we went to the unemployment and put our names in at General Motors. My dad and I went in to the Motors at approximately the same time. My dad came out of GM for a while and sold real estate. I stayed on working at GM. He had less seniority when he retired than I'll have, because I was quite young when I started.

I went into General Motors in a "Boys' Group." They were called "Boys' Groups" in those days in GM. It was rough. It was sub-assembly, and they paid you less wages because you weren't a man. You had to be twenty years old to get full pay in those days, or to be put on assembly. That was a ruling that they had at that time, so they made Boys' Groups out of them. They were making door handles, lock sets, what we call "CV groups" – those are different parts on cars. Sub-assembly sort of thing. I did that for over two years.

I took other jobs before I went to GM. I even worked for a dollar an hour when I first came here. I worked one time in a lumber company, nailing skids together.

Yes, in the fifties – especially '50, '51, '52 – that's when the great surge was up here. There were quite a few from around Kempt that came – Greenes, Prossers, Jefferys. There's Donald Ring, who just lives on the next block – he is a distant relative. He married a girl I went to school with. They lived next door in Kempt when I was a kid. The Jeffery brothers – they've done well. They're in the construction business. They quit the Motors and started in business. They were from East Kempt. And all the Greenes – there are six of them up here. Arthur Greene, he's president at the local dairy. He started off as a mechanic. He used to work in a saw mill. His dad had a mill in Kempt. Another brother is a supervisor over a cement company here – that's Gifford Greene, named after his father. And there's Sherman Greene, who lives right up the road here – he's in the refrigeration business. There's a lot that came from different parts of Yarmouth County. Les Gray from Carleton is a foreman in the Motors. Arthur Johnston from Carleton is in GM too. They all came here in the early fifties.

It was economics, I guess. You couldn't blame Nova Scotia for it. It's just the way things were.

A Banker and a Politician

ARTHUR CROCKETT – Westville,
Nova Scotia

The sixth floor of the head offices of the Bank of Nova Scotia at King and Bay in Toronto. The bank's president for over a decade, he is nearing retirement.

Sydney Frost from Yarmouth, Nova Scotia, I remind him, was president of the bank from 1956 to 1958; Rowland Frazee from St Stephen, New Brunswick, was chief general manager of the Royal Bank; and John Coleman from Joggins, Nova Scotia, was the Royal's executive vice-president. "Have you any idea why there seems to be such a concentration of Maritimers in the upper echelons of Canadian banking?"

He gestures with an unlit Matinée cigarette. "They tell the beautiful story of some years ago, when the late Leo Dolan was in New Brunswick Tourism,* and he was invited to speak in Toronto at the invitation of the then mayor, Hyram McCallum. In introducing him, the mayor said, 'You know of course that Mr Dolan comes from New Brunswick; he's a Maritimer. And I often wonder why the Maritimers ... they tell you it's such a beautiful place to live, and that they're such a brilliant race: so why do they have to come up here to make a living?' So he sat down and Dolan got up and said, 'Thank you for your kind words. Yes, we have a beautiful place there, and we are a brilliant race, but as to why so many of us have to come up here, the answer is that the competition is go great down there, whereas here they're not so bright.' Now that's exaggerated ..."

---

*   Leo Dolan, from Fredericton, was appointed director of the New Brunswick Government Bureau of Information and Tourist Travel in 1931.

I'm a depression baby, you might call it. I was going to school in '32, late '33, early '34 – those were tough days. And really, the economic end of my little home town of Westville, population four thousand, was a coal mine, which eventually went down. Now I had one of two choices – either go in the coal mines or go in the bank. I guess I was lucky. I went in the bank.

I went into the bank in Westville in 1934. Three and a half, four years later, I was moved to Charlottetown. The war broke out and I joined the navy. After five years the war was over – it was late 1945, and I thought I'd come to Toronto to see the head office. The bank didn't move me here – I made up my own mind that I would start off here. After the war I motivated myself and came here.

Do you recall that as being a hard decision?

No. I felt that I'd been in the Maritimes all my life up to that point, except for five years in the navy. The navy kicked you around the world, and you learned some responsibility, so I thought I'd go where the action was. I felt, at that time, having been in London, England, New York, and various large centres, that perhaps in my field there could be more opportunities, and learning processes, here. The bank was quite small then, too. But you could see after the war it was going to grow and expand – and as any company expands, up come opportunities.

I didn't go into the head office of the bank. I went into the main Toronto branch, which ironically I ended up being manager of from 1958 to 1964 – quite a long run. That's right here on the corner of King and Bay. That was very exciting ... And after that, the bank moved me around the world.

Take the legal profession. Many Maritimers, particularly Nova Scotians, are now senior partners in law firms right across Canada. Take for example Blake, Cassels [Blake, Cassels and Graydon], perhaps one of the larger firms here in Toronto. Alex MacIntosh,* who came from Stellarton, is the senior partner there. And Henry Borden,** from Halifax, was the senior partner for years of Borden and Elliot, another large law firm.

---

*   Alex MacIntosh has sat on the board of directors of such firms as the Canadian Imperial Bank of Commerce, Honeywell, and the Hudson's Bay Company.
** Henry Borden, in addition to his legal work, was president of the Brazilian Traction and Light and Power Company and, during the war, chairman of the Wartime Industrial Control Board.

There's a lot of personnel from Nova Scotia that've done well up here. Our senior fella in the Pacific, based in Manila, is from Newfoundland. And our vice-president in charge of Eastern Canada at the moment – he comes from down in the Valley somewhere. And the fella in charge of Western Canada comes from Dartmouth. So of the three vice-presidents that split Canada, two of them are from Nova Scotia. They've done well.

I guess part of the answer is that it's a great training and recruiting area. We're hiring young people all the time – both high school, senior matriculations, as well as university degrees – and they're excellent, I can say, from the Atlantic Provinces generally.

FLORA MacDONALD – North Sydney, Nova Scotia

The Conservative Member of Parliament's constituency office on Princess Street in Kingston, Ontario. She was the first woman to hold one of a handful of the most prestigious federal Cabinet posts in Canada when she was secretary of state for External Affairs in the Clark government of 1979–80. She chooses her words carefully when she speaks and pronounces them with exaggerated crispness. She is in her middle fifties.

I had been working in North Sydney for about six years in the Bank of Nova Scotia; and I suppose I had done fairly well for a woman in the bank at that time. I had started in as a clerk-stenographer and had become assistant accountant – a woman could not become an accountant in the bank at that time. In fact, there was a woman with whom I worked who had only been allowed to hold the position of *acting* accountant for about twenty years. So that was about it. There was no way for me to go any further in that field.

But I don't know that that in itself would have encouraged me to leave. I was enjoying my work. I had a great social life, all of which centred around the church. It was church clubs, young people's clubs connected with the church, all of that – so it was a very happy time in my life. But I'd always had a great desire to travel and I knew that sooner or later I was going to have to leave if I was ever going to fulfill that desire.

I had been to Ontario once, on a visit to a friend who had lived next door to me. Her father had been our church minister and they had moved to Ontario, and a few years after they moved I had gone up there to visit. This girl subsequently went on to college, to university, and when she graduated she wanted to work as a social worker with the Children's Aid Society in Peterborough. We'd always had the understanding that when she got through school and relocated, she and I would join up again, and then after we had saved some money we would travel and whatever – this was the idea. So she got a job in Peterborough and I was at the point in Nova Scotia of saying, "Well, I should really move on from here." And at that point she wrote and said, "Are you coming up to join me?" And I thought, "Well, fair enough." Being in the bank, one thing that I *could* do, since it was like a network, was to say, "Are there any job openings in the bank in Peterborough?" They wouldn't pay to transfer a woman in the way that they transferred men from place to place. But they would at least find out if there was an opening for you, and indeed there was. So there I was in North Sydney, ready to move, there was a job opening for me in Peterborough, and my best friend was there and had got an apartment for us – all of these things came together.

The one thing that I remember, of course, was being terribly, terribly emotionally upset at leaving Cape Breton, and that was a tremendous, a really traumatic, period. Just moving to Ontario. But once in Ontario, I settled into work, into a new job and a new group of friends and a new way of living. There was always a question of homesickness, because we're a very close family, but there were a lot of exciting things to do that I hadn't done before, and it was interesting. The things that I was able to get into, again through the church ... all kinds of sports activities, little theatre, musical events, all this sort of thing. So there was no spare time. And the first year that I was there, I persuaded the minister of the church and his wife to take their first visit to Cape Breton. There were by this time three of us from North Sydney who had come together in Peterborough, and I persuaded the minister and his wife to drive us all to Cape Breton. So we came down and stayed with our parents and helped pay for the gas.

Before then, my older sister – she had a more driving desire to get away from Cape Breton than I did – she had left and moved to Montreal. My two younger sisters had both gone to Halifax to train as nurses at the Victoria General. You know, we were leaving one by one ...

I never had any idea that I would settle in North Sydney for the balance of my life. I suppose if I had met somebody who worked there and married him, you know ... but that had never occurred to me. Oh, I knew eventually I would leave. My grandfather had been a captain of a clipper ship that operated between China and Great Britain and South America. My grandmother had sailed with him aboard that ship. My father had travelled widely to far parts of the world. I knew that travel was going to be part of my life.

Here to Stay

MARY JOHNSTON – Sydney, Nova Scotia

She works with a personnel-management firm in downtown Toronto. In her mid-thirties, she left Sydney in 1965. She, her husband, and their daughter live in the Beaches area of the city and they like Toronto very much. "I want to grow old here," she says. "I don't want to leave."

She is the daughter of John Johnston, a member of the founding executive of the steelworkers' union in Sydney.

I went to school at the convent. What could you do? I always had a lot of difficulty living within the mores of that society. I could talk to my father and mother, and I could discuss what I wanted to discuss, and my opinion was important. All of a sudden, locked into the sexual roles, you weren't allowed to do that anymore. It's very difficult. For a teenage girl at the convent, at that particular point in time, it was terribly restricting.

I used to pass the train station every day and say, "By God, I'm getting on that train and leaving." The possibilities, the choices, weren't there for me. There was nothing Sydney was offering anybody like me, and that's all there was to it. My father wasn't a lawyer, my family didn't have money. There was no employment. I went to the employment centre ... I couldn't even get a summer job there, but yet people who had contacts managed to get in to work at Zeller's [laughs] – or wherever, you know. I wasn't given those jobs. I mean, why not? I had the capability. So it was just a one-way street, right out of Sydney.

I left when I was seventeen. Toronto presented possibilities to me, and I knew that the world was made up of something, and possibly in Toronto I could find it. There weren't any choices as far as I was concerned. Could I return to Sydney? To do what? What would I do there? At least with Toronto, as big and as scary as it was, there could be something here.

I got an apartment and lived on my own, and found a job and got on with it. I had numerous friends who would say, "Oh, I've had enough of this, I'm going back to the Maritimes." Or, "I'm going to go home to Mom and Dad." I know that it's very difficult for a lot of people to assimilate into other kinds of social situations. It really is difficult ... Actually, I think it was as hard for me as it was for them, only they felt they had a choice and I didn't, and that was the difference. That was my perception of my situation at that particular time. Even now in retrospect – there's no turning back. What could I do at home? Was there any work? My parents, could they give me what I needed? The only answer I could come up with was no. Emotionally, I needed ... I was still very young ... But that was only a tentative thing, and I knew that if I went home to get emotional nourishment, that would only be – what? – two, three weeks? So I sacrificed the emotional for the practical in Toronto, and for six months, my emotional life was fairly poor. I cried myself to sleep every night, or whatever ... But I was surviving, and I knew it had to get better, it just had to get better. And it did.

Once in a while I get a call from someone much younger, kids I used to babysit or whatever. I get a call and they say, "This is so and so." [She mimes the mad panic of non-recognition.] And of course I have to string my way ... [Laughs.] "I'm on my way to Calgary." Or Edmonton. And there's a part of me that just dies, and I think, here we go again. Poor, scared, frightened little kids, running off to nothing. It's not as though they're actually going to work, you know.

We come back to choice. Is there a choice? If you're a Torontonian there's a choice as to whether or not – well, I mean possibly, depending upon what your skills are, or what your background is – as to whether you stay here or you decide to go to Calgary and live out west, or if you decide to leave the country. But for Maritimers there isn't a choice. That's how I felt – there wasn't any choice. And that's really sad.

PHYLLIS TRENHOLM – Coverdale, Albert County, New Brunswick

She had spent almost all her life in Moncton before her husband, Carman, a sales representative for Alchem Company, Ltd, was transferred to Burlington, Ontario in 1973. They have five grown children – Jo-Ann, Don, Carol, Barry, and David.

When we were told we were going to move to Ontario, the bottom fell out of our world. After all, Carman had been in town for twenty-five years and I had lived there all my life. Our first feeling was that we weren't going to go. But what were we going to do if we didn't go? We really had no choice.

But once we got here we found out how much easier it was to do everything. Even from the word go. I wasn't feeling well the last year we were in Moncton. There was nothing I could put it down to, nothing specific. I called the doctor in Moncton the first week of

September. The doctor's office said the last week in November, which was almost three months, and I said, "Well, we're moving to Ontario the first of November. Couldn't I have an appointment before then?" And she said, "No, we can't give you one. If an emergency should arise go to the out-patient department of the hospital and somebody will look after you there." That's what happened. Here, I called the doctor's office and the girl said, "The doctor gives medicals on Tuesdays and Thursdays. Would Tuesday at ten o'clock be all right?" There's the difference in your medical.

There was another thing in Moncton. I wanted to go to night school, but their night school taught English, business, and high-school courses. I wanted general-interest courses. There was nothing there I could get. When we came up here they sent out a booklet of the courses that they teach at night school – everything from flower arranging and macramé to oil painting, history, and book reviews. Everything. And they have their classes winter and summer.

It's just so much easier up here. Even the library. In Moncton, if you wanted a library book, you could get fiction – big print or small print. In the library up here you can get everything – technical books, magazines; you can get most any kind of a book, and if they haven't got it there they've got some kind of a computerized system with every library in Ontario, so if any library's got it, you can get it. And in their school system – Carol was amazed at the school library they had just in the high school up here two blocks away. They have a good library, and then when she wanted more information there was the McMaster University library only ten miles away [in Hamilton].

Even when you want to go shopping, it's so much easier. You don't have to go to Boston to do your shopping now ... And it's so much greener. Your trees are greener, your grass is greener. It lasts longer in the cities.

The people up here don't know how lucky they are. We were talking to a chap whose uncle was the first policeman in Burlington, and his father was the last person to have a milk route in Burlington, so of course he knows Burlington inside out. We were playing bridge, and he'd read the weekend paper and it said that Ontario had the least growth of any province in Canada in the last year. Therefore, he said, Ontario was a poor province. And I just looked at him. "You've got to be kidding!" That's the same as saying Gordon Sinclair is a poor man because he's not working as many hours. They don't know ...

And their school system ... The kids take it for granted. That's another reason I like it up here, is that our kids got an exceptionally good shake in school. David was twelve when we came up and they put him in a school with open classes. The first day of school there were all these kids, sixty or seventy kids, with their teachers: there were desks here and kids in the corner there and everybody was running around just like a zoo. I thought, "Poor David; he's never seen anything like this." He stayed and he soon found out that there were groups, those kids weren't running around willy-nilly. And David likes working in groups. He spent a year in that school, and they did tremendous projects.

The choice of subjects in high school here is tremendous. I thought Barry was crazy taking theatre arts. Wasn't there something he could take besides theatre arts? But I think in the long run ... Barry's a clown, he was always clowning around to get attention, and theatre arts took a lot of that away from him because he learned to feel he could be somebody without clowning around all the time.

At the same time they took their core subjects so they could get into university. And our youngsters were able to do any course they wanted in university. So I'm all in favour of their schooling here.

And you felt that positive about it right from the time you got here?

Well, for the first while we missed the people back home. But even though I was there all my life, my people were up here. My two sisters had come up, one right after the war and one in the fifties. One's in St Thomas and the other's in Wheatley. And Mother was widowed the year before we came up, so she came up with us. So more of my family is here. All of my cousins are up in Ontario somewhere.

I lived in Moncton all my life and had a lot of friends, but do you realize that all the people I went to high school with came to Ontario before I did? I went to Moncton High – one year at Aberdeen and then Moncton High. When the war broke out in '39, of course, there wasn't a boy left. The girls – a lot of them came up to Ajax, which is just outside of Toronto, and many, many of the girls went to Ottawa to work in the civil service.

What was in Ajax?

Munitions. I could go downtown in Moncton and not see a person I grew up with.

And, too, we knew that if we educated our children in the Maritimes we were educating them for the Ontario market. When you stop to think of it, if you have educated a Maritimer, if you've given him a university education or even a good technical education, where's he going to use it in the Maritimes? They're going to come to Ontario. Carman's brother is an engineer. He's been up here for many, many years. You take anybody except a teacher or a doctor, they come this way. There aren't that many jobs in the Maritimes. If a child stops school in grade ten he can pump gas, or work in small stores. But there isn't much for an educated person to do.

So you don't have any thoughts of moving back at all, then?

We could go back, but why? Our children will be here. I doubt very much if we'll ever go back.

When we were in Moncton, Carman was out of town most nights. His territory was from Rivière du Loup to St John's, and that meant that he was away at least half the time. He's only been away three nights since we moved. He's home every night. His territory was miles and miles, home, where here, his territory is Hamilton. He's home at nights and he doesn't bring his work home with him. He's here all the time, and he only eats about one quarter of the aspirins he ate down there.

I wouldn't go back, I don't think. And you couldn't get my sisters to go back to Moncton, I'm sure. Because it has changed ... Maybe it hasn't changed. Maybe that's the problem. It hasn't changed. No, I've got too much to gain by staying here. There's just so much more here. It's so much easier to do nice things.

MYRA JONES – Ecum Secum, Guysborough County, Nova Scotia

Originally a Davidson, she is separated and lives on her own in a fashionable apartment building near Bathurst and Eglinton in Toronto. She is a successful business woman with a Toronto-based real-estate development and property-management firm. Although she speaks with a discernible Eastern Shore accent, she is very much the city woman. "Only once in my life have I ever been homesick," she says. "And I was probably six years old." She is in her early forties.

I was seventeen when I left Ecum Secum and went to Dartmouth, where I was working for Canadian Pittsburgh. I married when I was nineteen. My ex-husband, who was in the navy, was from Toronto. When he got out of the navy in 1964 we moved to Ontario.

What did you think about leaving Nova Scotia?

I didn't want to stay there. I wanted to go places, do things, see things. I wanted to get away. I would have gone before I got married. I wanted my girlfriend to move somewhere to another city with me, but she was very attached to her family at that time. In 1958 I had put in for a transfer to Vancouver, expecting to move there in 1959. My plans were disrupted when my friends introduced me to their friend from Toronto. I eventually married and my girl-friend eventually transferred away, temporarily. Had I been single, I would have gone too.

Had you always wanted to leave, even as a kid?

Initially, not so much to leave Nova Scotia ... But to get away from Ecum Secum – yes! I did get away from home a bit as I was grow-ing up. I used to visit with my aunts who lived in Dartmouth. I was on the basketball and volleyball teams in high school in Sherbrooke. I often stayed in town with my girlfriend or one of the teachers when there was a practice or a game. I really enjoyed it.

But I remember at home, just going out for walks in the evening, and walking because there was nothing else to do, nobody to do anything with – and just wanting to get away. I packed my bag and wanted to run away when I was twelve, but nobody would drive me!

And you never felt nostalgic about it at all?

Never. I remember coming back to Toronto from trips down home and being so depressed I really didn't want to see anyone. It was a combination of things that got to me. One of the things that always depressed me was seeing kids in the village that didn't appear to receive any encouragement to go to school and who were allowed to drop out. You didn't need a crystal ball to know what their lives would be like – fishing when they could, maybe working a bit in the lumber yards and then drawing unemployment insurance. They had nothing or no one to motivate them. Those who managed to get to grade seven and junior high school might have a chance if they were willing to work. So many people seemed to be wrapped up in their own little cocoons, their own worlds. The most common thing to talk about was family and neighbours. There was little interest shown in anything else. Some people seemed to be always criticiz-ing others. I never knew if it was from lack of interest in what went on in the outside world or if it was just from boredom. I wanted more from life.

As a little girl, after going on visits to my aunts in the city, I used to dream of the day when I could leave Ecum Secum and get a job there. But now that I've travelled and seen other places, I wouldn't even want to go back to Halifax or Dartmouth to live. For the most part, I find Dartmouth depressing. It's almost as if the town was thrown together. There seems to be no order or organization to how and where the houses are put up. Maybe that's because it's an old city. Everything seems to move so slowly, even the traffic.

A lot of people say they find it kind of unfriendly up here compared to home, and the pace of life sort of hectic. You don't find that?

I thrive on it. I was always "go, go, go." Even when I was in Dartmouth, I worked a lot of extra time. I don't feel I'm cut out to be just a housewife and mother – I'd die of boredom. I have to be doing things. I've always worked better under pressure.

I've been in this apartment for almost eight years. It's only been in the last two or three years that I've gotten to know my neighbours. And that's fine; I like it that way. They would do anything to help you; they're there if I need them and I am here if they need me. But I don't like living in a place where people are constantly dropping in for coffee – it's such a waste of time.

I've usually gone home because of a feeling of duty and responsibility, not because I really wanted to. I like to see my family and friends, but I don't feel I belong there. There are things about Nova Scotia I really enjoy, and I don't feel I'm any better than the people back home. But I'm proud of what I've accomplished and I have no intention of ever living in the Maritimes again – although I do make a point of telling people how pretty Nova Scotia is and that it's a lovely place to visit.

LOIS VENIOT – Saint John, New Brunswick

A nurse at St Joseph's Hospital in Hamilton, she left her home on the West Side of Saint John in 1950. She is in her late forties.

There was nothing in Saint John for me. Nothing for anybody as far as I'm concerned. When you're born there, you don't know anything else. I'm glad I don't have to bring my kids up down there. I know they'd miss out on a lot.

I don't think that I ever liked Saint John, not that I can remember. It's so boring there, really. Even when I was growing up, you couldn't go and have a beer anyplace. There was no such thing as having a car or being able to drive. It just got people down.

We got married when I was sixteen. I think that's a lot of the reason why kids there do get married so young – for excitement. There's nothing else to do. Just to get away. Most of my friends in Saint John got married at a young age. Most of them broke up and married somebody else.

My husband Joe was born in Montreal, but his family moved to Saint John when he was two years old. He worked in a bakery, and wages were so low. At the time we were married, he was only eighteen and had no trade. We went to Montreal for six months, and then his parents came to Hamilton, so we came here. It just happened by luck that my husband's cousin was up here. He was a stationary engineer at the old cotton mill on St Mary's Street. He was quitting and told Joe about the job, so he went and wrote his papers and got it. Now he's a stationary engineer at the post office.

Joe could probably get a job down east. He likes it there for some reason – don't ask me why. He says he'd go and live there, but I tell him, "Don't expect me to go with you." Never. I have friends who live in Ancaster [Ontario]. She's Dutch, but her husband's from Saint John, and she says that he'd go back in a minute; so I said, "Send him and my husband back and we'll stay up here."

My mom would never go back either. She came up here just before we were married in '50, when my oldest sister was having her first baby in St Catharines. Mom liked it so well that she went back and talked Dad into coming up here. She says she would never go back.

I wouldn't care if they offered me $100 a day, I wouldn't go down there. I'll never, ever go back. I was never homesick. I probably wouldn't have started going down to visit if it wasn't for taking my mom down to see her dad. There was nothing there for me when I was growing up and it's got nothing for me now.

The Prince of Wales

STUART, VIVIAN, AND BETH WALSH –
Prince of Wales, St John County,
New Brunswick

The Walshes live on Charlton Avenue West in Hamilton. They have neighbours who came to Ontario from St Stephen, New Brunswick, Alberton, Prince Edward Island, and other areas of the Maritimes. "And there are several streets like this," says Stuart. "Just stuffed with Maritimers. There's so many you don't even know they're from the Maritimes, till gradually you get to talk with them."

"And you seemed to go together," says Vivian, his wife, who is originally from West Saint John. "Most of our friends, most of our closest friends, even though we've met them here, are from the Maritimes."

Stuart and Vivian have four children. Beth, their eldest daughter, is a nurse in her mid-twenties. She was six when the family left New Brunswick.

One of the Walshes' favourite stories concerns a confusion about Stuart's origins when he first came to Hamilton. The family had bought the house on Charlton Avenue, were living in half of it and renting out the other half. The Walshes' and the tenants' mail all came to the same box, and the address on Stuart's redirected letters from New Brunswick gave the other occupants of the house something of a start.

"You see," he says, "the right mailing address for Prince of Wales was RR#3. But I didn't know it, so I said, 'Well, everyone knows where Prince of Wales is,' so I just put 'Prince of Wales' at the post office. So everything just came 'Prince of Wales' when they rerouted the mail. 'Stuart J. Walsh, Prince of Wales' – and that was the address. And you know what it's like, it's typed on there, and it looked as though I was the Prince of Wales. And this guy did a double take. He figured, 'Man, I'm renting from a Prince!' And then later he said, 'Here I've been thinking you were a prince.' [Laughs.] I said, 'Well I am, aren't I?'"

STUART   I have three sisters here. One lives in Burlington and two live in Hamilton; and a brother in Guelph. I was the last one up here. The first time I ever visited Hamilton was in '48, I guess, with my father. Then I was here again in '53. In '62 I came to stay.

I worked in the railway in Saint John, CPR. And when the diesels came in, they cut everything right to pieces. There was just no work. I ended up here.

VIVIAN   He only worked half the year anyway ...

STUART   In the wintertime, the winter port was going; business was good. And then during the summer you got a little bit of work on account of holidays. But the period in between that ... you got nothin'. In the spring and the fall you would be off for sure. Really, all it was, was the winter months you were workin'.

VIVIAN   So you just survived in the summer. And then you made the money in the winter to catch up. So then he'd be off all the next summer.

STUART   That was my main reason for coming here. When I first started I worked at National Steel Car for about five months. And then I went to the TH&B [Toronto, Hamilton and Buffalo] Railroad and then to Stanley Steel ... getting laid off different places, eh? And I went back, on recall, back to the TH&B. And then I got a job at Dofasco – the Railroad Division. It's pretty well permanent. There's an awful lot of people work there. If you took all the foreigners and east-coasters out of Stelco and Dofasco, they'd have to shut the doors.

VIVIAN I know when I went and got a job down to Woolworth's – not when I first came to Hamilton, but when the kids got older – I think that's one of the reasons I got the job: because I'm a Maritimer. Because the woman that hired me was a Maritimer, and she said, "They're the best workers. They don't last, but when they work, they're the best."

Did all the family come up here together?

VIVIAN No, he came up first ...

STUART I came up with my sister – she had been here for a good many years. We drove up.

VIVIAN And then we [she and all the children] came up on the train. I was talking to him on a Wednesday. He said, "Come on up – and he didn't even have a house. And I came up on a Saturday, something like that, and he had just bought this house, but we couldn't move into it yet. So half the family stayed at one sister's house and the other half stayed with another sister, for three days, and then we moved here. And then I was here a week, two weeks, and I got pleurisy ...

BETH First time in our lives we ever saw her sick, ever.

VIVIAN That was the only time I ever *was* sick. What a time, what a time. See, we never moved. He grew up in his home. The same house he was born in, he grew up in. Same with me. We spent our whole life in one house – till we were married, and we had an apartment for three months, and then we moved into another house. And then this big move. I mean, we weren't used to doing *any* moving.

I got to Toronto, and you're supposed to come down from there on a certain train ...

STUART She got the wrong one ...

VIVIAN I came CP up from New Brunswick. And we ended up in a different station! The conductor, he said, "Get on *this* train ..."

STUART Out of Saint John it's only CP. So naturally she came up out of Saint John on CP to Montreal. And then, CN and CP had a pool going from Montreal to Toronto, so it could be CN you're travellin'. But then you revert back to CP when you come from Toronto to

Hamilton, depending on what kind of ticket you bought out of Saint John. So she bought a CP ticket, but she ended up coming CN from Toronto to Hamilton. She should have come up to Upper James Street, CP, but she came up to Stuart Street, CN.

VIVIAN I got into Hamilton and there was no one there waiting for me. I had to phone. I was early or late ... I didn't know what I was!

And I didn't have anybody up here. I didn't even know Stuart's sisters. I'd met them once. I've got a sister and two brothers up here now. But you didn't know anybody. And you know the worst part of the whole thing? You're boxed in this little, wee house, and houses on each side of you. And the noise! And I can remember finding it so hard to understand the fella on the TV. He seemed to talk so fast. And the radio ... And it's so dirty up here ...

BETH I hated it. I probably hated it because I was the only one [of the children] that had any establishment. I had a girlfriend there, and at six you really don't have too much ...

I remember everything about it. I had my sixth birthday just before I came. I started school down there just before, it might have been two weeks. At that point in my life it seemed like a long time. There was this one little room, and there were maybe twenty kids there. Two, I think they were either thirteen or sixteen – they seemed big, big to me, 'cause I was only six – and they sat in the back. And then they had them in rows to the front to the littlest kids. Myself and a girl that lived by me were the youngest ones in the class.

When I came to school here, when I first got here ... well, I spoke differently, that was one thing, because I had an accent. But it wasn't just that ... like, some of the words I used: I used to say, "Where is Christine at?" "Where's it at?"

"What 'at'? You don't say 'at'. What are you sayin' 'at' for?" But it didn't make any sense to me, because that's the only thing I ever knew. Or "seen it." Everybody there said "seen" instead of "I have seen it," for before, or "I saw it." Which is wrong – but it's the way people talk down there.

VIVIAN Different words ... Like "erasers." They call them rubbers. When the kids first came home and wanted a rubber, I said, "What?"

BETH But people up here didn't have a good attitude. If you were from down east you were ... [searches for the right word] ...

VIVIAN [Emphatically:] You were lower!

BETH You were lower class, and for some reason you were a little bit simple.

STUART Well, a guy was tellin' me, he says, "You're not too bright from the Maritimes." And I said, "Well it seems to me it's the opposite. They're not too bright from Ontario." I said, "How many premiers?" I said, "You've got ten provinces, and at one time, I think it was six out of the ten of them had east-coasters running them." So I said, "You can't be very smart if you have to get east-coasters to run your provinces for you. And when you're speaking of Hamilton," I said, "the mayor that was the longest-serving mayor ever in Hamilton," I said, "he wasn't an east-coaster, but he had to marry an east-coaster to get the job done" – Mrs Copps.*

BETH It's a real thing, too [To Stuart:] Like the man who brought you here, Dad. Dad said to him about "If you took the foreigners and east-coasters out of Dofasco, they'd have to close the doors." And he said back something about "Then the *real* Canadians," about how they'd all be gone out of here, and "then you'd have the *real* Canadians left." This guy was born here, in Brantford. And my mother is a staunch New Brunswicker. Always sticks up for it and Dad always tells her to shut up. [Laughter.] 'Cause she got up and said, "What do you mean, *real* Canadians? *We're* the real Canadians."

VIVIAN Canada was started down there, not up here!

* Victor Copps was Hamilton's mayor from 1962 to 1977. He married the former Geraldine Guthro, whose parents were from Sydney Mines.

PART THREE

Alberta

So I bade farewell to the eastern town I
never more will see.
But work I must, so I eat this dust, and
breathe refinery.
Oh, I miss the green and the woods and streams,
and I don't like cowboy clothes,
But I like being free and that makes me
An idiot I suppose.

    – From Stan Rogers, "The Idiot"

A Miner, a Mechanic, and
a Driver

DONALD MacDONALD – Reserve Mines, Nova Scotia

In his seventies, he is a retired president of District 18 (western Canada), United Mine Workers of America. He lives in Calgary, although he spent most of his working life in Wayne in the Drumheller Valley.

I was only sixteen when I left Nova Scotia, and it was a good many years before I returned. It was a long walk, by golly, and the twenties were pretty rough out here.

A lot of us fellas, we came out here in the first place on the old harvest trains. There were two trains, about eight or ten days apart, and if you stayed two months you had your return, the same old ticket brought you back. But I didn't go back. I gave my ticket to a fella that had been out here for a year or two.

What made you decide to leave Cape Breton?

I entered the mine as a workman, ten hours a day, at thirteen years of age. Just having heard them talk down around there for years, their conversations relating to years and years of how tough the going was, some way or another I got the impression that as I was, I would always be. It's about as simple as that.

Although many times, in the first year or two or three, I wished I was back. At least while I was there, I was eating. I had to be very careful about eating out here, there were a few times. That first winter, I just barely survived, even though I was single and so on. And that summer was awful tough. You take in the thirties here, my God, there were people that lived on freights. Oh yes, I rode freight trains. I remember I wanted bridge work up in Churchill. It was a rough trip up there, I'll tell you. The snow was terrible – I rode the box car all the way up, four hundred miles. That was 60¢ an hour, but it was a godsend. That's how bad things were.

You never thought of going home?

No. Well, I knew there was nothing there. I knew that opportunities were seventy to one out here.

Even then?

Well, not exactly in those years, but after the war and so on, wages were better. As a matter of fact, living was better. The standard of living was better nearly everywhere out here, if you had a standard to go by. When you had no job, it didn't matter too much where you were.

But I can remember my brother and some of the fellas I knew when I was down there, talking about the strikes, how they'd go and dig into a hill to get a little bit of coal – really a hell of a time, especially during that '25 strike. And then before I ever left there, I had all the news of the 1909 strike,* because I remember we had to have people rent our upstairs – see, my dad went all through that strike – and I was just a little fella, two or three years old, and I often wondered what the heck they were doing up there.

No, you had to watch yourself. If you got drunk every second week when it was pay day, well, you may just as well have stayed down there. But if you watched yourself, no two ways about it, you could do better here.

There were fifty-some-odd coal mines in the West. I worked in four of them. I was in three mines when they closed them down. But there's not one mine in Drumheller any more, not in the whole Valley. During the war there was coal all the time, because there was great demand for coal, but after that they closed, one after another.

Were there a lot of people from home working in the mines out here then?

In Drumheller at that time, I would say there were about seventy-five. [Pauses.] They're quite a great bunch of fellows, the Cape Bretoners. I've roamed around some, all over Canada, but of all the people, I've never seen any to leave home and be as lonesome. Most Cape Bretoners I've known, even the first two or three years I was around Drumheller, they went back. They'd go back, even though there was nothing to go back to. Somehow they just didn't seem to be able to give it up. They think an ungodly lot of that island. [He trails off.]

The Cape Bretoner that I replaced in the UMW, Angus J. Morrison, was one of the best union people I ever met in my life. He was the district secretary and was from just outside Glace Bay, Myra. A

---

* The 1909 strike of District 26, United Mine Workers of America, against the Dominion Coal Company, lasted from 6 July 1909 until 27 April 1910. On the 1925 strike, see Ann Hyde in Part One of this book.

good fella on the platform, and a great guy. If you ever met Angus Morrison, and if you were hungry, you'd eat.

This Angus, he spoke fluent Gaelic. In Drumheller there were two locals in the United Mine Workers, and he used to come down there every once in a while. Well, on the street, you might be talking to Angus, and you might be a bitter son of a gun, and he wouldn't know it. But while he'd be talking to you, some Cape Bretoner would walk by and say in Gaelic, "The sonofabitch is no good." Then Angus would tear into you. [Laughs.] And that's a fact.

[Pauses.] In Canada at that time a coal miner could only work in Cape Breton or Alberta. Where else could you go? There was coal in Stellarton, up around those places, and there were two little mines in New Brunswick. There was nothing in Quebec in the way of coal. And then Ontario – lots of rock, but no coal. Manitoba – there was one branch on the border, a little mine. Mediocre. But then Alberta was the coalfields. And British Columbia.

But Cape Bretoners' mining experience was different. They had to get broke into it to some extent when they started in the mine out here, especially at the coal face. In Cape Breton, they had air at the face of the coal, so they had drills that were run by air. But when you took a six-foot auger, and you had to know how to sharpen it yourself, and there was a breast plate on it, and you had to drill that in – that was a lot different.

I remember one time at Reserve Junction when I was a little fella. My dad died when I was very young. There were six of us, and we had a very, very hard struggle to exist. I used to sell papers at Reserve Junction. There were three street cars, and they met there at the junction – it was central between Glace Bay, Sydney, Dominion, and so on. And the *Gazette*, *Record*, and *Post* were 2¢ each. When those cars came in, if there were two or three minutes between them, that was good for me. But sometimes they just used to land all together, and I used to run in my bare feet getting to the cars to sell those papers. So one evening, I held this car up maybe two minutes or more – fellas inside wanting papers, you know? A fella from Glace Bay, his name was Doucette, was driving the car, and by golly he bawled me out for holding the car up. He jumped off the car with me, took me and hit my head against the car two or three times. Didn't hurt me altogether, but he was pretty mean.

There was another fella by the name of Tommy MacDonald, and he lived in a place called No. 11. It's on the edge of Glace Bay. Now this Tommy MacDonald, I was a little bit late too with him a few times, but he'd always say, "Don't worry, kid, you're all right. You sell your papers. Another minute won't hurt." Very nice guy. I thought that was all right.

And by golly, it must have been sixteen or seventeen years later – by this time I was a mine boss and in charge of night shift, about seventy miners and drivers – and I went into this place and took a look at this fella. I looked at him, and we talked for a minute. Right away, I knew he was a Cape Bretoner. But I said, "Look, your name just couldn't be Tommy MacDonald, the conductor from one of the street cars?"

"Yes I am. Who are you, anyway?" I told him the story. So it just happened that he had a real bad place, a lot of impurities. He'd only been in the mine two or three days out here, and he was drilling with this auger, and the perspiration just falling off his forehead. "I don't think I can make her," he said. And I said, "Now, you just hang on, Tommy, we'll fix all this." I showed him how to sharpen the auger, drilled a couple of holes for him, and I sent one of my men in to stay with him an hour or two. If he had a good miner with him, he'd be OK, but he was working alone.

So about four or five days after that, a better place showed up and I got him moved over there. This place was much better, and after he got to know how to drill the hole, and the fire boss told him how to shoot the coal, how much powder and so on, by golly, Tommy got by not too badly.

But Doucette, I looked for that man for thirty years. I never did see him.

DON BISHOP – Gaspereau Forks, Queens County, New Brunswick

A large suburban home in a residential area of southwest Calgary. He came to Calgary in the mid-sixties, more than a decade before it became the thing to do. He is in his forties.

"I remember when we were young fellas out running around, if you didn't go to Saint John to work, you were nothing. Everybody, as soon as they graduated from school, 'Where you going?'

" 'I'm going to Saint John to work.' Got to get to Saint John.

"Then the thing changed. Maybe ten years before I left there, there was a big drive – go to Toronto. You were nothing if you hadn't been to Ontario. When I said I was coming out to Calgary, they figured that was the end of it right there! They thought that was terrible."

I used to do a little bit of everything, work in the woods in the wintertime and work in the mill in the summer. What else was there to work at back there then? In the fall you'd look forward to going to the lumber camps. We'd have to portage the stuff back in with teams and build the camp. We'd stay there for the winter and then we'd come out until the time came to stream-drive the logs down. Then we'd go back in and we'd stream-drive the logs down into Chipman. I'm telling you, it was hard work. But a guy was young then, and healthy. I enjoyed it. I really enjoyed getting up in the woods and getting the good old fresh air. You ate well, and nights you'd go to bed at 8:00 or 8:30, and you'd be rested by the time you wanted to get up in the morning. You could stand a hard day's work.

I worked for the government back there for a couple of years. And I had a service station in Nashwaaksis. I'd have had a good business going if I'd looked after it. But I was just a young fella, couldn't get settled down. Parties every night. I was out for a good time and that was it. I was single – I think I was around thirty before I ever thought of getting married.

My wife's from St Stephen. She was married before and lived out here. She said she wanted to go back to the West again. She's a teacher – she wrote to the School Board to see if she could get a job, and they said, "Sure, come on back." I thought I wouldn't mind going out for a year to see what things looked like, so out we came.

We drove out here in a Volkswagen. We went from St Stephen to Boston and up to Fort Erie, Ontario, then came up the Lakehead and into Winnipeg and Brandon, Manitoba. It cost us forty-eight dollars for gas. It was 1966. I'll never forget that as long as I live. Four of us – myself, my wife, and two little boys. Forty-eight dollars.

I had written out here to the Goodyear Tire Company. My wife knew somebody out here who sent the Calgary *Herald* back, and I discovered this ad for work with Goodyear Tire in a service station on MacLeod Trail. They wrote me back and told me they'd give me a job. I started for Goodyear, and I was making $1.75 an hour. I thought that was big money.

I was there for three or four years with them and I kind of got itchy feet. Moving from job to job. When I went to work for Goodyear, I thought I'd be there till ... but it doesn't work that way out here. I worked at tire work for a few years, for different tire companies, busting truck tires and stuff. And then I worked at Oland's Transport. Now I work in a shop repairing alternators and starters. We get the parts and fix them, generally on big units – big trucks and cranes, stuff like that.

"I've driven back and forth across Canada eight times. And I've done stupid things, too. Like trying to break the record. I left here one Friday night at seven o'clock – there was something going on Monday in St Stephen – and we were home Monday morning about nine o'clock. I never stopped. Did most of the driving myself. I came to Montreal before my wife took the wheel. My eyes were so bad, I felt like somebody was putting sand into them. I was so tired that I imagined there were two elephants – they were really two women running down the road alongside of us. Well, I drove all Friday night, Saturday, Saturday night, and Sunday. And we got home Monday morning.

"I had an Oldsmobile, a 1970. If I hadn't have had that car, I would never have done it. I put heavy-duty shocks and coils on her, and that sucker would really hang to the road. The harder I drove it the better it seemed to work. A 455 motor – seventy-five mile an hour was just a joke for that on the road. And I just poured the coal right to her.

"You can drive home cheaper than you can drive out. It takes more gas to come out from the east than it does to go back home. It's about 3,000 feet higher out here. Coming out, you're climbing a little bit all the time. You can almost figure it'll cost you a tank, maybe two tanks of gas, more than it does to go back home."

I only said I was going to come out here for a year and then I was going to go home again. But I've been here ever since. I like it here. But I miss back home, too. I miss the hunting and fishing. I used to do a lot of that. If I wanted to go out fishing, I didn't have to worry about going out and buying a fishing licence. I just went out. And hunting was the same thing. But here you've got to drive so far.

You know, it's a good pace back home. They don't give a damn if the world blows up at their ass or not, and that's a good way to be. Out here, it's such a pace, pushing all the time, you've got to do her in a big smash. Back home, they work hard, but if they don't get it done today, they'll get it done tomorrow. They're super people back there. I can't say enough good about them.

I liked Calgary, but I don't like Calgary now. When I first came here, it wasn't near as big. It's the traffic. On a bad night here, I know darn well I could go from Fredericton to Chipman quicker than I can get home from work. Lots of nights it takes me damn near an hour to get from my shop to home. It's fifty-eight miles from city limit to city limit in Calgary. And there's so much pollution. Some mornings you get up here, especially if you're going to work and the sun's just getting up, and you think, "My God, look what I'm breathing."

After so many years away, do you still like getting home as much as you did before?

I enjoy going home very much, for about two or three days. Then I get bored. Everybody's working down there, and here I am just sitting around. And I don't like to go somewhere, then they'll think, "What the hell did he come for? He's gone, you never see him." At night you sit around, bullshit with the people, then the same thing the next day.

But it's sure changed. On Brookside Drive in Nashwaaksis, there's a big shopping centre up there now, and a funeral parlour. None of that stuff was up there before. Not a thing. There used to be houses and a big asphalt plant way out there, that was all.

I find it more with the people. I used to know every Tom, Dick, and Harry around there, but now I don't. I don't know this younger generation coming up.

I went to school back many years ago with a guy named Charlie Tyler, and we used to be the very best of friends. One summer when I was home, I went with my brother-in-law Vincent in the truck, and he had to go over to the welding shop. Charlie drove in, and it was the funniest thing. He never spoke. I thought, "Well, that's funny." I heard him going over to Vincent: "Who's that guy with you?" "Well," he said, "you must know Donnie Bishop." In kind of a way we both felt stupid, I think. I suppose the last time I'd seen Charlie would have been close to twenty years. I recognized him as soon as I saw him, but he didn't recognize me ... until afterwards.

[Pauses.] It's really too bad. If there was only something to get going down there to draw people. There's lots of work down there, but there's just no goddamn wages. Some relations of my wife there, one of them is a carpenter, and he has guys working for him. So I said to the guys one time, "What's the top wage here?"

"Oh, five bucks an hour." Building houses! I've got two boys, they drive for an outfit here in town, and I think they're getting around eleven bucks an hour.

Somebody is making a pisspot full of it, and the people there are suffering for it, that's my way of thinking. I blame a lot of it on that damn old Irving. He's getting bigger and bigger and bigger, and the people there, they're the ones that are making him. I saw him on TV, they had I think it was the ten wealthiest men in Canada, and he was one of them. The government doesn't tell him what to do; he tells the government. If it was spread out to different outfits, I think it would be a lot better. But when one guy's got the control of all the province ... that's a pretty powerful man.

For example, they've got a mill there in Chipman. When I was home last, the guys thought they were going to fix him – they'd go on strike. It was over some kind of a skidder in their lumber yard down there. They brought a machine in and put three or four guys out of work. So they all thought, "We'll go on strike." Irving just told them, "Listen, if I didn't have this boat to load in Saint John, I wouldn't give a shit if this mill ran again this year or not." So they had to haul their horns in and go back to work.

Out here, it's just a different ball game. Because you could quit a job here tomorrow morning and tomorrow noon you'd have another one. But back home, they figure they own you. You've got to work for them.

RON MacNEIL – Conway, Prince County, Prince Edward Island

Fort McMurray – the home of the Syncrude and Suncor tar-sands plants. He and his partners Steve Barr and Alf Askew own Sun Taxi – by far the biggest cab company in town. It is hard to stand on any street in Fort McMurray and not see one of their black-and-orange cars within five minutes. They also own Sun Tire, which services their fleet.

As we talk in the cab company's business office, Steve offers the odd clarifying comment and runs interference on the phone. An English Quebecker, he bought into the company when Ron's original partner, Jerry MacDougall, moved home to the Island in 1981. The calls are mostly from people looking for work driving.

Ron is a friendly, talkative go-getter in his late thirties. It is obvious as he speaks that these are subjects he has thought about many times before.

I didn't leave home till I was twenty-five – in the fall of '69. I came out to BC, and I ended up going right up on the border of the Alaska Panhandle – Stewart. I spent six months in the payroll office, computer programming, and then transferred to underground, running the computerized electric train, a Mitsubishi, that hauled the ore through a ten-mile tunnel from the mine. They couldn't build a road to the ore body because glaciers surrounded it, so they drove this ten-mile tunnel. It was really quite an undertaking. They had about fifteen or eighteen miles of roads to keep open, and it cost them a million a year to keep the snow off it – just that one stretch.

Oh, it was weird. Beautiful, beautiful country – the most beautiful part of North America I think I've ever seen. Rugged mountains and glaciers. For hunting and fishing, it was paradise. You could fish salmon there – spring salmon, dog salmon, Dolly Varden, and steel-heads. Halibut, land-locked rainbow – they all ran through there. You could hunt goat, three kinds of sheep, deer, moose, black bear, grizzly, caribou, all in that same region. I shot an eight-foot silver-tip grizzly when I was in Stewart. It was just exciting to be there – a boom town. People were making big money. They worked hard and they played hard. I was just going to spend six months there, but I ended up staying.

I quit for the summer in '75, went home, and met Gwendolyn Johnston, my wife. Her parents own Maple Leaf Dairy in Summer-side, though she at the time was nursing in Prince Rupert, BC. She bought a car and drove back across Canada. I bought a new Honda 1000 and toured down through the States, and then in the fall came back out to BC.

But I found I couldn't get back on my job. When I was home that summer, they had had a train crash. The guy ran into a dead end – survived by a miracle. They went back through the record books, of course. And when they checked back through my records, they saw where I'd been putting in caustic comments about the condition of the brakes, and why the cars were being switched out. Legally, if five percent or more of the brakes malfunctioned, you had to start switching cars, which I always did. When they did the tests after the accident, fifty-some percent of the brakes in the period since I had quit had not been properly repaired. But of course I got a "No Rehire – Poor Attitude" slip.

They blackballed me, and I couldn't get a job in BC. I just couldn't. I tried for I guess about four months. It'd look good – go in, and "Sure, no problem." They'd look at my work record – "Great." And all of a sudden, two days later, "No, sorry, not hiring." Gwen had since moved to Prince George, so I drove over there and tried to get a job at Logan Lake, BC. And the same thing – it'd look good, and all of a sudden, it'd be gone.

So then I came with a friend, Bruce Grant, to Fort McMurray. A priest, Father Paul Thompson, who is still a friend of mine in town, helped us get a job with Suncor – actually, Great Canadian Oil Sands then. I spent I guess about ten months in camp, paid off all my bills and got everything straightened around, and then Gwen came over and started nursing here. We went back in '77 and got married in PEI. Then back out.

When I was working at Suncor, I started out in the lowest position in the mine, walking the belts.* Then we were transferred to 75-ton trucks, then to 150-ton trucks, then to 170-ton trucks. I spent three years minus three days at that. It's a lot of boredom driving the equipment. It's interesting the first while. But after a while – utter apathy. Round and round. No sense of accomplishment at all. I'd come home and my wife would say, "How'd it go?" "Oh," I'd say, "round and round like a mouse in a pisspot."

So I'd spent five and a half years underground on shift work, and then just about three years here, and I just couldn't handle it anymore. There were two suicides in my department out here that fall. Young family men – just too much pressure on them. My wife was on shift work and I was on it. It just got depressing. So I said I had to quit.

We bought a mobile home in Gregroire Park [Fort McMurray], and took a holiday to Hawaii just about a week after we moved in. When we came back I bought a cab and went driving taxi.

I drove for Fort Taxi for five and a half months. I got in there because of my partner, Jerry MacDougall, who I ran into out at the plant. He was driving cab longer than me.

The people who were running Fort were more or less a little on the shady side. A lot of people knew it, and they made no bones about it themselves. They had company cars and were feeding them – giving them the preference trips. The company car would get four trips when you got one, and their four trips were all the best trips. There was a lot of discontent.

Were they the only game in town?

Between them, Fort Taxi, and Your Taxi, they had her pretty well tied up. Then Sun Taxi became available. Fort was thinking of buying it but they said the price was too high. So I thought, "Those SOBs. I'll show them how to run a cab company." I borrowed some money against the properties I own back home, put a down payment on it, and we took Sun over. We had eight light blue cars on the road then. We changed the colour to black and orange and went from eight cars to about fifty-three in a matter of two and a half months. We took eighteen cars off the Fort fleet alone.

We have about ninety-eight percent of the business here in town. We're probably the only operation in town here that runs twenty-

---

*   "Walking the belts" means continuous inspection, for bad rollers and the like, of the belts the tar sand is conveyed on.

four hours a day, three hundred and sixty-five days a year. The oil-sands plants run on that schedule, but I don't know of any other businesses here in town.

That seems like a lot of cabs for a place this size.

See, the average age in this town, out of 30,000 people, is twenty-three. So it's a young town. A lot of the people – a lot of the girls – don't even have their licences.

Another reason the taxis are so busy is the satellites [areas of Fort McMurray]. Area Five is way up one little loop, then you come way back down, cross the bridge, and go up to Area One, is another loop, then Area Two and Area Six. They're spreading it out well.

STEVE And there's nothing up there to service the area. There are no stores. They come down, number one, to do their banking in the Valley, and once that's done, they do their shopping.

RON This is the busiest liquor store in the province, and it's down-town.

STEVE Take into consideration that the Syncrude and Suncor plants are twenty-five miles north of town here, and occasionally men miss their buses, are called in for overtime, or are sick. And we're servicing the tar-sands plants, the airport, and most of the major hotels and businesses here in town.

RON Suncor spends about $400,000 a year just in cabs alone. Just one contract.

STEVE People have the money to spend. They're making good salaries, good wages.

RON These guys make very good money. Look at some of the cars we've got. Loaded. Power windows, power seats, velvet interiors. We had a Cadillac on the other year. You never see cabs like that in the city. If you want to come up here and put your own cab on, drive it yourself, and hustle, if you can't get yourself forty a year ...

But they work hard. It's not an easy job. Driving cab's not the job people think it is. A good cab driver's got to be on the ball, and he's got to know the town like the back side of his hand. I've had people come in here who've been in town for ten or fifteen years, and they say, "Oh, I don't have to take the course, I know the town." And I just rhyme off ten addresses or ten trailer courts, and they can't name one of them. And after they take the tour, they're impressed. They've seen sections of the town that they didn't even know existed.

But it's been interesting. I enjoy the cab business. There's always something new. Cab drivers, if they don't hear a good rumour by noon, they start one. And by four o'clock, they believe it.

Do you have many Maritimers driving for you?

A third of the population of the town is from the Maritimes. And I guess there are 6,000 or 7,000 Newfoundlanders here. Oh yeah, if I fired all the Newfies, I'd be out of business. They're not scared to put in the hours, and they'll work. And there are no problems with them. The same with the oil-sands plant. They'll hire a Maritimer over a British Columbian or even an Albertan. They'll work, and they'll stay – they're making bigger money than they ever have in their lives.

Well, even up in northern BC when I was there, there was a phenomenal amount of Maritimers. I life-guarded on the national team on PEI for two years – at Rustico Island the last summer. There was a guy there named Fred MacDonald, who worked on the gate at the Rustico Island campground. In the cookhouse in Stewart one night this guy walks in. "Gee, that guy looks familiar. Where the hell have I seen him before?" And of course two or three days later I met him: Fred. And there was a Corrigan there – Bill Corrigan from Charlottetown. And Kendall Forbes, a friend of mine from Summerside, he came out and stayed one winter. A buddy of mine, Ken MacQuarrie, came out with me from the Island to BC in '72. He stayed there for a couple of years. He and his wife Colette, daughter of J.A. Doiron, the lieutenant governor of PEI, ended up here in Fort McMurray. He's got his own taxis on the fleet now.

Still, all the ones I talk to, they're all thinking of going back home ... But once the oil firms get them up here, and they get them into their own housing and stuff, it's pretty hard for a guy to pull out. It ties a guy down, let's face it.

Let's say Suncor – if you want to buy a house through Suncor right now, you have to sign up with the company for eight years before the house is transferred to your name. That's a long stint. They own Athabasca Realty, who control the housing in town for them. It's just a separate branch. You have to work for the company for eight years, and make payments to the company for eight years, before they'll turn title over to you. You don't even have title to it. The people that do tough it out, lots of them, the last day of their stint, sell their houses and they're gone. That's all you'd hear there – "I've got a year and eight days to go till I get my house paid for. I just can't wait."

Syncrude has sort of a different package, I think. As long as you've got the cash to buy it out, if you quit, you can buy it out.

But if you want to sell it, they'll pay market price for it, but they have first option to buy it back.

I'd like to go back, I really would. When I used to go to PEI in the summer, when the plane used to fly in over the Island, I'd cry. The tears would come to my eyes. I'm not a very emotional person. I can hold a pretty steady line. But I used to go in and it would fly over Cavendish there, and tears would come to my eyes. Weird feeling.

I remember I went home there one fall, and I had a lot of things to look after, and I didn't get down to Cavendish. My buddy runs a Honda dealership there, and I got a motorcycle off of him. I nearly froze my fingers riding down, just to see Cavendish. I just wanted to take one fast run down and take a look. Parked the bike, went over and stood there for about twenty minutes, then back on the bike and headed back. As a matter of fact, my hands got so cold, I had to stop in at Hendersons' in Clinton to get them warmed up.

I was born in Conway, right in my parents' home. My parents, Oscar and Edna MacNeil, were general merchants there. Conway's pretty well dead now. It's funny. We went back one spring when we were home. I had to really stop and look to see where I was at. The big MacKinnon and Adams farm houses were gone. And Gwen said, "Well, where were you born?" And I really had to stop and look. The store was even gone, and it was the focal point of the village. The whole village just died out and disappeared.

I remember J.W. Palmer, my grandad, coming in still, and getting the winter groceries. They'd get icing sugar and dates and mixed peel, kerosene oil, molasses, and staples you couldn't get on the farm itself. They did that one shopping deal just as the first snow hit – then they went home and stayed for the winter. They had the basement full of oysters in seaweed, and waxed eggs. My grandmother picked every kind of wild berry you could find. And there were pickles, salt pork, and salt cod, and potatoes and turnips. They'd fish eels and smelts through the ice. They visited. They worked hard, but they enjoyed one hell of a good lifestyle, to my mind.

The Island is absolutely ... it's beautiful. And you know what the sad part is? The people on the Island, a lot of them, don't appreciate it. They don't appreciate it worth a sweet tweet. I don't know if it's because they're not shown how ... I don't know how to explain it. They never get away to take a look back maybe. They never got on the outside to take a look in. I don't know if you have to get away to see it, or what.

I think if people get out and move around a bit, and see a bit of the country, it says something for them. I've got some good friends on the Island. They all left at one time. They might have only been gone a year, they might have been gone two years. But the ones that go back seem to do all right, because they've got a different outlook on life. They get away from that damn pettiness.

It reminds me of a story, I can't remember who told me, about a woman who died at the age of ninety-two at a place on PEI. She was born in Ontario and came to PEI at the age of so many months. She had married there, had raised five children there, and had so many grandchildren and so many great-grandchildren. And the notice in the paper said, "The former Ontarioite was interred ..." After ninety-two and a half years, she still wasn't an Islander. She was born in Ontario – she was an "Ontarioite." And that's just exactly the way it is – she was "from away."

Actually, I quite enjoy the Islanders. I own two buildings – a fourplex in New Annan and a threeplex in Kensington. When I was home the other year, I got some storm doors through the government insulating program there, and I had this elderly gentleman helping me put them on. I had three of them to put on, and we were going up to the other building to put up a couple others. All the way out, he wants to know my business. Like, "Who owns the building? Did you buy that? Do you own this? Who owns that?" He's pumping me all the way. And I said, "You know, it's funny. My wife and I were talking the other day. We'd like to come back and settle on the Island, but my God, Islanders are nosy. They want to know all your business." So he says: "Isn't that true." And then right back into Question Period. Sixty Questions.

And they haven't looked after their people there either. They've been paying them peanuts. My mother taught school for thirty years there in PEI and the first year she was on pension, she made more than she ever did teaching. And that's a piss-off. Something's wrong.

I think basically the Maritime people are just too busy earning a living to appreciate life. It's the same thing as being in business or making money. Because making money's a game. And if every cent's got to go for your power bill, heat bill, your house mortgage payment, and your car payment, just for subsistence and clothes on the kids' backs, you can't make money. That's the way they've kept the Maritimes.

And what ticks me off about the Island economy is the fact that when they do pump a lot of money in there, all the rich people in Charlottetown and Summerside get it. They build more hotels. They build more motels. The people who really need the bucks – who need year-round industry – are getting three months, and they're back on the pogey. It's a joke what the money has gone into.

I used to see the rich kids of the prominent families around Summerside, and they really used to tick me off. Because they really do run the show. I'd see myself go up for a speeding ticket on the Island, and I'd get nailed thirty bucks. And I'd see one of the doctor's sons come up, and he's got five speeding tickets, and it's a little slap on the hand – "Don't do it again, Sonny." No goddamn justice. They buy, they run the whole show. They really do. There's just so much social injustice there. I see some of it here, but I've seen it more back there. It all goes back to the petty bullshit.

The reason most people leave the Island is frustration. Because you know damn well unless you're a doctor or a lawyer or whatever, and you set up your own trade and get at it there, or the family has money initially, your chances of getting ahead there are just about zip. Because the old families have the money; they have the land; they have it all tied up. They talk about the absentee landowners of the nineteenth century! The landlords are there today, and they've got everything tied up tight. Go down through the courthouse and see who owns what. They got her tied up tight. They talk about monopolies in BC in the forest industry here, but they don't even know who owns what back there. They got her tied up, man. Tied up tight.

The Maritime Reunion Association of Alberta

An abandoned schoolhouse just off the Crowchild Trail on 5th Avenue in northwest Calgary. In the windows hang the flags of Prince Edward Island, Nova Scotia, and New Brunswick. These are the offices of the Maritime Reunion Association of Alberta. A huge yellow-and-blue sign – brought out to each of the many social functions the MRA runs in the city – sets out the Association's purposes:

To conduct a social and recreational association for Maritimers in Alberta.
To develop facilities and programs for Maritimers coming to Alberta to help them find employment and accommodation.
To advance, develop and foster friendships among people.

KEITH McELWAIN – Riverview,
Albert County, New Brunswick

The president and co-founder of the MRA. A big man in his late twenties, he exudes the kind of confidence peculiar to the successful salesperson. "Negativity," he says scornfully, "I live with it every day. My attitude is the most important asset I have. I look for positive people. If you can't find them, you've got to look somewhere else." He is a distributor, an independent sales manager, for Bondel water filters. He and Linda, his wife, live with their daughter in northwest Calgary.

What happened to me I assume happens to a lot of Maritimers when they come here. They're coming because they're not happy with their lives in the Maritimes. There's no money. People are all the same. I just said I had to get out of there, to go somewhere, do something. Things were going to be better in Alberta.

I never finished grade ten. I quit at Christmas time. So I came here with no skills, no trade – I mean anything. In '71. I arrived out here in a Volkswagen with everything I owned, and no money. I moved in with one of my brothers and he put me to work laying carpet. An absolute menial task, as far as I'm concerned. If I ever had to get down on my knees and kick in another piece of carpet, unless it was a personal favour for a friend, it would kill me.

Went through a lot of crazy times, you know, loaded and crazy parties. Always on the tear. I had three Harleys. Worked the rigs, travelled around. And booze all the time.

A buddy of mine from Riverview and myself moved into this apartment. We had a bed for each of us and two dressers. We bought those out of a hotel, the Westward Inn, that was changing to redecorate a bit when I was laying carpet there. So we bought those, and that's all we had. We didn't have any kitchen furniture, we didn't have any living-room furniture, we didn't have anything. But we did have a spot, and that was more than what most people we knew had.

The day we moved in, the buzzer rang, and it was Linda. She's a Moncton girl from the West End. She was eighteen and I was nineteen. She and a girlfriend of hers were passing through town on their way out to Banff. They were looking for a place to stay for the night, and I said, "Come on down." And she never left. She's been with me ever since.

I remember when we first set up house. How we kept it together under that roof, I don't know. We had fourteen in the house at different times. A small bungalow with two bedrooms upstairs!

Sleeping in the basement, sleeping on the floor in the living-room, on the couches. For years we did that. Finally we got ourselves a one-bedroom, beautiful hillside kind of place with a glass front. It was nice. It was small enough that nobody could live with us. That was why we got it.

Is Calgary home now?

Well, my whole family's here. There are five kids in the family, and all five of us are here. We've all been here for quite a few years now too.

One of the most difficult things I've had in my life was thinking where I wanted to be was where I was at. You know, "I'm in Calgary." I drove across the bridge the other day and I said, "This is my town. You got her. I can do anything I want here." I feel very comfortable in this town. I do like it. We've got a little girl. We've set down some roots. We're going to be a family here, and I enjoy that.

I've been home. I went home for a month in '79 and stayed for four. I remember the thing that really got me when I was home was that in Calgary I could do eight or ten calls a day – go out and see eight or ten people. In Albert County if I got to see one or two people, I was doing well. You know, you can't get out to anywhere in the afternoon but you have to stay for supper. It's all right, but it took me a while to get used to that when I went back home.

Out here, it's a big, exciting new town and everybody's flying. It's not like that at home. Moncton's a small town.

My dad's twenty-seven years there. He did really well. He was with Electrolux of Canada – and now he's with Royal Trust. He's a very positive-minded guy. He keeps saying, "Well, things are going to move. Things are going to move." I hear them out here saying the same thing: "When things get going in the Maritimes, I'm going home." I don't want to be negative, but my God, they were saying that when I was three years old.

How did you get started with the Reunion Association?

Well, a fella by the name of Paul Savoie from Moncton came to me one day and said that he and another fella wanted to bring the Minglewood Band in and have a lobster dinner. They thought I had some money, and they wanted some financial backing. I didn't tell them any different. So I said, "Fine, we'll back you." Actually, I never put a penny up. It was never needed. The money always comes out of ticket sales. You pay the boys after they play the "do," you pay the arena after, and you pay everybody after. The whole show was sold out two weeks in advance without a word of advertising, so there's no money needed.

Now, I have a good friend, Rick Beers. I said to Ricky, "Geez, three of us are bringin' in the Minglewood Band for a concert and lobster dinner. I'm going to back it. Do you want to take half the load?" Well, what happened was that Ricky got involved, and about two weeks prior to show time we'd sold about a thousand tickets. We were trying to get a booze licence for the night from the Liquor Board of Alberta, so we could serve liquor there. "We'd love to give you a liquor permit," they told us, "but you need to be incorporated as an association." "Well," we said, "we are." And they said, "Yeah? What's your name?" We called ourselves the "Moncton Reunion Association of Alberta," just to have a name. We didn't get the liquor permit, but that's where the idea came from.

The do was a fantastic success. I couldn't believe it – twelve hundred Maritimers all in one room. I remember the fear. We were in a big arena, and I went upstairs and looked down, and I just thought, "My God, there's nothing you can do now." We had security. We had a rugby team – people from down east who had played college rugby and formed their own rugby team out here. They all had a thousand friends there themselves, and so they all got drunk. It was pretty hairy, but nothing happened. We never had one incident.

Ricky and I were watching the whole thing and we said, "Look – there are people coming out of the woodwork to go to this thing. They're not only from Moncton. They're from everywhere, all over the Maritimes." We got excited and started thinking, "Why not start something? Why not have the Maritime Association?" So we started taking people's names at that do, that first one – people we could get in touch with after. The do went off really well. We came out of there with the idea of the Maritime Reunion Association.

My wife and I got married the next day – that was June 6, 1980.

We've gotten a lot of positive responses from people in the business community and the media. They said, "Hey! This is a super idea. This is just great." And it is. But the idea, the end goal – you can't go anywhere without a goal – is just to help those that are coming in that don't know where the hell they're at. Can you imagine coming out of Salisbury and moving into Calgary? "Where am I? I'm in Calgary. I just got off the train. I've got seven dollars in my pocket and things are not the greatest." They've got no idea what Calgary's all about.

We're economic refugees. If you come in here from Laos or Indochina or something like that, they give you two years tax-free.

They give you all kinds of benefits. They help you get organized. What the hell do they do for the Maritimers that come here?

I'll tell you how I see a lot of Maritimers coming here. I see it this way because I lived it this way. And when I was living it that way, I saw hundreds of others living it that way. I've been into a thousand houses in Calgary where there's anywhere from five to twelve guys living there. We call them "townie houses" now, not because they're town houses but because they're full of everybody that's in town. I could take you right now to half a dozen places like that. A lot of talent getting wasted. Because if you've got three of them that are boozin' it all the time, if the rest of them aren't, they're going to be soon. They never get any sleep. People are going through jobs because they're not going to work because they're up all night. And telephone bills! I've heard that if you tell them you're from the Maritimes and you want a telephone, they want a double deposit. People calling home ...

I don't want to downplay the talents of the Maritimer coming here, because there are some very talented people that come here. But they're still in the same boat as far as getting relocated. Your average Maritimer comes out and moves in with friends. A house like this where Linda and I are living [a bungalow], there'd be maybe ten Maritimers – and as it is, we have a bedroom downstairs that's rarely empty. And so you get five or six or eight or ten or twelve or fifteen moving in a house. The partying that goes on and that sort of thing. Not only is the talent wasted to the rest of society but it's wasted to themselves. Their impression of themselves is lowered. Like, "My God, I've been here six months and nothing's happened." The attitude is that they're going to come out here and get rich. Like the joke we put in our [MRA] newsletter: There's a guy in Cape Breton, and his grandfather says, "Why don't you go to Alberta – they're picking money up off the streets out there." And so he and his buddy, they come to Alberta, and the first day in town they're walking down the street, and on the sidewalk he sees a twenty-dollar bill. He starts to bend over to pick it up, and then he straightens up. And he goes again to bend over to pick it up. And he straightens up again and looks at his friend. And the guy says, "What's the matter?" "No," he says, "I don't think I'm going to work on my first day in town." [Laughs.]

They lose their identity. They're in a kind of situation which isn't all that good. Because they're either living with too many guys or not enough. There is that too. There are Maritimers living all by themselves in the city. They don't have any place to go and they're alone. So where are you going to find companionship? In the bars.

I had a guy come out one time. He laid on my couch for four months. He wouldn't even get up and go to Banff. He said, "You guys go and tell me about it when you get back. I can see it all on TV." And never did a thing. Never left the house. I didn't realize then how sick he must have been, inside, and how much pain he must have been going through, and how much fear was in the guy that he wouldn't even get up off the couch and look for a job.

There are some other things too. The average Maritimer comes here and is going to be here for two years at the outside. Going to make a bunch of money and help Mom and Dad pay the bills. Go home and take over the farm and all that sort of stuff. What they don't do, is they don't join community associations. They don't join the Elks and the Lions. They don't get active in politics. They don't get active in anything. "Why should I? We're not staying." They don't know who their Member of Parliament is, who their rep at City Hall is.

We're hoping, and one of our goals in the Association, is to fill in and be able to take people from the train and put them through and make them members of the community. Not to take the identity of Maritimers away by any stretch of the imagination. But make them aware of what is actually going on here and help them get involved.

We could be a big association in the city. We could have 10,000 members. Help people find places to live. Help people find employment. You know, we've got in the neighbourhood of 50,000 Maritimers here in Calgary. My philosophy is either we go for it or we don't. I'm not into a maintenance situation; I'm into a growth situation. Piddlin' around is not my bag.

DANNY BATHERSON – North Sydney, Nova Scotia

He helps the Reunion Association organize concerts and dances. He was the full-time MRA coordinator for a period, but, introduced to the water-filter business by Keith McElwain (above), he resigned from that position to devote his energies to independent sales. Throughout our conversation he is interrupted by calls about an evening he is putting together in the West Hillhurst Community Centre, Calgary, with Cape Breton fiddlers John Campbell and Carl MacKenzie. Danny is in his twenties.

I went up to Fort McMurray in 1973 – worked a year up there. I was in the first two hundred that worked on that new Syncrude place. It went from two hundred in one kitchen to about eight thousand in camp. She was a big project.

After a year in the Fort I went home. Summertime – you know, summer in Cape Breton, you've got to go home. So I went home, and stayed for about five years or so. Went back to the College of Cape Breton. I got my Recreation degree and then I went to Toronto. I spent a year working at a Boys and Girls Club – I was the arts-and-crafts director there – and left there and came out here. The reason I came here is that I knew all kinds of people. Half the town is out here in Alberta. An incredible crowd. There's just hundreds.

I was framing houses when I first arrived in town. I had some tools and had done a little carpentry work before. I was in an apprenticeship program for a year. I never was much of a carpenter – but, you know, make some quick money banging them together. And do they ever bang them together! They're all slapped together the same way – as fast as they can get them together.

I had heard about the Association, because Matt Minglewood's my brother. I had heard through him that they played out here for the Maritime Reunion Association. I saw a little ad in the paper when I was working for a job in Recreation – got the job [as coordinator] with the Association, and it's been the highlight of my Calgary stay.

I came in just at the right time. We ran a big outdoor concert, that was my first job. I knew all the promoters through Matt. The Reunion Association wanted to bring out Buddy and the Boys, and I knew the boys personally. So we flew Buddy and the Boys out, and we had a great concert. Our idea was that we didn't want to have a rock 'n' roll concert. We wanted to have sort of a picnic. Thirtieth of May [1980], and we had a great crowd. Seventeen hundred. There were kids and dogs and coolers ... We gave them all the lobsters they could eat. We flew out about three thousand pounds of lobster from Ocean Delight in Shediac. Cost us about $10,000. The hill was red with lobsters! We had all kinds of lobsters left. We bought enough for 2,500. I was going around the next two days knocking on doors, giving away fifteen pounds of lobsters.

We had it at the riding stables out here. Out in the country – beautiful sloped hill ... you would swear it was right in Nova Scotia. There was an incredible feeling in the field. You know, right here in Alberta, she was all Maritimers.

A beautiful write-up Suzanne Zwarun gave us. She writes daily columns.* Of course Suzanne's a member. She started the article off – I thought she was going to butcher us. The column started, she

* In the Calgary *Herald*. She is from Dominion, Cape Breton.

was out in the country, couldn't find the place. She came down the
road and she stopped ... Here was this guy lying in the middle of
the road, and the car there. She figured she had found it. Some
young red-headed fella lying across the middle of the road, waiting
for his buddies to come back to haul the car out of the ditch. Typical
Maritimes, you know, she had it in her head. She'd found it. Lo and
behold, she was ten miles in the wrong direction, and it was a
couple of local boys. So she got it on track and she just ... families,
dogs, cats, ... It was a good show.

We kept it pretty low key in the afternoon. We opened the show
with a piper. Some Irish music, and then a local band, a band from
Ontario called High Country. And there was another band from
Cape Breton here – Billy, Cornelia, and Nick. They're a great band.
And we had Buddy and the Boys. The music started about 2:30 in
the afternoon, and finished about 2:30 in the morning.

Did you break even?

Oh, we made $4,000. A lot of work. Oh, my Jesus. I never slept for a
couple of days for that show. It went rather well. We were lucky. I
had three weeks to do it. We put her together in three weeks.

And you've kept on organizing those kind of do's?

Yeah. A few of them have been rock 'n' roll, and we advertised one
as an Irish Ceilidh. I think we have to keep that Maritime flavour.
Ryan's Fancy played last year, and had 650 people. We had Cornelia, Billy, and Nick. They're from Arichat, that way. They're a
good troupe. They have their baby on the road with them. They're
hard working. They don't go home anymore. They go home, they
work a little bit. But they work mainly here in Alberta.

All the Maritime groups are headed this way. The groups come,
and the Maritimers are the ones that pack the clubs. And usually
when you get a Maritime group in, and a room full of Maritimers ...
it's in the air. So you can't help but get a half-decent write-up. I
know Matt always gets great write-ups here in town.

But we have plans. We put a booth in the Stampede. We had a
list of about forty volunteers who were down and put their time in
at that booth. We just scheduled a week and filled in the time slots.
We had a real nice booth, in the Round-up Centre. We had lobster
traps, fish nets, pictures of the tours people provided, and information – we had all kinds of information from the tourist departments.
The federal government sent us down from Edmonton – geez, they
sent us down boxes and boxes of maps of Canada. They gave us
about $1,500 worth of maps. We had about 15,000 people going
through a day, I think, in that whole building.

So that went quite well. And from there we went to the baseball game. We had a Maritime night at the ball park up here, with the Calgary Expos. Set up our booth, you know, and the flags and display.

You must have quite a membership for all that.

I suppose we have about 400 members. That may be stretching it a bit. We have a board of directors – a dozen. And then you get the people that help out at do's. Oh, we have a good group.

JEFF MILLER – Bathurst, New Brunswick

Miller's Donair on Centre Street North in Calgary: one of the main ticket outlets for Maritime Reunion Association dances and concerts. Jeff operates the business together with his brother Kirk. He is in his late twenties. I ask how the donair business got started in Canada.

That happened in '77. There was a guy from Halifax and another guy from Dieppe [New Brunswick] who opened up virtually around the same time. The guy from Dieppe owned the Pizza Delight franchise, sold it, and went into this company called Greco Donair.

There were three donair places in Edmonton when we opened here, although I didn't know anything about it at the time. We were the first in Calgary. We got ahold of the recipe and the know-how and came out here. There are so many Maritimers out here – it's a good area.

Did you start into this business when you first came?

Well, not really. We came out with the idea in mind, but we didn't have the capital. We weren't sure what we were going to do to obtain the capital. It wasn't going to be given to us. So we went out and did bar jobs, and bought a taxi, and sort of busted our butts for a year. And then in August, '79, we started on the mall, the 8th Avenue Mall, with a little trailer. It's a little project they had called "Mall Days," and it runs from the first of May till the end of September, so we were on there for basically two months. It was just a little trailer we put together for about $5,000, to see if the product would go over. Got the equipment, got the recipe, knew the know-how, and away we went.

We were fortunate to be on the mall. It was a real good bet. We had incredible line-ups – literally half-hour line-ups. We just couldn't pump them out fast enough. Made a little money and went to see the bank. We showed them our cash flow from it, and what we thought we could do. They said "Fine, go for it," so we went ahead with it. At the end of the summer we both worked in the bar for another couple of months – I stayed on until March and my brother quit around Christmas time – and we started building this [Centre Street] place.

Are you the only donair outfit in Calgary?

A month after we opened, there was another company opened. It's called "My Donair." We opened up in August '79, and they opened up I think around December of that year, in the Marlborough Mall. And they had a good location, so they've done quite well.

Are they from home too?

No, they're Calgarians.

Would their clientele be mostly Maritimers?

I don't think so. Their clientele is probably about forty-five percent, fifty percent Maritimers. Ours is definitely eighty-five percent. No doubt about it.

Because of the connection with the Reunion Association?

Yeah, a lot of it. And we're also from the Maritimes. It helps. And when we first opened, my brother and I did all the work ourselves, so we were there to talk to the people ...

We've had a lot of response from the Maritime Association, and they've been like gold to us. There's been a lot of sort of free advertising – word of mouth. We've helped them out as far as selling tickets and stuff like that, but there has been a lot of talk about our shop, and they've given us a great boost.

It's really – you know, the whole Maritime idea – it really strikes home once you do leave. It's like that saying, "You don't know what you have till it's gone." And it's a good feeling. It was the same when I was working in a bar. I was working at The Highlander – and that is a Maritime bar. You can go in any given weekend night, and I'd say eighty percent of the people there are Maritimers. And out of that eighty percent, I'd say fifty, sixty percent are from the Cape. I love them. My mother was born in Louisbourg.

How did you ever decide to come out here and try this in the first place?

My brother and I were going to open up a Kelly's [record] store in Bathurst, and we had this guy doing his masters on sort of a feasibility study for a Kelly's outlet there. He did it. He got A-plus, and all systems were go. We took this in to the bank. We had, I think, around $7,000 to invest ourselves, and we needed the capital backing. I don't know if this is just politics where I come from, or what happened, but the bank manager emphatically said, "No. No way." We were really upset, because it was there on paper. Funny thing, though. Three months down the road Sam the Record Man opened.

So I don't know. We stuck around for about a year and sort of salted away a little more money and actually went on sort of a big gamble, into a bar in Bathurst. We went for it, and we lost. We lost a fair amount of money. It was at that point that we packed our bags and said, "Let's get out of here. It's not going to happen for us here."

And I had no intention of going back to university. I subbed at the local high school for a couple of months and was approached to go back and get my education degree and come back and teach there. [Pauses.] But I don't know, it's just tough. There's not a whole lot there, you know – not unless you go into some type of profession, you're lucky, or it's given to you.

LARRY MacDONALD – Mulgrave, Guysborough County, Nova Scotia

He is in his early seventies. In sales, consulting, and public relations all his working life, he came out of retirement in 1981 to work as interim coordinator of the Maritime Reunion Association.

He is friendly and outgoing, and anxious to set the record straight about Albertans' opinions of people from home.

They take us for a bunch of ignorant clots. Either farmers or fishermen. But Maritimers are the most brilliant people in the world. Nova Scotians, I'd say, particularly, are the backbone of Canada. And I don't care who says they're not.

I went through so much of this. See, my company represented thirty-five mills, and an awful lot of them were in the States, and I was constantly up against that. It's still the same. I mean there are a lot of offices where if you say you're a Maritimer ... No way. I'll tell you the ones that are saying that around here, too, and it was the same in Toronto – the quick rich. They've no more cultural background or moral background than an alley cat.

Nearly all the guys that I knew that felt the same as I did, we'd fight over the Maritimes at the drop of a hat. I've got in fights. Of course I was half lit. In a hotel, as a matter of fact, I hit one of the guys who was one of the chiefs at one of our mills. I was tighter than a coot. But he said all we were was a raggly bunch of ass-out-of-our-pants Maritimers ... I'm telling you, I get awful heated.

But you can take any profession. Take the legal profession. Vaughan Hardigan from Sydney Mines was chief agent to the attorney general. He's down in Lethbridge. Some of the best criminal lawyers we have right in Alberta are from Nova Scotia – went to St FX and Dalhousie. And Dalhousie in Halifax is still one of the best law universities – I won't say in the world – but it's the best in Canada, bar none. No, the legal profession is adequately represented from the Maritimes out here.

And the intelligence of the people that came out of there. Take my class in school. There's not one failure in it – unless it's me. Not one. Ryan was captain of the *Bluenose*. Johnny – Dr Stanton – did a lot of research work. I think he was out here for a long time, in Victoria. You can just name it – the oil business, professors, judges, teachers, and so on. *Dedicated* teachers. I mean to humanity, to other people. I think that as a group of people that I've met, as far as intelligence goes – I couldn't put a percentage figure on it – but we're well, very well, represented in the Maritime Provinces.

They used to call the Maritimes "the brain factory of Canada." Like the people that first came out here. There were a lot of young fellas at home – oh, I know many of them – that hauled out here on the harvest trains. My Uncle Anthony came out here after World War I. He was a civil engineer. He was one of the engineers that built the first snow sheds for the CPR.* The very first snow sheds. I get a great feeling going through the Rogers Pass.

What I'd make a comparison with is Boston. I'm half-Irish, and a great many on my mother's side were Irish, and they really made a name for themselves. Uncle Mike was in Salem, and Uncle Leo was in Portland. Uncle John was in Boston. My dad was killed in World War I, at Vimy Ridge, and Grandmother and Grandfather brought us up. But every year I went with Grandmother for two months, on summer holidays, to visit the relatives. My Uncle John became vice-president of John Hancock Insurance Company and in later years went to Harvard Business School. Huge companies like John Hancock – it's one of the finest insurance companies in the world – they recognized where the abilities were. And that's about all that any Maritimer needs, I think, is somebody to recognize the ability and give him the opportunity to develop it.

A lot of people that came out here – and I can go right back to Uncle Anthony and those snow sheds – they were idea men. They'd

---

* Snow sheds provide protection against snow slides for trains in mountain passes and rock cuts.

make things work. It's happened in this little Maritime Reunion organization already. They made it work, because they have the energy, they have the ideas. Betty MacLennan for instance [MRA vice-president]. She owns her own management-consulting firm. Brian Appleby [treasurer, from Moncton] – Brian came out with McCain's Foods and left to participate in a business of his own. He's a real smart boy – all the attributes of a very successful man. Another one I met at a meeting was Robert MacLeod, who took over from Brian at McCain's. Now, there's a boy that studied political science at UNB. Wish you could hear him. Steve Read manages a Safeway's store. Go in and see his store. It's an old store, and it looks as good as new. I bet you it's an example to the Safeways in the city. And it really delights me to know young people like that.

"I remember as kids in Mulgrave, all the boats used to come – from Arichat, from Guysborough and Canso. That was a daily deal. Well, Whint MacDonald was a shipping magnate for years. He bought a royal yacht – the Surf – and I think it was King Edward VII's yacht. It was old, old, old. But you know how they keep them in repairs. He bought it at an auction in England, and sold the silverware off it and paid for it. That's the kind of stickhandler he was. But he put that on the Canso run. Geez, a beautiful boat. And as kids, when I was sixteen, we had excursions on that. My friends Hadley and Bud Keating and Clancy and I would do like Keith [McElwain] and Danny [Batherson] and these fellas have done – we'd go around and hustle tickets. Two bucks, I think, or five bucks, and we got Tony MacIntosh's orchestra. Tony MacIntosh – I don't know if he was from Sydney or Glace Bay – was the best pianist that I ever heard. It was always a condition when you hired the orchestra that somebody sat on the piano stool with him, because he'd be so drunk that he'd fall off the stool. I'm not kidding. But we'd get the newspaper to give us a little ad, you know, and then we'd go across from Mulgrave and pick them up in Hawkesbury, and we'd go into Arichat and into Canso ... And we were doing that when we were kids!"

Well, I suppose at the time I was a young fella there, there were about 1,200 people in Mulgrave. There were only the two industries – the people that worked in the fish plant, and the people that worked on the railroad. And Mr Loggie – the general manager of the fish plant – was the mayor. But the railroad supplied the majority of the jobs, because they had the roundhouse and the shops there, and the machine shop which was necessary to maintain the two ferries that carried the train across. So there was the crew on the two ferries, and then there was the roundhouse, which maintained the engines, and of course the regular yard crews for moving the freight and the trains. And it was really, around the railroad, a hive of activity.

I wish more places in the world were like Mulgrave during the depression. If we could only inspire a few today to get some of that old feeling, things wouldn't be in the hellish mess they're in. I can remember our parish priest, Father Patton. Father Dan bought a seven-passenger Buick, and my job on Saturday morning was to drive to all the stores. I was thirteen, fourteen years old. I didn't have a licence till I was about eighteen. Nobody bothered. He used to make a list for me. He'd have a list for each of the real poor families in the parish. Whether it was clothes or groceries or hardware or whatever – coal or wood or a part for your stove – Father Patton would have the list. I'd pick up a couple of my friends, and we'd go to the different stores, fill up the old car, and go deliver it. It was a good place to live as a young fella. They were just wonderful, kind people.

I was back in Mulgrave a few years ago. It hasn't changed very much. Mulgrave is still a fine place. Some people I went to school with are still living there.

But the Canso Causeway, although it was a wonderful feat of engineering at the time, it sure destroyed Mulgrave as far as industry goes. There's scarcely any young people. Soon as they get old enough ... Well, of course, I did the same thing in my day.

I left in 1928, when I was sixteen, to go to Halifax. They sent me to school down in Halifax, but I didn't like that very much. And I had a little trip going to sea for a little while – as a pot-walloper, peeling potatoes – and I didn't like that much either. And then I came back to Mulgrave.

Well, they thought the Causeway was going to be such a help. It really caused more depression than already existed, which was ample. But the Causeway did – the preliminary surveys on the Causeway and for the new line of the railroad to come down and meet it – it did provide jobs, mostly during elections. And I went on the Canso Causeway, on the preliminary surveys.

I had a great friend, who was their chief engineer, Bill Thomas, and he always kept a job open for the four of us that were on the original survey crew with him. He was from Halifax, and when there was nothing to do in Mulgrave, Bill would always get me a job doing something.

Incidentally, Bill died on that job and his brother Barney came out here and became commissioner of works for the City of Calgary. The best commissioner of works we ever had.

Through the connection with Bill and some others, I applied for a job with Victoria Paper and Twine in Halifax. They had the old Wilson Warehouse down by the Dartmouth ferry. I didn't get it. There were about a hundred applications in for the job, which was to assist a Major Kelly. He travelled from Montreal east, and he was one of the very successful commercial travellers of that day. But he wasn't what you'd call a true company public-relations man. He was crochety. He didn't drive a car – he used to hire a taxi and keep it all day at every city he was in. The only thing about it was that he was so financially successful that people looked up to him. That was about it. Well, that was one reason why I was after that job. Because it was just as well to go after a good one as a mediocre one. But in any event, I kept calling about the job. Mr Atkinson was the manager with Victoria Paper and Twine at that time, and he came to like me through my persistence in calling, knowing that the job wasn't there. So finally, after about a year of this, he said, "Look, Larry, if you can get a job with a company, travelling New Brunswick and PEI, it will greatly enhance your chances of getting a position with us when Major Kelly retires."

So eventually I did get a job, with Cutahay Packing, travelling the three Maritime provinces. The biggest part of that job was cleaning windows and hanging signs – grocery, meat, and vegetable signs. So I can safely say that I cleaned every dirty window in every over-stacked pantry in the Maritime Provinces. But I enjoyed it.

I had to make my itinerary out with Cutahay Packing, in quadruplicate. I had to make it out three weeks in advance and re-cap it once a week, so the company could phone me any hour of the day from Toronto, Chicago, or Montreal and find me. I made five copies instead of the four and sent the extra copy weekly to Victoria Paper and Twine. My report was made out on a legal-sized form. Every bit of my sales story was on it, and it was all on that one sheet. The file had just been an ordinary letter file of applications for the job. So when these sheets came to Victoria Paper and Twine, they had to fold them to put them in the regular file. And then they got too many, so they had to start a special file for Larry Mac-Donald. So when they came down to hire the new man – I've forgotten whether it was the vice-president or the president that came down – he said, "My God, this MacDonald must be interested in working with us."

So that was my start. To make a long story short, I stayed on that territory for nearly thirteen years. I had northern Nova Scotia and some accounts in Halifax, but I had all of New Brunswick and all of PEI. I went from $22.50 a week, and a very limited expense account, to $75.00 a week and a real generous expense account. So I was in heaven. I had the best job of any young fella in the Maritime Provinces.

I don't know that there's any company that had the feeling, and the way their people were treated, as at Victoria Paper and Twine. I think they were one of the finest companies in the world. But there was a big upset. International Paper took over our company, and many others. Things did change some after the new management took over. Because I was in the Maritimes, and they had given me free rein down there. Our new president was a management consultant and owned his own firm in New York. So it was a little different, with a high-powered guy like him coming into the Maritime Provinces, and our slower method – and real method – of operating.

I came out here in 1957 with the polyethylene plant. I was with them, and then I started on my own, as a packaging consultant, and I retired on my own.

What kind of a place did you find Calgary in '57?

I compared it a lot to Saint John and Halifax, although it was more modern than both. But in the reception that I received – the people – it was no different than home. I just met the same type of people that I'd left. They were kind, and it was kind of an easy-going city, and people were very friendly. I had no trouble at all with business. I called on the same kind of people – made some marvellous friends and I still have them.

Being quite aggressive when I was young, and interested in growing businesses and new ideas, research ideas, I was full of admiration for the way Calgary was growing. And I still am as far as that goes. But it just became a big city – practically overnight. I suppose what you'd call sane, safe living, that's sort of gone by the wayside. Because we have so many people that come here for a quick buck. We don't get the solidarity of people that are coming, well, seeking worthwhile, life-long job ambitions.

I was on helping, counselling down at AADAC* – the Alberta drug-

---

* The Alberta Alcoholism and Drug Abuse Commission.

recovery centre. There was a bunch of the boys came in there, quite a few of them, from Newfoundland. Most of them had been on the oil rigs, got their first big pay cheques, came back and got loaded; bought a car and lost their licences. So they couldn't get back up north. The judge usually sends them to AADAC on a probation set-up. They put in a little tour there, attend the meetings for a while, and if they pan out all right, then we recommend them to the oil company they were working for.

Well, I can put myself in the same position, had Calgary been in existence when I was a young fella. You know, there were just hit-and-miss jobs in the Maritimes, and then they were poorly paid. If you did have a full-time job, it was at the lowest salary scale that you could possibly get anywhere. And then they come out here and get on the oil rigs, and they get big money ... but they're isolated. And then following the example of a lot of the old hands – quick money; easy come, easy go – the boys get their first big pay cheques, get down into Edmonton, and get drunk.

I know what it would be like if I got three or four thousand bucks in one crack. And maybe we're a little more aggressive and perhaps get in a little more trouble. It could have happened to me, because we all got pretty handy with our dukes down there, and you settled your arguments right there and then and were good friends the next day. That's not an understandable trait these days. And so the guys end up quickly in jail.

And we get blamed for a lot of people that come from Central Canada and Vancouver and from all over. I'd like to see that image changed, of young people from the Maritimes. Because there are so many Maritimers that have helped build this country, that have been a marvellous asset to any community that they've been associated with – everywhere that they've ever been, and I don't care where it is in the world.

Of Jobs

ALAN WADDELL – Crapaud, Queens County, Prince Edward Island

A big, friendly man with red hair and a moustache, Alan is in his late twenties. He lives in the Silver Springs section of Calgary. He is in training to become a bus driver with Calgary Transit.

I don't know whether I'm going to enjoy the bus driving or not. Everybody growls if you're late – "How come you left me standing in the cold?" If you're early everybody growls that you left too soon – they missed the bus. You can't please anybody. I haven't put in that many hours driving, but there've been a few moments when I've just wondered to myself, "Is this job worth it?" Like in the evening, if you're running Route 1 from Bowness to Forest Lawn, you haul drunks both ways. You get the Forest Lawn Hotel at one end and the Bowness Hotel at the other. You get the fellow coming from the bar with a box of beer, who when he goes to dig his money out for his ticket drops the beer right at your feet. Crash! He's half upset, and you've got a big stink of beer all over your clothes and the front of the bus. People come on and they wonder, "Is it you or is it on the floor?" I haven't quit yet, but I don't think it will be my life-long business.

What made you decide to pack it in, home?

I'd been trucking, basically, for eight years. There was just nothing going on. I was making the same money in 1980 as I made in 1974, and that's no good.

Who were you hauling for?

Stabilizers in Charlottetown. They haul liquid asphalt, basically, for the government, and around the Island they haul fuel for Texaco, Shell, and Imperial Oil. We get paid mileage, and we just weren't running any miles. We just weren't busy. If you don't turn a wheel you don't make a cent. You should have 3,000 miles for a good week, and if you want to make it real good you should be getting into 3,500, 4,000. We were getting about 1,500, 2,000 miles a week.

We hauled liquid asphalt to contractors who were doing work for the government. So if the government was issuing no contracts, the contractors weren't working, therefore there was no asphalt being used. We sat. Rather than working from Saturday one week until Saturday the next week, you'd be working from Sunday till about Thursday, maybe Friday morning. But you might work Sunday, Tuesday, and Friday and that'd be it. Fifteen hundred miles and you'd be on home.

Did you quit there to come out here?

Well, I didn't quit. Somebody was going to get laid off and I told them they might as well lay me off, I'm going west sometime anyway. I got laid off at Stabilizers the Wednesday before Hallowe'en, 1980, and left home Thursday morning for the West. Got into Calgary Saturday night, laid around Sunday, filled out a couple job applications on Monday, and Tuesday got up and went right at her like a business. I was into quite a few places on Tuesday, and Tuesday night I got a call to go to work for a landscaping company – Cedarcrest Lands. Then December twelfth the landscaping company shut down for the winter, so I figured I'd go east for Christmas and come back after. I'd been in Calgary seven weeks – made enough money to pay my trip out and my trip back. I think I was ahead about a hundred dollars.

When I was leaving to go home, the fella said, "You'll be all through for Christmas."

"Yeah." What I understood was that I was all through – period. Anyway, in January I go phoning from home wondering where my separation slip is, and he says, "You have to be laid off before you get that." "I what?" "You have to be laid off before you get that." "Oh?" "Yeah. I meant you were through for Christmas. We were shutting down landscaping, but we wanted you in the shop." I could have had a job for the winter. I should have stayed in Calgary.

When I went home at Christmas, I got a job hauling fuel. But there was nothing going on. Very, very quiet. One of the lads that was working in the shop servicing equipment, that winter he got put on the road. They were cutting right back on the shop because they hadn't used the machinery all that much all summer. They were laying off people that'd been with them for quite a few years. I don't know where you place the blame. There was just no work.

I said, "I'm packing the bags and going. Who's coming?" I wanted at least three people so there'd be a pretty good split on gas. I ended up with four. We stayed overnight with my sister in Montreal, and we packed a lunch there. When I travel, if I'm going from Point A to Point B, she's all business, and I don't want to spend five hours a day in a restaurant. Thirty-nine hours and we were in Calgary. When we stopped for gas, everybody went to the bathroom, we switched drivers, and on our way. It worked out really well. We were tired when we got to Calgary, but not too badly. And we didn't waste any time. A lot of people don't agree with me – they want to see the country. Well, if I want to see the country, I'll go on holidays when I can afford it.

I was sort of looking for something a little more permanent this time. We got into town Wednesday morning and I went to work Thursday night for CN. I applied on Thursday afternoon and went to work Thursday evening, but the job I applied for, I got bumped before I got to work. I was supposed to be running Express* from

---

*   CN Express, freight.

Calgary to Red Deer. I ended up working in the warehouse. About four weeks later the closest I was getting to trucks was loading and unloading them, and no sign of anybody dying or anything – which was about the only way I could get the position – so I found another job.

Hauling fuel for Westcan. Bulk transport. They're branched all over Alberta. Out of Calgary you go as far north as Red Deer, south to the US border, west to the BC border, and east to the Manitoba border. Most of the runs are just over the border into Saskatchewan. That was a fairly good job. Put a lot of hours in.

I was at Westcan for a month, and I quit there to go to Transit. Fewer hours, and the money was looking better.

I find in Alberta there's lots of work around. If you work, and do what you're told, you'll have no trouble getting a job in this town. No problem at all.

In the East, when they're working, they're thinking a five-day work week. If you're working construction, or pretty near any job here, the day of the week means nothing. Saturday or Sunday is just another day you go to work. In the East, if you're working six days in a row, everybody's looking at you: "Are you ever drivin' 'er ... hogging money." But like this landscaping company I worked for, I started on a Thursday, and I think it was twenty-one days before I had a day off.

You take working for the City here in Calgary – they do most of their work on Saturdays and Sundays. When they were laying the cement for the Deerfoot Extension* – the cement base below 17th Avenue – it was one continuous pour. They never stopped till they finished. They were laying cement for forty days.

They were putting a water main in on McKnight and Edmonton Trail. I was going to work one morning, it was thirty below. There was a bunch of people there lighting bales of straw. They set fire to straw to soften the ground, and they worked there all week – just the same as a day in July. The first sign of snow home, they shut down. It's just a different way of living.

Are you looking on it out here as kind of a long-term proposition?

Well, there's nothing to go back to, so you have to. Things aren't going to get any better in the East, not in the near future.

---

*   The Deerfoot Trail is the main north-south highway running through Calgary's east side.

What sort of options would be open to a person in Crapaud?

Well, if you don't teach school, and you don't farm, you would either sell gas or be a bartender – at the curling club, which is not a full-time occupation. Other than that, there's a poultry plant, but that is not a high-dollar operation.

Hubert Harvey runs the store in Crapaud. His son lives in the northeast of Calgary. There's a Boulter from Victoria – David Boulter – he's in the northeast. David Foy – he's from about a mile outside Crapaud – he's in the northeast. Just in Cochrane, Jo-Ann Oakes, she's from Crapaud. She has two brothers in Mission, BC. They were here for about two years. My sister just moved here. My next door neighbour and his wife, from the Island, were here; another next door neighbour's been here for about three years. Blair Francis, Eric Francis – out of the Francis family there are five or six of them here. They live just up Edmonton Trail. From right around my home, there must be thirty people in Calgary.

A lot of people come west and probably get the same job they had in the East. Somebody working in a warehouse for $4.50 an hour in the East is working out here for $7.00 an hour and paying twice the rent. Like a fella I know, on a good week he'll probably make $500. But he'll not go home and tell people his hourly rate. His hourly rate is $5.00 an hour. He works twelve, fourteen hours a day, seven days a week.

But there are some now ... A fella I worked with haulin' potatoes – this was haulin' potatoes for about $80, $90 a week around 1972 – he works for a company in Calgary. I don't know exactly what kind of money he makes, but he bought a $110,000 home. He's not hurting too bad.

Another fella I worked with haulin' potatoes, he's a pipefitter out here, and he takes home $600 a week. Which is not too shabby.

When I was leaving the Island, I was into the club at the fire department, and one of the lads there – the only time he's ever been off the Island any further than Moncton, he and I went to Toronto – he couldn't see why anybody would want to leave PEI and go anywhere. You know, he figured you come out here, you make $100 and spend $105. So I sent him a postcard back, told him I was making $200 a week, just to make him happy. But if you don't leave home you make no money at all.

The crucial question is, are you here so you can make some money and go home, or are you saying, "This is going to be my home, this is where I'll be at least until I retire"? [Pauses.] The thing is, you've got to drive for fourteen hours here to go to the beach – one way. If you're going the other way to the beach, she's a hard fifty-hour drive! Mountains are nice, but when you're used to waking up in the morning and listening to the waves rolling in over the beach, mountains don't do a thing for you.

I find driving around on the prairies is very boring. It's a killer. I can't stay awake. Go to bed, sleep ten hours, wake up in the morning, and drive to Saskatchewan – about a five-hour drive one way – and I'm falling out of the seat. Around home, I could run back to back to Halifax, eight, nine rounds a week, and it wouldn't bother me all that much. Here ... Lord! You sit there and you sit there – you don't touch a gear and you very seldom make any adjustments of the steering wheel. You rest your arm. It's very hard work.

Another thing here, most people are colour-blind. It doesn't matter what colour the lights are, if people are in a rush they don't bother easing up at all. Downtown, it's just out of this world, people running red lights. The same thing with pedestrians – they'll start across the street any time at all. In Montreal or Toronto, you don't do those things. If you run a red light in Toronto, it's an instant trip to the hospital; do it in Montreal, you go to the morgue. But here, it's just a common everyday thing.

Even potatoes – the difference in potatoes is unbelievable. Alberta potatoes, when you peel them, you throw forty percent of the potato out. They're all beat and marked. If you're boiling potatoes here you pour the water off them and mash them, then you pour the water off again. They're very wet. If you don't eat them as soon as they're cooked, there's nothing to them at all – they'll be all gone soggy. Potatoes that we buy in the stores here, in plastic bags that you can't see through, you couldn't get that stuff out of your building home. The inspectors would have you turned down flat. I know farmers that have spent a small fortune on claims on much better stuff than we're buying in the stores here. It's out of this world. When you're used to working on a farm where if it happens to be a poor year, the farmer will throw out thirty percent of his crop because it won't make the grade, and then you see some of the junk in the stores that they're charging big prices for ... It's disgusting.

I know some people in the northeast [of Calgary] that have been here for years, and when I came back out the last time I mentioned I'd brought a friend out some potatoes. "You didn't bring us any?" "Well, no." "Does your friend have any left? Would he mind giving us some?" It seems like a small thing, but at least they're decent spuds.

Another thing too is seafood. People here – they go to a restaurant for lobster, they're probably buying rock lobster, the warm-water lobster that has all the flavour of dead tissue paper. And they think they had a hell of a feed of lobster. They've read about people that ate lobster and enjoyed it, and they think it's delicious. But they never had a nice green lobster and watched it turn red and ate it, right an hour out of the sea. They don't know what good seafood is.

I don't know. For me to say I'd be here the rest of my life, I think I might be lying. Unless they brought the ocean closer to me. [Pauses.] But there's one thing they can't take away from Alberta. There are plenty of jobs.

DAVID BONA – Halifax, Nova Scotia

He and his brother sub-contract plumbing jobs in the Calgary residential-construction industry.

I first came out here in '76, working in the summertime when I was in high school. I had two brothers here, and they were sort of saying, "Well, if you're looking for summer work, here's where it's at." So I just came out like that. That's when I started learning a little bit about the plumbing trade.

I continued on into university after that, into engineering, but the interest wasn't there a hundred percent, so I fell back on the plumbing trade. I could always go back. But I'm going to try this out, anyway. I'm trying to make the transformation into building homes.

Till now you've been plumbing for contractors?

Yeah, for four or five homebuilders. We sort of sub out of them. It's called "piecework." One fella gets the contract, he gets the materials, and he pays you on a sub-contract basis, instead of paying you by the hour. That's a little incentive for you to work faster when it's needed. So that's what we're doing.

Do you mind being in Calgary?

Well, I worked on the rigs one summer and I couldn't take it. I was in southern Saskatchewan and southern Alberta in these little holes in the wall, small towns, and I just didn't know anybody. You'd spend half your day working, the other half sleeping, and what little time you did have to yourself, there was nothing to do. There was maybe one bar in each town. And why go to a bar if you're going to be alone? So that kind of life is really hard. In Calgary it's not so bad. I know a hell of a lot more Maritimers than I do Albertans or westerners here. So you sort of feel at home. And I've got three brothers out here. I come from a family of ten, so it's almost half the family. That makes a big difference.

I've been here long enough that I almost think of it as a second home. I'm comfortable here. One of the most important things is that you feel like you know your way around, you feel comfortable in your surroundings. I'm to that point now. You can't have everything, you know. There's a trade-off. There's a lot of things I like about Halifax. I like the smaller city. I like the trees. I like the water, the ocean, stuff like that. The beach in the summer. You miss all that, but you're trading it off for a little bit of work [pauses] – and trying to get ahead sort of thing. I guess that's most of it.

There are a lot of little things that are wrong with Calgary, but I guess that goes with prosperity – because there are just so many changes that it's hard to control. People have a lot of grudges about that kind of stuff.

There was something interesting on the radio the other day. I was listening to a talk show. They were talking about the municipal government here putting ads in the Toronto and Montreal newspapers saying the streets aren't paved with gold, and the rental situation is bad, stuff like that – trying to keep people back home type of thing. And part of the radio show was, "Why do these people come and take the money from Alberta and take it home?" And I felt like calling up and saying, "What are you talking about? I haven't taken a cent here that I haven't earned." Haven't I put something back into this economy? Whether you're an engineer or a plumber or whatever you're doing, you're contributing something. I mean, granted, there are people that are coming out here and committing crimes and stuff, but that's to be expected ...

They blame that on Maritimers?

They blame it on the influx of people, and they tend to say, "easterners." But people are just a little careless with their terms. When they say "easterners," they generally mean the Ontario-Quebec area. Anything from Winnipeg on is just "the East." And there's a lot of people here that haven't been east of Winnipeg.

I'll tell you, there's an incredible amount of tradesmen here from the Maritimes and Ontario. I'm only in housing. I don't know much about commercial, but I'm sure it's pretty well the same thing. If you took all the easterners out of here, I don't think you'd have that many houses going up.

SHAWN MULHERIN – Grand Falls, New Brunswick

A graduate in business and economics from the University of New Brunswick, he is in his early twenties.

I was working for my dad back east – he was in the grocery business for a long time. He was wanting to sell out, and I really didn't want to stick around Grand Falls. I just finished university at the same time, so I was kind of willing to do something different. So when he sold out, I came out here. I had a couple of sisters out here too. I hadn't seen them for a while, and I wasn't doing anything, so I said, "Go try it out west for a while."

When I came out, I sort of took the summer off, and then I needed some more cash to get going again. My sister was working at Safeway, and they were paying nine-something an hour for someone that had experience, which I thought was the greatest. I didn't think anybody made that kind of money! In 1977–78, I was working at Tingley's Save-Easy in Fredericton, part time. I was at university and I sort of ran out of money. He was paying me about $5.50, $6.00 an hour.

But then I got tired of that. Actually, it's kind of boring work. I travelled for a couple of months, and then in 1980 I started working in the oil patch. I'm motorman on an oil rig. We drill holes all over the countryside — it takes us between two weeks and a month and a half, sometimes, to finish a hole. You have five guys that work on the rig – actually work the rig twenty-four hours a day. First of all you have a driller. He's in charge. He's the boss while he's there. And then you have a derrickman, and he's just a step lower than the driller. He works running in, like running pipe in and out of the hole, from up in the derrick. He takes care of the mud system also.* And the motorman, he takes care of the motors, because it's run by diesel motors. I'm not saying he's a mechanic – he just more or less changes the oil. And then when he's working the floor, he's sort of in charge of the two roughnecks that are on the floor. And he's the one that's supposed to handle the chain. The roughnecks have to do stuff like dig ditches and keep the rig clean. It's sort of less responsibility as you're going down. I started out as a roughneck.

I work for Laredo Drilling. We've been drilling around Drumheller, Strathmore, and all kinds of little towns around there. We usually do that in the summertime, and then wintertime we move up north, because that's the only time you can drill up there. It's really swampy up there – you can't move anything in the springtime or in the summertime. When it's wintertime, everything freezes over, and you can just move in.

This company has just been drilling for CDC most of the time I've been with them – the Canadian Development Corporation. They

---

* "Mud" is an oil-patch term for drilling fluids.

contract the drilling services from Laredo, and we drill wherever they want us to. We're just responsible for drilling the hole straight, and the machinery of the rig. They're responsible for everything else that goes into the hole – like testers, loggers, cementers.

So what do you do when you're not on shift when you're way out at the end of nowhere?

We usually live in camp, so unless you're right next to a town, there's not really much to do. We work a day shift and a night shift. After twelve hours, you come in, you shower, then you eat supper. If a town's close by, everybody just jumps into the truck and we go into town as fast as we can and have a good time. When you're up north you can't go anywhere because there aren't any towns around, and nobody has a vehicle up there because you get flown in. I mean, you play cards, you watch different movies – we have a video machine. There's lots to do. When you're down south in the summer, after work it'll still be light for a couple hours almost, so a lot of guys have four-wheel drives, and we go out four-wheelin'. Or we just go for a walk. You're out of the city. It's kind of nice just to go for a walk. We used to have one girl that worked there, she was one of our cooks, and she just loved to fly kites, so I used to go flying kites with her. You make quite a few friends too.

You work two weeks on, and then one week off. And the pay is pretty good. That's one reason I haven't quit. I find it sort of interesting, too, because I had never seen a drilling rig before I came out here. I only planned to do it a few months, and I'm still doing it.

When I got my first pay cheque, I just couldn't believe it. I thought I was making good with Safeway. I'm making $11.71 an hour. I get taxed more than I made back home. If I work six days, they take off about $300. I wasn't *making* that back home.

It's a lot of money, but I still think we're underpaid. You take a guy that wants to work construction in this city, with no experience at all, just a labourer, he's going to make twelve-something, because of a union. It takes you a while to be a motorman, and I'm only making eleven. We work twelve hours a day for fourteen days straight. In a two-week cheque, you make just as much on overtime as you do on regular time. So if you didn't have your overtime, you'd just figure, "I'd be making half that." Which isn't *that* great.

Do you like the work?

As far as the work goes, I don't mind it. We have a lot of fun working there. And it's a lot of responsibility. Because the rigs are usually worth on an average about $5, $7 million. They leave a bunch of guys out working ... most of us between the ages of twenty and twenty-five, not too many over thirty, anyways ... It sort of gives you a good feeling.

The only thing that bothers me about it is that there's really not that much future in it. A lot of guys are scared of getting laid off, because there's no union. And if the guy just doesn't like you, he'll run you off. Myself, I get along with people pretty well, and I've been around for a while, so I've got no problem there. But the only thing is, we shut down. This summer we were shut down for about a month and a half. And they don't give you any prior notice. I worked for about three months straight, and we had spring break-up. That's usually a month and a half off. And then I worked for about a month and a half after that, and we shut down for about a month and a half.

Do you go on unemployment?

You could, I suppose. But if you worked a few months straight, and you were smart with your money, you really wouldn't need that. But let's say you were going to be a full-time rig worker or what-ever, you wanted to build a house, and let's say you had payments to make all the time. What would happen if everything shut down? You could go looking for a job somewhere else, which you'd prob-ably get, but if everything's shut down, somebody's going to have to lose somewhere.

Another thing about the oil patch, there are so many divorces and family problems because of the way it goes – two weeks in, one week out. It's a pretty rowdy place to live, I'd say. You sort of go up there around small towns, go to the bar and have a good time. I guess for a guy that's got a family or a wife, he'd be tempted ... I'm not saying just cheating and stuff like that. I'm just saying there gets to be a breakdown in relations.

But the money's so good that nobody ever quits?

Most guys either get fired, or they work at a goal. Like a guy will say, "I'll try and work six weeks, and then go to Hawaii," or something like that. Go to Europe.

If a person uses discretion and is sort of thrifty, he can work on an oil rig for five years and get a start with the money he's saved. Then again, I've seen guys that work on rigs, come out on their week off, and spend everything they have.

Every now and then you get kind of fed up. Let's say it's 3:00 in the morning, it's freezing out, and you've got a dirty job to do. You just say, "I'm going to shut this down. This is not human." But then you come out, go down to the office, and they treat you good in the office. Have a coffee ... bullshit ... get your pay cheque. Feel good again – everything's great.

How tough is the work?

It's overrated. I laugh when I look at magazines and stuff like this. They had an article in *Weekend* one time, and they were going on, saying, "You work twelve hours a day and you don't stop working till that twelve-hour shift is up," and all this stuff. It's not that hard. It's hard when you're moving a rig, because you've got to take everything apart and put it together and everything. But then once you're drilling ... If you drill faster wells, you have to make a lot of connections, but inevitably it gets to slow drilling, and you only have to make a connection once every hour.

A "connection"?

When you're drilling a hole, you put a bit on the end of a pipe, and you send her down. It's called a "kelly" that pushes it down. And you drill so far, and your pipe's sticking out, so then you break off the kelly and add on, put on another pipe. At the first of the hole, you just sink 'em down, because it's pretty soft. And then depending on what formations you hit ... We worked up north for a while last year, and we'd only make one connection on a twelve-hour shift. The middle of winter, you know, and cold. Nobody's going to want to go outside and do too much work. And we'd sit inside, bullshit for twelve hours, and go out and make the connection. I've had two weeks' work where I never did anything so easy. On the other hand, I've had two weeks' work where I never stopped. Let's say if you go in a hole, and you're testing. Let's say you run five or six tests. You're just pulling your pipe out, putting on another test tube, running it down. And you'll have problems, or you'll get stuck in the hole. Sometimes you'll be really busy, and then, "Wow, it's dinnertime already!" A lot of times it'd be time to quit, and I just couldn't believe it. You'd just eat supper, and the next thing you knew, three hours had passed. That's why, when you get slack times on the rig, you really enjoy them.

Are there a lot of people from home working on the rigs where you are?

Oh yeah. I never met so many. Well, a lot of Maritimers are known for being good workers on the rigs. We had a rig party not too long ago, and we figured out everybody that was working on it. There are three crews there – and the engineer, the geologist, the cooks, and everything make about maybe twenty-two, twenty-three people.

Out of all those, there were only two that were from – not just Calgary – but from Alberta. There were five of us from the Maritimes, I guess – mostly New Brunswick.

Every now and then you'll have an engineer, or some real hardcore Albertan, start saying, "Aah, easterners!" and all this. And we just look at him: "Better watch your mouth, boy. You may be in Alberta, but this camp's an easterner camp." It's kind of funny to see somebody, you know, givin' her for Alberta ...

Have you pretty well given up, then, on eventually working back home?

Well, back home it's almost stagnant. People aren't really looking forward to too many things, except for working for so long to get on unemployment. If your parents aren't in farming, or in some kind of business ... Let's say your parents work at CN. Well, their children will work at CN. If they don't like it, that's about all they can do. If you don't have any contacts, I guess, you'd have to work at McCain's or go on unemployment.

Where I'm working in the oil patch, at least once every two weeks some boss is being a real ass about something, and the guy just says, "Take your job and shove it, boy. I can find another job." And that's better for a person. I'm not saying it's good to walk out all the time. I'm just saying that it's good to be able to have a choice.

It's bad. Seems like when I was growing up, most people had a choice. But then when I was grown up, there was no choice, really. There were, I suppose, a few – but there's a lot of people that I know had to leave. There's just not a lot going on. They definitely need a restructuring of life down there – or economics anyway.

Halifax Sells Alberta

LAUREEN BOWNESS – Halifax, Nova Scotia

She is in her twenties. Her family owns a sporting-goods store in Halifax. When we spoke, she had been in Calgary ten months. Her tremendous enthusiasm for the city and rapid-fire presentation of its virtues and advantages is almost overwhelming.

I came here of course, like everybody else, because of money. And I was bored with the people in general. They weren't motivated. They weren't successful. They were dead. Out here people are money makers, they're career-oriented, they want to go places and they're doing it. I just find it exciting. I love being around them. It just motivates me to no end. I love it. The people at home, I found, didn't motivate me to do anything. I'd talk to them, they'd either be unemployed, or they'd have jobs that were no big deal, going nowhere with their companies. I came out here and I'm meeting all kinds of people that are really successful, that are making big money, and I just find it exciting. I love it.

How did you come to leave Halifax in the first place?

There was absolutely nothing in the city for me. I had college background, I had seven years' sales experience, and I started Dad's [sporting-goods] shop from scratch, so I thought I knew a lot about business. But there was no way I could get a job.

When Dad opened the store in Halifax, he had four kids at home, most of them were going to university, and he couldn't quit his job. So he opened up this business and said, "You run it, and if it goes well, then I'll quit my job and come to work, and if it doesn't, we'll just pack it in." I was living in California at the time, and I jumped right on a plane and flew home immediately. We started from scratch. We built shelves, we stocked the store, and we watched the business grow. It just went super. Within nine months, it was so successful I couldn't handle it by myself. Dad quit his job and came into it, and it's become a very successful business. But after seven years working in a family business, it got small for me. I wanted to expand, get into bigger and better things, open up stores all over the country, and he wasn't into expanding. I just got really bored, so I left. And I thought, "I'll have no trouble getting a job with all this experience and education behind me." I left at Christmas, and it took me three months to even find a job. And I just beat the roads, beat everything. I tried to get a job in sales, but they would take one look at me and say, "Are you kidding? There are hundreds of *men* out there looking for sales jobs." Then finally Coca-Cola offered me a job as an accounts-payable clerk, and I lied even to get that. I didn't have any clerical experience. So I took this job, and I hated it. I couldn't stand it. I worked there for two years, going nowhere. They knew I'd be bored so they promoted me really quickly. I climbed to the top of the office, but that was it, that was as far as I was going. I told the manager I'd like to get into sales. "No way. You have to drive the trucks first. We only take our sales boys right off the trucks." There's no way I could drive a truck and start hauling all these cases of pop, so I just got absolutely bored and started goofing off. I'd say I was sick, leave, and go out looking for other jobs. I ended up being fired, because I was goofing off and I hated it. He called me into the office one day and said, "This isn't for you. Why don't you get out and get into sales?" I said, "There's nothing I'd rather do, but nobody in this city wants to give me a job. There are too many men looking for jobs, and men never get sick, never get depressed, they never goof off, so they hire men over me."

So I got disgusted and tried a few things on my own. I bought into a company, Maud Lewis Art.* I used to sit in malls for twelve hours a day trying to sell those products. We did all kinds of art shows, the whole bit, but nothing was selling. There was just no money in Halifax. I was getting so upset, thinking, "Is it me? Are they not buying because of me?" I was getting so discouraged.

So finally I took a vacation and came out here. I looked in the papers, went for job interviews, and was being hired on the spot. People were saying, "Yeah, we'll take you. No problem." So I went home, put my house and my car up for sale, gave everything I owned away, jumped on the plane and moved back to Calgary. I didn't take any of those jobs I was offered. I looked around for about five weeks and found the job I have now, and I just love it. I'm a sales rep for National School Services – selling yearbooks, athletic wear, football shirts, and stuff like that. I have one of the best territories in Canada – Innisfail [Alberta] south to Montana. And I was the first female to be hired by the company, so that excited me. I was a new thing for them. Everything just sort of fell into place and I just love it.

People here will buy. The market's there – these kids have money. In Halifax, it didn't matter what you had to sell. When I was working for Dad, I went and called on a few schools trying to push our product, and people just hummed and hawed and started price bickering. Here, I go show my product, they're ecstatic, they're glad to see me, they want to talk to me. They've got the money, and they can afford to buy them. I never get *no*'s. In sales, *no* is "see you later" – it doesn't make any money. Here it's all *yes*, no matter where I go. I can't stop selling. It's unreal. In Halifax, it was totally negative, a waste of my time. I don't know how many schools I called on, and I never made a sale. Here I very seldom go into a school where I don't sell. Very, very seldom. It has not happened to

---

* Maud Lewis was a painter from Marshalltown, Digby County, Nova Scotia, known for her simple paintings of farm and domestic scenes.

me. I have not had one *no*. I had half a *no*, she had doubts, but I talked her right back into it and off she went. It's just unreal. Success has never happened to me like it's happening here. It just doesn't stop, and I guess it's because my attitude's changed. Now I'm hyper, I'm excited. I go in and I say, "This is what I've got. What do you think? Isn't this great? Don't you love it?" And people will answer to that, whereas if you go in Halifax they say, "Oh, come on, Laureen, Joe Blow's down the street, and we're hearing you guys all the time." I just find people are happier here. They're more business-minded. They say, "Do you have a product? Sure, I'm willing to listen." And once they listen, if you're a good sales-person, you'll make a sale. And selling is very important to me. I'm on commission, so I only make money when I make a sale. But I took *no*'s at home. Out here I don't take *no*'s. I just hang in there. You're not going to get rid of me that easy. I'll be back. I go back, and I go back, and I conquer them. I'm much more motivated here. I just slipped and slided around down there.

I've got no regrets about coming to this city at all. Not one. I love it. I don't miss Halifax, because I know what I was like. I was stagnant, I was boring, I was ho-hum just like everybody else. Just existing, trying to pay the bills and just getting along. Whenever I think of Nova Scotia I think, "No money, no job, no future, no nothing." It's a drag. When you're young, you should be in a place where everything's happening. When I'm ready to retire, I might end up there, but now it's too motivating to be here. And I find that I don't miss the small things that other people miss. I don't care about the beauty, that doesn't matter. I'm young, and if I don't make it now I'm never going to, so it's important to me to be here and go as big as I can. I love it. I just think it's dynamite. I never wanted to be as high in a company. When I lived in Halifax, if I could just have been an office manager, that would have been fine. Now I definitely want to be vice-president of a multi-divisional company. My scopes are wider, because the future's brighter.

MIKE HASLER – Halifax, Nova Scotia

Jasper Park Lodge, the CN hotel in the midst of the Rockies on the Alberta-BC border. In his mid-twenties, he is Jasper's assistant convention manager and sales director. He is from Leiblin Park in Spryfield, a town that was amalgamated into Halifax in 1969. He is quick to explain that he is not the only Nova Scotian there. "Our chief security officer, CN Police, Norm McAuley, he just went back to the Maritimes. A fascinating man from Cape Breton – and his daughter's working here now. Jo-Ann Black up in

Personnel, she's from Dartmouth. Our rooms division manager, Michael Hunter, his dad actually grew up with my mom in Jollimore."

Looking out across the Lodge through the large ceiling-to-floor window in his office, we talked about the number of people from home of Mike's age group in sales and public relations in Alberta. "There's no question in my mind what the reason is," he says. "I can go in and adjust to any given situation. I can read people. I know how to approach people. It's a gift. I think a lot of Maritimers have that gift. You have two different kinds of salesmen. You can have a salesman who is successful, but is a salesman – he's gimmicky, a go-getter, a real hustler kind of thing. And then you have a salesman who is that sincere guy – believes in his product, and is an honest and sincere person. Not particularly over-honest, but sincere – not putting on airs and not trying to be anything else. People see that in you. It's not a rip-off attitude. It's sincerity, and Maritimers are sincere people. You can feel it."

Back in 1977 I was attending Saint Mary's University, and the first semester I dropped out. I just didn't feel like going to school anymore. I drove a truck for awhile. My best friend and I, we'd heard about Jasper, so around January that year we decided we'd go down for an interview – in the basement of the Hotel Nova Scotian. We thought we'd come out for the summer – I had planned to return to university and go into political science. We got offered jobs as "steward's helpers," which we found out after we got here was dishwashing. That was kind of a shock. At first I said, "I'm going." And then I said, "I'm all the way out here, so let's stick it out, see what happens." So I'd just been working a couple of weeks and I heard that they wanted part-time people with bars – like a banquet bar. I'd done that at Saint Mary's. So I did that part time. You worked your eight-hour shift in the dishwashers, and then you worked from six o'clock until one o'clock that night. You'd clean up and get out of there around two or so. After about my fifth week there, I was offered a position in that department full time, as a bar porter. A bar porter does all the heavy work, like lifting all the cartons and counting all the booze. It was good. You were out with the public, meeting the people. But as it turned out, after about a week of that, we were almost at the end of banquet season, getting into "A la carte," or high season, and an opening came up in The Moose's Nook, one of our bars, as a bartender. I became assistant bar supervisor. I was in there about two or three weeks and was asked if I'd be interested in being the bars manager. It took me back a bit. This was in July, and I had arrived in April. Everything's happening pretty fast. It was classed as a mid-management position, and I didn't really know if I was ready for it. Besides, I had planned to return to university. Then just on the spur of the moment I said to myself, "Why not? Let's try it, see what it's like." And so I did. And I've never, ever thought about going back to school since.

All our sub-department and department heads are usually laid off for the winter, so then I was laid off. I had done quite a bit of wrestling and gymnastics, and when I got home I was approached by a friend of mine who was working for the Institute for the Blind and had a wrestling team there he wanted me to coach. I did that for the winter, and returned in April, as assistant to the bars manager. But I'd had enough of bars. I found myself being bored. I decided I'd get into the food end of it. So they hired me as a captain waiter.

Is that the same as a maître de?

No, it's not. You have your maître de, who runs your room, and he usually has an assistant. Then you have captains, who run sections. You run small banquets of fifty-five people. It was a good job. And then later that summer I moved over to Golf Clubhouse, which is our gourmet dining-room, and I was the assistant.

That was 1979. That was the first time that I stayed with the company full time all winter. I was transferred to Edmonton – the Mac* – and that was one of my most interesting years, because I really got into a lot of the nitty-gritty. I got into a lot of accounting, helped to organize some of their banquets, and just different things. It really gave me a good insight into the business. I came back the next year in charge of banquets. A lot of things happened to me that year. I was married. We had a child. I stayed right up till December, and they put me in accounting. But they just wanted me because, well, this is only a seasonal operation, and they don't want to lose you. I had a family. I was looking. I figured that they were just keeping me on the payroll, and I didn't want to do that. So I had some vacation time, and I took six weeks and went home, took some time off. When I got back, they asked me if I wanted to go on a course – an incentive program out of Cornell University.** While we were there the maître de at the Lodge accepted a position in town [Edmonton] – and I was next in line for that position. So that's what I did. Maître de is the biggest department in the whole hotel – some eighty staff, and you're doing conventions of up to a thousand

---

*   The Macdonald – the CN Hotel in Edmonton.
**   In Ithaca, New York.

people, breakfast, lunch, and dinner. It's not as if they're eating some place else. They're free, they're here all the time. You're not in the city where they can go and shop for things. You organize everything. So anyway, the season was quite successful, and I really enjoyed it.

What kind of conventions would you be looking after?

The Oilmen Convention – that's every second year. We get the Alberta Law Society every year. We have a lot of international companies. We have the International Food Brokers, and tours from all over the world. We can accommodate approximately 720 guests, and we have a staff of 550 – so it's almost a one-to-one ratio.

But ever since I decided that I wanted to try hotels for a while, I wanted to get into the public-relations end of things. Now I'm the assistant convention manager and sales director. It's like a convention coordinator. We go out and sell the convention, but we also cater to all their needs. We do all the food, all the menus, the dances, the meeting rooms, all the organized functions they may have. It's interesting.

Is there any kind of a recruitment program that gets people from the Maritimes to come out and work here?

Not just Maritimers. Twice a year, the first time in January, our personnel manager goes and starts recruiting in Halifax – because of all the universities there. Then she goes to Montreal and Toronto and the surrounding areas, and that's her winter program. From there she comes back here, and then in the summertime they go again. We have two kinds of people we bring: our students, who come at the first of the summer, and our fall staff, who are people who either have just finished high school and don't want to go to university, are in between university, or are people who are just out working for a living, don't have a job, and want to try something new.

A lot of the kids walk away grief-stricken. They find it a rude awakening. Well, they say a good waiter or waitress is up in the top five pressure jobs in the world, in there with a neurosurgeon, believe it or not. It's a pressure field. You're constantly bombarded, especially in a place where people are paying big money. They want service. Good chefs, but the chefs are temperamental. They have to run on food costs, and they have to be productive. They're under pressure, your superiors are under pressure, you're under pressure.

We're open from the second week in April till the end of October – we get about three days off, maybe, and we work anywhere from ten to eighteen hours every day. What happens to a lot of these kids when they come out – when they get in the dining-room, particularly, and see that they're working a lot of shifts, a lot of hours, and the maître de is not so nice all the time, and they can't understand why the chef is cursing and swearing, or why these people are so worried about having coffee, one milk, one sugar, or lemon – they get disillusioned by the whole thing, and they say, "Why did I come out here?" As a result, a lot of them walk away unhappy.

What kind of a reputation do people have that come here from the Maritimes?

I find that either they are *good*, or they're no good. Either we have good ones, or we have bad ones, there aren't really too many in between. They're probably our most likeable people, and they don't let the pressure bother them as much as others from around Canada. They don't let it get them down. I think they're a lot more flexible – maybe "hardy" is the word.

But I'll tell you, it's an experience. I'll have my kids come out here for sure. You're meeting people from all over the world. You rub shoulders with everybody, from royalty – which we have a couple times a year, usually – to prime ministers, senators, garbagemen, construction men, salesmen, you name it. That's what makes it so interesting. You meet all walks of life in the hotel business. I think that's what's kept me here so long – that every day, no matter if you're doing the same job, it's different.

But I want to live back home. We're going to move back. I've always had in the back of my mind that I want to go back there and show them that I made it, and so can they. Let's face it, Halifax is a rich city for a certain few. There's a lot of animosity in Halifax. It's a real class distinction. The classes are definite. You can see it. There's no reason why all of us can't do it right in Halifax. It's got everything to offer. It should be *the* city. And the only reason it's not is the class distinction – there's a certain class of people in Halifax that don't want it, because they have the money and they don't want it to be taken away from them. And why shouldn't it be?

The rich people in the South End are scared. Scared of the competition and of losing their money. They're on the defensive all the time. They know that they got it on a silver platter, that they didn't have to work for it, and they don't want to lose it, because they'd have to work to get it back. That class distinction is bad. You feel it in the air.

I felt that growing up. I played a lot of sports, and I felt that I was under pressure because this guy had money, and I didn't. I felt the pressure all the time. I felt it when I was older, going into bars. But when I was that old, I didn't put up with it, because growing up in Spryfield, I didn't want to put up with that. It was a fight, and that was all there was to it. A lot of the guys who grew up in the South End never went down to the bars, because they knew better. They stayed in their house parties and they wouldn't go out.

When I go back, and one of these guys says something, I'm going to say, "You piss off, buddy." I still sometimes have an attitude where I'm going to deck the guy first, you know? And I don't mind doing it. If I feel justified, I'm going to give the guy a shot. I still have that attitude. Because most of those guys need a good shot. They've never had a shot, and they need one.

I grew up fighting. It was tough. You could take people's attitudes from Spryfield and put them in Harlem, and they'd fit right in, no problem. Where that kind of situation occurs, those people build up a wall against everybody else. That's the way in Spryfield – we were against everybody. We wouldn't let anybody in, and we wouldn't go out, and when we did go out we went with a gang. It's not good, let's face it.

Is that why you left?

I didn't know what I was going to do, but I knew I was going to get out. I said, "Man, there's more to life than Spryfield and Halifax." There was nothing there for me any more. There was just nothing. I started going to bars when I was fourteen or fifteen, and I'd been that route. I worked part time since I was thirteen, full time in the summer, and there was nothing there that could hold me. I wanted to do something else. I was going berserk. That's probably why I didn't finish university – because the city had nothing for me. I think if I would have gone to university in another city, I would have stayed.

Some people say that if a person really wants to make something of themselves, they have to get out. What do you think? Can you do it at home?

Very few have. Back home – and when I say "home" I don't mean Halifax, I'm talking back in Spryfield – yes, you can do it. But I think you have to leave your element. Especially if you grew up with the circle of friends that I grew up with in central Spryfield, you just can't say to your friends, "No, I'm not." "No, I'm not going out"; or "No, I'm not going downtown"; or "No, I'm not going to the tavern"; and "No, I'm not going to go and throw rocks at a cop car." There's too much pressure.

I changed, and I'm glad I did. But I know a lot of them didn't.

And you reckon you'd still be there otherwise?

Oh, I know I would be. And I'd be at the Green Dory, or at the Spryfield Tavern, or I'd be working on the docks for four or five months, and I'd be on unemployment the rest of the year, and that's the way of life down there. It's really tough. But there's no reason why anybody can't do it, can't get out of there.

You know what it is? I think the people lack confidence. All these buddies of mine – talented, funny, smart – but they have no confidence. They can't come out of their shell – I don't know what it is. They haven't got the drive for some reason. They haven't got that drive. It pisses me off, because I see my buddies, my good buddies, and I say, "Oh, my God." It hurts. Really, it hurts, when you see the guy's got more talent than you, but he hasn't got the drive to bring it out of him. That's the thing that gets me.

But I don't care, where I grew up, that's part of me, and I don't want to lose that. It's there, and if you run from it, then I think it's wrong. The whole thing is bad down there maybe, but it's wrong for you as part of it to bad-mouth it. If you're down on it, then go and change it. Do something about it.

That area is the first place I'd start looking if I moved back. I have eight brothers and sisters and Mom and Dad back there, and Mom's brothers and sisters, and Mom's mother. Out of, say, ten of my friends, eight of them are there. I wouldn't hesitate to move back there tomorrow. There are places down in Herring Cove – nice ocean, beautiful homes. I'd move back tomorrow.

I'm going to go back. I'd like to be part of a change in Nova Scotia. I don't want to miss it. I want to be there, and I want to help it, because I know it can be done.

COLIN LOGAN – Halifax, Nova Scotia

The sixteenth floor, 505 4th Avenue SW, Calgary – the offices of Symco Drilling Fluids. More than twenty-five oil companies have offices on this one block alone. Colin is in charge of Symco's sales.

I was brought up in the North End, but I was born just down behind the lieutenant governor's mansion on Bishop Street. There were some old houses behind what is now the stevedores' hiring hall. They're no longer there. It was just a run-down, dirty old shack – something less than the upper crust, you know?

I came here in 1976. There really was very little uncertainty for me because I came to a job, and I had a place to stay. I had a sister here.

The reason I came is very simple. It was twofold. First of all, I wanted some adventure. I wanted to live somewhere else. I wanted to see other parts of the world. Quite frankly, even at this point I'm not satisfied. I'd like to go to the Middle East and live there for a while. I'd like to go to Southeast Asia.

Were you in sales in Nova Scotia?

I was training for management to work at Simpson's. I just got fed up with it. I didn't want to work there anymore. It really was a dead-end job. I could have been there for the next twenty-five years. Who needs it? I wanted to do something else. I saw too many guys who were forty years old and were twenty-year men at that point, working for Simpson's. And I thought, "These people – their priorities are screwed." They had no idea what life is all about. There's too much out there to see and do.

Anyway, the second reason I came out here: I was the youngest in a family of eight. Both of my parents were kind of wrapped up in me because I was the youngest and the last to leave home and so on. And I wanted to stand on my own two feet. I went home to them one day and announced that I was leaving. I got on my own feet and away I went. I had everything lined up. That was before Christmas – my wife and I left the third week in January and were here by the second of February. Drove during the winter. We got stuck in a snowstorm in downtown Chicago. Then we got into a place called Fargo, North Dakota, and it was so damned cold that the wheel bearings froze up on my car. The grease froze on the bearings and they broke up in little pieces when I tried to drive. So I had to have them replaced. The wind chill factor was 130 below that day. It was just incredibly cold. You couldn't get the car started, obviously. This guy came from the garage with a super-charger on the back on his truck. He was running current from the engine for about ten minutes before we could even get it to turn over. When we got to Winnipeg it was a little warmer – 120 below. We were a little upset. My wife cried every day. She wanted to turn around and go home, that was all there was to it. She was brought up on the Bay Road [in Halifax], and she just wasn't all that excited about coming.

I would sooner be in Nova Scotia too, but I've got other things that I want to do first. There's all kinds of the world out there to see. It's not that I dislike Nova Scotia. I don't. I like it there. I enjoy it there every time I go home, and it becomes increasingly difficult to come back to Alberta to live. There's no question about that. But it makes a lot of sense for me to be here, and it's a very broadening experience. I'm a very restless sort of individual. I want some adventure. Go and see the rest of the world. Nova Scotia will always be there.

I'd like to be involved in the oil patch anywhere in the world that it's operating and viable. It's kind of an exciting industry to be in. It's kind of a do-it-now, get-it-done-as-quickly-as-you-can type industry, and I'm an industrious sort of person. When somebody gives me a job, I like to get my head down, my ass up, and get after it. And it's the kind of thing I enjoy.

This company I work for now is a mud company. We provide drilling fluids to the drilling industry, and we also provide the engineering service to make sure they're doing the job they're supposed to do.

When I first came here I went to work for a small oil-equipment firm, as an accountant, a cost accountant. After about a year or so I got into sales with them, selling separators, line-heaters, pump jacks, dehydration units, and all things that have to do with oil-and-gas production.

And then I went to work for International Drilling Fluids as a mud salesman. I worked for them for about two and a half years, and they sent me through mud school – a technical course outlining the drilling fluid system.

I worked for IDF for two and a half years. And the fella who runs this company [Symco] also ran that company. He quit, came here, and he hired me to work for him. That's how I got into this job.

The premise on which I base my job is that I don't work for this company, I work for my customers, and when my customers are satisfied, then I get satisfied. I treat them as well as I can and as a result I'm very successful. This job is not a dead end for me. This will be a means to an end. Someday I'll own my own company – hopefully in Nova Scotia – and I'll be involved in the oil industry. Some kind of a service company – marine service or a mud company or something.

To me, Nova Scotia – the Maritimes in general – represent so many good investment opportunities. All the power is centred in the hands of a very small group of people, and they're all wealthy. I mean you've got the MacCullochs, the Olands, the McKeens ... whomever. All of those people now have what we would consider by North American standards to be "old money." They don't work anymore. I mean, they've got a hundred million dollars and they can live quite comfortably off the interest on their investments. It's beneath them to work for a living anymore. And I think a little new entrepreneurship in Nova Scotia would make a world of difference. Once you get people working and start kicking ass from time to time, the attitude is contagious – "Hey, there's a buck to be made here, so let's get after it." It certainly is contagious here. Everybody here wants to make money. People here are very aggressive. And I'm very aggressive. I always was. That's why I ended up here.

2506 4th AVENUE NW

2506 4th Avenue NW, Calgary. The stereo is cranked up a good deal of the time, and the corner is piled high with Molson empties. On the bulletin board in the kitchen, cut out from some newspaper headline, are the words, "New Brunswick." The house is divided into apartments, and everyone who lives there is either from Florenceville, Centreville, Glassville, Hartland, Grand Falls, or Bristol, except for one young guy from Vancouver, and he seems pretty well assimilated. Lloyd Wallace, Alan Shaw, Duane Lee, and Vince Buchanan are all in their late twenties. They've worked and lived together over five or six years in Toronto, Saskatchewan, and Alberta, and have been the best of friends since going to school together in New Brunswick. Lloyd and Vince drive trucks delivering building supplies for Winroc Gypsum. Duane drives a cement truck. Alan works for the City of Calgary.

LLOYD WALLACE – Centreville, Carleton County, New Brunswick

He has a brother in Calgary, a sister in the Queen Charlotte Islands, and a brother in Goderich, Ontario. Out of the whole family, only his parents are in New Brunswick. He has the thick, muscular arms of a man you want to speak to with respect, and the quiet, friendly manner of someone you'd like to know better.

I've come out here and gone back three times. This is my fourth trip. The first time I was here, in '76, I worked on seismic testing. In '78, I was working on a wheat farm in Saskatchewan. We had to stop on our way out and take a guy to this town in Saskatchewan, because he had a job lined up there. The guy we stopped in to see, he said he probably could get us a job planting – it was planting season. We figured, "What the hell, it's only for four weeks" – but I ended up staying for four months.

Since I started moving around, I've never stayed in one place more than a year. I've been landscaping, testing gas wells, delivering gyproc; I've lived in Saskatchewan, I've lived here in Calgary and I've lived in Vancouver. This is the best place I've found so far. I guess I know more people here than any other place I've lived. Vancouver was nice, though. I like the city a lot better because there are a lot more trees and stuff. It's a prettier city, but I don't know that many people there.

I've been here about a month on this last trip. We left home on a Saturday and got here on a Tuesday morning – driving right along. We'd stop two hours every morning and have a little nap, get up, and go at her again. She's a long haul through northern Ontario, but once you see that Manitoba border – zip, you're right here.

I like going home in the summer. The summers back east – can't beat them. I wouldn't have come out this time, but we're planning on getting married, so we wanted to get a little money ahead.

Are you going back after you get married?

We're going back there to get married, and maybe to Newfoundland for a honeymoon, and then we're coming back out here to work again.

There's nothing to get going back there. I worked on a farm all year. It was a good job, but geez, we worked upwards of a hundred and five hours a week. Cleared $380 or so. I went to work one morning at seven o'clock, got back home at ten o'clock the next night – on that tractor for forty hours. Just straight time, no overtime or nothing. I figure if a man puts anything in over forty-four hours a week, he should get a little something extra besides a sore back and a sore ass.

Is there no work at the McCain's plant in Florenceville?

Oh yeah, you can always get work there pretty well. They usually start you in at around $4.25, $4.30 an hour. They could afford to pay $6.50, $6.75 an hour. Sure they could. Just look at the money they're making off the farmers.

Is the money that much better out here?

It's a hell of a lot better than what I was getting when I was working back home in the summer. I was only getting $4.00 an hour. What I'm getting right now's not that good. It's only $6.75. But I'm waiting to go with this company I was working for before, Wildcat Production Testing, testing gas wells. When I was working there before, I was clearing about $1,600 a month. This time I should be able to clear about two grand a month.

I figure they should put something in back east to keep the people there, some industry or something. I know I'd sooner live back there than out here any day.

ALAN SHAW – Bristol, Carleton County, New Brunswick

He has shoulder-length hair and likes to party – neither of which sits particularly well with the older guard of Bristol Baptists. He tells this story of the 2506 4th Avenue boys when they were back home in the early seventies:
"A bunch of us got together and bought this old dance hall in Glassville for $3,000. It was out in the middle of nowhere – they used to have dances there a long time ago. We got dances rolling there and we used to have anywhere from three hundred to five hundred people. They came all the way from Fredericton to Edmundston – all young people. We never used to advertise, just word of mouth, and everybody just rolled in there and had a great time. There was never any trouble, never any fights, nobody ever got hurt or anything like that. We had a sign saying, 'Recommended Donation – $2.00.' Two dollars is pretty cheap to have a good time. We used to keep half the money, and we'd give the other half to the band. The money we made, we'd take and turn it back into the building. The first year we put a new roof on. That cost $1,200. Then we built a fence around it, and slowly we were fixing it up. Then they shut her down. The old people were complaining. What it boiled down to was that they didn't like seeing young people have a good time. They came out with a law that said any wooden structure of that particular size wasn't allowed to contain more than sixty people at a time. You could apply that law to just about every church in New Brunswick – it was more or less just to shut us down. That's the Bible Belt for you."

I worked for Irving for five years at the tree nursery in Juniper. I'd work there the rest of my life if the money was right. It gives you the feeling that you're accomplishing something, because you're replenishing nature. But I started there at three bucks an hour, and after five summers I was making $3.95. In the spring, when the rush was on to get all the trees out for reforestation – before they bud, because you have to plant them before they bud – we used to work between sixty and eighty hours a week, and we never got any time and a half because it was classified as a farm.

How'd you make up your mind to leave home and come here?

I worked every summer, and every winter I did nothing but lay around on unemployment and drink beer. I got laid off, and I kind of got the feeling that I was being a burden on my parents, because you're not working, and still you're eating meals and stuff. Vince [Buchanan] came out first, and he called me up and said, "Come on out." There was nothing back home, so I figured I might just as well go and check it out.

How long have you been out here?

Two years, right to the day.

What do you think of it?

I have to go home once a year or I can't handle it out here. I'm getting laid off in two weeks, and I'm beatin' 'er to New Brunswick just as soon as I can. I'm just waiting. [He trails off.] Back home, we're all really clannish, we all stick together. You don't find that out here.

Another thing that really pisses me off about people out here is that they have no conception of the East whatsoever. I've said to people, "I'm from New Brunswick." And they say, "That's right next door to Newfoundland, isn't it?" Or, "What do you do, fish?" I say, "I live two hundred and fifty miles from the ocean. I never even saw the ocean till I was eighteen years old." Everybody out here thinks the country ends right at the Quebec-Ontario border. That's it. There's nothing beyond.

LLOYD They don't give a goddamn for the East. It's just like that Sydney Steel – they pretty well moved it all out and put it in Ontario. They don't know what's going on down there or anything like that. If a lot of these people would take the time to go down there and look at the place, they'd probably have a hell of a lot different opinion. Take them through the middle of New Brunswick somewhere and say, "You see any ocean here, everybody making a living fishing?"

ALAN And something else, they figure that people from the Maritimes, or even from Ontario, are coming out here and taking Albertans' jobs.

LLOYD I find the guys at work, they won't say it to your face, but they talk about it. I know what they're talking about. I'm not foolish.

ALAN But it isn't true, because there aren't enough Albertans to fill those jobs. The unemployment rate in Alberta is three-something percent, which is nothing, because you have to have mobility, so actually there's no unemployment here at all.

Do you think you'd like to go back?

ALAN I'd like to get on permanent with the City here next year, work a couple years and go back to Fredericton and try to work for the City back there. I'd be a hell of a lot happier. It just boils down to whether you want to make money or you want to be happy.

I make good money. I make over $10 an hour, but still ... I have lots of money to live with, but I don't bank any. The only way you can make money out here is if you get into something out in the bush. Because if you're in town, after you pay all the bills, you're still broke.

This is a really bad place if you want to go out to a bar at night, because you can't go to a bar without it's going to cost you at least a hundred bucks. If you're drinking something like double Caesars, they're five bucks apiece. We hardly ever go out to bars because we just can't afford it.

Another ridiculous thing, where I work for the City, they're going on strike for a two-dollar right-straight-across-the-board raise. That'll put me up over twelve bucks an hour. And they want a thirty-two-hour work week, for the same money – get paid for thirty-eight hours, but only work thirty-two. And I'll tell you right now, at the City, you wouldn't believe how slack it is. I used to work for the federal government in Ottawa, and I thought that was bad. I don't work any more than two hours a day; nobody does. You just get to the job site and it's time for break. There could be something really serious going on, but when break time comes, it doesn't matter, you shut her down and stop for a break. It's a good job, for sure, but it's just such a waste, because you're just not doing what you should be doing for what you're getting paid. You're not putting back in what they're giving you.

The same in Ottawa. I was a "silly servant" there for a year. I worked for Statistics Canada. I was coding small-business income-tax forms – say, a general store would be 637, manufacturing would be three-something-something. They had a quota: you had to do two hundred a day. I'd have two hundred done by 9:30 in the morning, and just talked on the phone to New Brunswick all day. There were about 10,000 phones in the building, and there was a special code to call New Brunswick. You only had to dial five numbers and you had New Brunswick right there.

But it's ridiculous. They don't even *have* time and a half at the City – it's double time, and triple time on a holiday. One guy worked Remembrance Day, and he got somewhere around $32 an hour. You can make $300 just in one day. Every two weeks I lose $145 in income tax. That's more than a lot of people in New Brunswick make in a week.

DUANE LEE – Glassville, Carleton County, New Brunswick

A tall man with long brown hair, a beard, and an earring in his right ear. He has mechanic's papers, but prefers working outside his trade. "Too greasy," he says. When we spoke, he'd been in Calgary almost two years but was about to lose his driver's licence for six months. He was planning to move back to New Brunswick for the duration. I ask about Glassville.

In the main town there are maybe two hundred people. Maybe three hundred in the whole Glassville area – Centre Glassville, West Glassville, East Glassville. There's one general store, one post office, and one service station. It's mainly a farming community. People there either work for lumber or work for a farmer or work for the government. There's a government garage there, a snow shed and stuff – they have maybe twelve. A lot of people travel to Florenceville to McCain's.

I've got one brother, that's all. He lives here in Calgary. My parents live at home. In their generation of my family home, out of four brothers, all live in Glassville. Out of their families, there are seventeen kids – two of them are home. The rest are away, from Australia to New Mexico to Norway. There are five here in Alberta. It's bad. All the young folks are going to move out here, have their families here, and you'll have nobody left to replenish the place.

There was once a cheese factory, three hotels, and two blacksmiths' shops in Glassville. And one blacksmith shop was capable of boarding fifty horses at one time. They were thriving businesses. There was a tailor shop, two or three general stores – there were probably close to a good five or six hundred people living there, and a good thousand people coming and going in the course of a week. Just a thriving little town. My grandmother used to sell meals for a quarter – just an endless supply. People coming through, they knew where to go. She'd just cook all day.

One hotel burned, and they never did anything with it. People moved out, other businesses went, and when their families didn't want to take them up, they just petered out. All private family businesses. They supported the family. You could do the same today, but people took off, moved to bigger towns. Probably just the same as me ...

I've been away from New Brunswick for three or four years. The reason I left was to go to the Northwest Territories. Going to make some big money. A town called Port Radium in a mining camp – a hundred and eighty guys, two chicks. You had to sign a contract for four months – sign your life away for four months. I couldn't stand it that long. I stayed there for ten and a half weeks, that was enough for me. My brother, he got up there and got to be foreman. He got me the job. When an opening came he phoned me and asked if I wanted to go to work. At the time I was on unemployment, I think, so, sure. If people could stand to stay there they could make themselves some money, but you can only play so much basketball, lift so many weights. You get really bored of it after a while. It's bad, really.

After I got out of trade school in New Brunswick, I worked almost two and a half years in Centreville. Used to drive fifteen, sixteen miles a day, one way. I was working for an International dealer – apprentice mechanic. I started there for $125 a week, and I worked from seven till five with a half hour for lunch. When I quit two years later, I was making $150 a week. I quit to go work in the woods. I was making more money in the woods running a chain-saw. I was clearing $430 every two weeks. Well, I was working a lot harder too, but of course I was getting in shape and I was feeling a lot better. I didn't mind the work.

And I worked two and a half years for the provincial government operating heavy equipment – a land-drainage tile ditcher. It puts underground subsurface drainage tile in farmers' fields to drain the excess water off. I was getting $7.10 an hour, guaranteed forty hours a week whether it rained, snowed, got stuck, or whatever, all expenses paid, a half-ton to drive, everything. I was prepared to stay there and keep that job, but you were always away from home. Sunday night I was always leaving one side of the province to go to the other side, work all week, leave Friday, and then come back. You'd have to leave Sunday because you had to work eight o'clock Monday morning, and you'd have to leave at three o'clock in the morning if you didn't. And they'd always lay me off at Christmas time and I wouldn't be able to go back to work till March.

But you could get unemployment from it?

Yeah, but you sit around three and a half or four months, it's bad. I don't mind sitting around, but not for an extended period of time. Living on unemployment, I was spending a good $50 a week in gas, just visiting around. You get tired of watching television. I don't like TV much anyway, so you go out visiting. Always in the car. Come time to go back to work, you have to scrounge around for money, because you have to pay two months' expenses before you get one expense cheque back.

After the Territories I went to Toronto, then I came out here ...

What'd you do in Toronto?

Drove a dump truck. Well, I worked for this battery place for six days – Mallory Battery, they make the Duracell batteries. I don't know. I'm just not the type of person to work inside in a factory, walking on a cement floor all day. I said, "No, got to do something different." I had my licence and everything, so I went driving truck. I didn't know the city very well at all, but I learned pretty fast. The only reason I left – or I probably would still have been there – was that it was coming winter and it was a construction excavating type of deal, and there wasn't any work. I was getting maybe twenty-five hours a week, $6 an hour; and I was paying $365 a month for an apartment. So I came out here.

By yourself?

With three other guys and a girl. Some friends of mine came from Centreville to Toronto, just stopped off to visit for a while on their way out here. Thursday night they said, "Well, let's go. Want to go to Calgary?" They more or less talked me into leaving. I wasn't getting any hours, and the other two guys I was living with – one guy was from Juniper and this other guy is a cousin of mine whose father moved from New Brunswick a long time ago and has been in Toronto for twenty years – they weren't working, so we said OK. Friday morning ten o'clock we were on the road. We all came out here in a van, and I've been here ever since.

"I've driven across three or four times now. When we came back last year, we were five of us in a half-ton. January, just after Christmas – two people in the back of a half-ton all the way from Toronto to Calgary. That's not a word of a lie. There were three guys and two chicks. This one chick was with me, and this other chick was with this other guy, and this one other guy, it was his truck. He stayed in the front all the way, but the four of us, two would go in the back for like twelve or fourteen hours at a time. We had six inches of foam on the bottom and a furniture mat wrapped around it, and then a flannelette blanket, and then on the top we had a sheet, three or four sleeping bags, and another big furniture blanket. We had lots of insulation. It was forty-eight below in Thunder Bay. You'd have to wear a toque, but it was really no problem. Just crawl in there. Oh, just nice. Sleep! I slept there one time about fifteen hours. I'd driven all night, and by about one o'clock in the afternoon, I was so tired ... I layed down, and that was it until the next morning. We covered something like a thousand miles, and I just slept in the back.

"I was pretty dubious when we left Toronto. What were we going to do when we got to northern Ontario? The coldest spot on record in Canada is up there. But it worked out just fine. It was just great. We had a bottle of rum – if you were cold, just take a few hits. Getting in and getting out was pretty cool, boys, but once you got in there, after about ten minutes it was just like an oven, just no problem. You had a chance to lay down, stretch yourself out, and sleep, and it wasn't a bit warmer in the front than it was in the back."

I drive a cement truck here. Some days I get nineteen hours, time and a half to ten and double time after ten. I clear $2,100, $2,200 a month. I don't work hard but I put in a lot of hours. Contending with traffic and all that, it's pretty tiresome. We earn our money. I deliver mortar to masons and stuff, and it has to be there pretty well on time, because you know bricklayers – when they run out of mortar and they're just standing around, they get all upset.

You like Calgary?

It's a really easy city to find work in, that's for sure. If you've got a trade, you can have a different job every day of the week if you want one. When I was looking for a job down at the Manpower Centre, just take your pick, there's everything there. Welders, pipefitters ...

I'd like to start my own business here. I figure a construction company. I'd like to have a backhoe, a dump truck, and a little, small bulldozer and do landscaping around houses and stuff. The guy that bought the company I'm working for, he told me, he said, "I never made any money till I quit working with my hands." He owns twelve sections of land and half a construction company in Saskatoon, and half of this company here. He's always in between here and Saskatoon. Comes here, picks up a cheque for twenty thousand, goes there and picks up a cheque for twenty thousand, stops at the bank afterwards. Every day I go to work I make him nothing under five or six hundred dollars. It should be me driving that Cadillac car, you know?

I really like New Brunswick. I never left there as far as moving away to live till I was twenty-two years old. If I'd have had a business there with my parents, and if they were willing just to sort of pass it over to me, I'd never be here, and that's a fact. I'd be there supposin' all I did was make a living.

VINCE BUCHANAN – Centreville,
Carleton County, New Brunswick

Vince has been in Calgary for two and a half years, although he has been leaving home, travelling back and forth, for ten. "When I was sixteen, Alan [Shaw] and I took off hitchhiking and we went to Toronto. That was the place to go."

"Told our parents we were going to Davison Lake [New Brunswick] for the weekend," Alan laughs. "The next thing we knew we were in Toronto."

"I lived in Toronto three times in a row," Vince continues. "Go up and live for a while and then ... go back home. And then ... back to Toronto for a while. I think the most I ever lived there was eight months.

"You can take the Maritimer out of the Maritimes," he laughs, "but you cant' take the Maritimes out of me."

I came out here with three other people, three girls. One Saturday afternoon, I was sitting on the front step drinking beer, and we just got up and left. We didn't have any special destination in mind, but we headed for Calgary. I was going to go to Saskatchewan – Lloyd [Wallace] and a bunch of the guys were out there farming. But as it happened, Lloyd's brother was living here then and he gave us a place to live. We all found work and I've been here ever since.

Did you quit a job home?

I was working in the woods driving skidder. It's a good job, but there wasn't much work, and I had a hard job getting money out of the guy.

What other kind of work could you do around Centreville?

You can be a farmer or work in the woods. Right around where I live you can work for farmers while you're drawin' pogey – they don't take anything out of you. Or you can work baggin' potatoes or taking them out to railway cars. Those 110-pound bags get pretty heavy towards the end of the day.

I told myself when I left that I would never hay or pick potatoes again. But I was home the other summer for about two weeks, something like that, and I was hayin'. I've done enough of that. And pickin' rocks.

Have you got a trade?

Truck driver. I deliver gyproc. $7.50 an hour. And you earn your money too.

Would the wages be close to the same if you were working at home?

[Pauses.] You would probably make more if you were driving trans-port ... Yes, you could. [Pauses again.] What the hell am I doing here? I could go back home and get a job driving in Centreville. On the highway, too. That's what I want to do anyway. I think that'd be great. [Laughs.] What am I doing? Should get the hell home.

POSTSCRIPT Alan Shaw was laid off five days after we talked, and not wanting to wait around, put an ad in the paper and got a drive east. Duane Lee and Vince Buchanan left for New Brunswick in a '66 Chev half-ton two weeks after we spoke. "It's time," Vince said. "Can't help it. It's in the blood."